TEACHERS AS CURRICULUM PLANNERS
Narratives of Experience

F. MICHAEL CONNELLY
D. JEAN CLANDININ

Foreword by Elliot Eisner

The Ontario Institute
for Studies in Education

Teachers College
Columbia University

Published simultaneously in the U.S.A. by Teachers College Press,
1234 Amsterdam Avenue, New York, NY 10027 and in Canada
by OISE Press/The Ontario Institute for Studies in Education,
252 Bloor Street West, Toronto, Ontario M5S 1V6

Library of Congress Cataloging-in-Publication Data

Connelly, F. Michael.
  Teachers as curriculum planners.

  Bibliography: p. 215
  Includes index.
  1. Curriculum planning. 2. Teacher participation in
curriculum planning. I. Clandinin, D. Jean. II. Title.
LB2806.15.C67 1988   375'.001   88-2272
ISBN 0-8077-2907-8
ISBN 0-8077-2906-X (pbk.)

Canadian Cataloguing in Publication Data

Connelly, F. Michael.
  Teachers as curriculum planners.

(Research in education series; 15)
Bibliography: p. 215
ISBN 0-7744-0317-9

1. Teaching. 2. Curriculum planning. 3. Story-
telling. 4. Experiential learning. I. Clandinin,
Dorothy Jean. II. Title. III. Series.
LB1027.C66 1988   371.1'02   C88-093465-4

Manufactured in the United States of America

93 92 91 90 89   2 3 4 5 6

Contents

Foreword

In *Teachers as Curriculum Planners* Michael Connelly and Jean Clandinin provide a narrative built upon the premise that experience is the primary agency of education. This premise is one that enjoys no place of privilege in an age in which technological approaches to teaching and learning are dominant. The reasons are not difficult to discern.

First, experience is slippery; it is difficult to operationalize; it eludes factual descriptions of manifest behavior. Experience is what people undergo, the kinds of meanings they construe as they teach and learn, and the personal ways in which they interpret the worlds in which they live. Such aspects of life are difficult to relegate to a technology of standardized observation schedules or behavioral measures, yet what people experience in schools is central to any effort to understand what schools mean to those who spend a major portion of their lives there.

Second, our efforts to improve education have been focused upon finding practical methods. In the words of the U.S. Office of Education, we should employ "what works." Since teaching is defined as a profession, it seems reasonable for professionals to know what they are doing. Knowing what one is doing means knowing how to get from A to B. Educational research conceives of its major task as providing the route. The job of the professional teacher is to employ a technology of instruction that will take him or her on that route as expeditiously as possible. Using the "best method" has been the way one becomes marked as a professional. However, since the "best method" cannot, by definition, be idiosyncratic, the effort has been toward standardization.

Using "best methods" has also been tied to the measurement of outcomes. If there is to be evidence of effectiveness in teaching and curriculum planning, the effects of those methods must be measurable. Further, those effects must be standardized or common across students. If the method is idiosyncratic, it is likely that the outcomes will be as well. If the effects are idiosyncratic, comparability across students is complicated, and the assessment of teacher competency is made more difficult. Thus, conceptions of "best method" are supported by conceptions of measured outcomes. Both require standardization; both focus on what people do; and both neglect what people experience.

Given this context, Connelly and Clandinin's book swims upstream. It is not in the mainstream of the images of practice that have been salient in schools in the United States or in Canada. Yet, its focus on experience places it among the works of scholars such as John Dewey, William Pinar, Madeline Grumet, Philip Jackson, Maxine Greene, and others. More significantly, perhaps, this book provides us with a reminder that it is more important to understand what people *experience* than to focus simply on what they *do*. It is possible to get teachers and students to perform, and at the same time to scuttle any interest in what they teach and learn. It is possible to develop observation schedules for rating teacher and pupil behavior with perfect reliability and yet miss most of what counts in their lives—what they make of what they are doing.

At a time in which feigned interest has become a high art and accommodation to the expectations of others a common form of politics, we need not only to *see* what we look at, we also need to *interpret* it. This interpretation requires a willingness to listen deeply to what people have to say, to see beyond what they do in order to grasp the meanings that their doings have for them.

One of the strongest aspects of *Teachers as Curriculum Planners* is the use of teacher narratives. The metaphors by which teachers live, the way they construe their work, and the stories they recount, tell us more profoundly about what is going on in their lives as professionals than any measured behavior is likely to reveal. But to use such data one must have courage. Narratives are regarded as "soft," and soft data do not inspire confidence among the tough-minded. Narratives are often riddled with metaphor, with individual cadences that convey personal meaning, and with those expressive features that do not lend themselves well to truth tests. The willingness to pursue these elusive but informative aspects of educational life is not common within a framework that seeks "best methods" and measured outcomes. One must be willing to understand by participating sympathetically in the stories and in the lives of those who tell them. One must be willing to vicariously participate in scenes that one cannot enter into directly. One needs to be able to trust on the basis of coherence, utility, and the often ineffable sense of rightness that true stories display. In short, one secures meaning from material such as the reader will find in this book not by seeking correlation coefficients, but by opening up to what teachers have to say to us.

The use of narratives, and the epistemological frameworks through which these narratives embody and convey meaning, not only provides an important way to think about curriculum and teaching, but also is vital to understanding what goes on at school. Connelly and Clandinin take teachers seriously; they seek to understand education by understanding how teachers conceive of what they do. Their book offers to prospective teachers a view of "education with a human face."

Perhaps the most important contribution of *Teachers as Curriculum Planners* resides in the way it exemplifies a mode of inquiry and a view of knowledge that has gradually been establishing its legitimacy in the field of education. As scholars increasingly employ the approach used here, two important contributions can be expected: First, we can expect to acquire a fuller, more replete view of what curriculum and teaching means within schools; second, we will continue to legitimate personalistic, idiosyncratic, and experiential approaches to educational research. By doing this form of research we build a literature from which others can draw, and we strengthen further the foundations upon which new work can be built. Connelly and Clandinin have done both. They have written a book that makes the fullness of practice more vivid and one that pushes the frontiers of inquiry a little further. To do one is an important achievement. To do both is rare.

Elliot W. Eisner

Center for Advance Study
in the Behavioral Sciences

Acknowledgments

This book has been an exercise in collaboration between two university teachers working together but at different ends of the country. Collaboration has been through computer links, phone calls, and infrequent meetings. Writing this book has taught both of us much about the nature of collaboration.

Our collaboration goes far beyond the two of us. We have both collaborated with many other teachers with whom we have been fortunate to work in our graduate classes and in our research schools. The teachers with whom we have worked taught us a great deal about teaching and learning as they shared their classrooms, stories, journals, letters, and biographies. They worked with us as we wrote and thought through our ideas of the practice of teaching. They helped us to read their texts of classroom practice and thereby to better understand the centrality of experience in teachers' lives.

Evidence for the important role that collaborating teachers had in this book is found throughout as we use their words to make points and illustrate ideas. They shared with us the lessons they learned from their experiences with children. When we asked these teachers if they wanted to have their names used, most wished to remain anonymous, some with a pseudonym, some with no name, and some with a first name only. With caring insight some said their stories belong in part to their students with whom they learned in their classrooms. We express our gratitude to the teachers who have shared in this project with us and, through these teachers, to their students.

The work has also been collaborative in other enriching ways. Several scholars have given us direction, encouragement, and guidance at important moments. We are particularly indebted to Joseph J. Schwab, Professor Emeritus, University of Chicago; Elliot Eisner, Professor, Stanford University; and Mark Johnson, Professor, University of Southern Illinois at Carbondale. These scholars were able to "play" with our ideas and show us possibilities we had not seen in the work. They too taught us about collaboration.

In our collaboration with each other, with teachers, and with other curriculum researchers, we have continually engaged in a reflective process on our own personal practical knowledge. We have both come to new understandings of the ways in which we know our teaching and learning situations. Writing this book has helped us see new narrative threads in our own lives and, in this, the book is a beginning for new explorations into personal practical knowledge.

Finally, we are grateful to the National Institute of Education in the United States and to the Social Sciences and Humanities Research Council of Canada for their financial support of the research program on the Narrative Study of Teachers' Personal Practical Knowledge, on which this book is based.

Last but not least, we wish to thank Rita O'Brien, JoAnne Squires, Marie McMullin, and Gary Pyper for the collection and entering of field records into the computer and for working so carefully to help us produce a finished effort of which we could all be proud.

F.M.C.
D.J.C.

Introduction

This is a book for teachers. It is a book for preservice, novice, and experienced teachers. It is a book that celebrates the experience of each and every one of us who teaches. We show, often in the words of teachers with whom we have worked, how reflection on our narratives of experience helps us make meaning of our lives as teachers.

Partly this book grows out of opposing traditions of school reform in which there is a never-ending tension between the demands of authority with its prescriptions for what should be taught in the curriculum *and* the primacy of teachers and students, who live out and ultimately experience the curriculum. At various times, over the years one or another tradition gains the upper hand. Of late, those who would control teachers and the curriculum appear to be gaining support. We share in the other tradition. This book sets out one way of thinking that stresses the legitimacy of each teacher's personal knowledge of classrooms.

All books, as Elliot Eisner once wrote, have an autobiographical origin, and this one is no different. In our work with experienced teachers, both in classrooms and in graduate level professional development programs, we have been impressed with the centrality of teachers' life experiences and how they know and live out their lives in classrooms. This is not a new or even a remarkable observation. To the contrary it is commonplace. But it is a commonplace that is mostly ignored. In proposals for the reform of schooling, radical reformers of one persuasion tend to think of teachers as helpless reproducers of inequitable social structures, and radical reformers of another persuasion tend to think of teachers as conformists unwilling to implement new ideas, policies, and programs. In all of this talk about school reform, there is little sense of the tremendous power and potential in the experience of classroom teachers. We understand how spirited teachers may revolutionize their practices through reflection on their own experiences and new ideas, and how they can transform new ideas into powerful curriculum programs through this reflective process.

More than this, however, as we learned to listen to teachers we realized the ways that each of us, not only teachers, keeps telling and retelling stories about our past. And in the telling of our stories we work out new ways of acting in the future. Curriculum reform, as we listened to teachers, sounded less and less like either of the traditions and more and more like a process of living out the stories we tell ourselves in order to make meaning of our experience.

And as we listened to teachers we realized there was a lesson in this, a kind of metaphor, for how teachers need to listen to the stories of their students. Just as reformers need to listen to teachers, teachers need to listen to the stories of their students. Looked at this way, we imagine a classroom as a place where students and teachers tell stories to one another to make sense of where they have been and to help them grow and develop in the future. The more we listened, the more we have come to believe that the essence of reform is nestled in an interacting matrix of life stories within the classroom.

The book is organized into four main parts, Understanding Curriculum, Understanding Yourself, Understanding Influences on the Curriculum, and Understanding Your Narrative: Curriculum Planning in the School. Understanding Curriculum contains one chapter, which develops an experientially based idea of curriculum. The part titled Understanding Yourself contains five chapters, in which the ideas of personal knowledge and narratives of experience are developed. Chapter 3, Narrative: Your Personal Curriculum as a Metaphor for Curriculum and Teaching, states the book's central theme. Chapters 4 through 6 develop a set of tools and integrative ideas by which individual teachers may reflect on their narratives of experience.

The third part, Understanding Influences on the Curriculum, looks outward from the individual and shows how it is possible to integrate one's context into the reflections on one's narratives of experience. Chapter 7, Recovery of Curriculum Meaning, is, therefore, a key chapter since it relates the personal and the contextual in methods of reflection, which we call recovering and reconstructing meaning. Subsequent chapters in this part treat research, curriculum literature, influential persons and groups of persons, and curriculum materials as contextual influences on one's personal knowledge.

The final part, Understanding Your Narrative: Curriculum Planning in the School, consists of four chapters containing a great deal of case material. Teachers report on the cycles and rhythms in planning lessons, on planning as curriculum inquiry, the administration of a school curriculum, and working with students. Teachers and students have the final word in Chapter 15.

We hope that teachers, and others, will read this book primarily for purposes of reflecting on their own narratives of experience.

Part I

UNDERSTANDING CURRICULUM

Curriculum is often taken to mean a course of study. When we set our imaginations free from the narrow notion that a course of study is a series of textbooks or specific outline of topics to be covered and objectives to be attained, broader and more meaningful notions emerge. A curriculum can become one's life course of action. It can mean the paths we have followed and the paths we intend to follow. This broad sense of curriculum as a person's life experience is behind the idea of this book captured in the subtitle *Narratives of Experience*.

1

The Idea
of Curriculum

People who come to curriculum studies for the first time usually ask one of two questions. If they are students coming to a class, they often ask "what is curriculum?" and if they are teachers assigned to a curriculum committee, they are likely to ask "how do I do it?" These are important questions, and it is not surprising that teachers and students—who may also be teachers—ask them. But the answers are not at all easily given, and when they are given the question asker is often unhappy with the answer. Sometimes teachers come to the study and doing of curriculum because they want the practical side of teaching. These people tend to be unhappy with airy, theoretical discussions of curriculum conceptions, theories, and policies. Others may be experienced teachers who want to understand curriculum at a deeper level, and they may be unhappy with an answer that talks about strategies, techniques, and tactics for selecting, organizing, and planning curriculum. It is, in fact, impossible to give an answer to the two questions that will satisfy everyone.

Undaunted by this difficulty we set out a view in this book, which, if not satisfying for every reader, will help, we believe, all readers to understand not only their own answers to these two questions but also the answers given by others.

We have a bias. Almost all of the books that you might read on curriculum these days take an eclectic, comparative point of view. These books organize and classify the different answers that people give to the questions, and, as such, yield a kind of taxonomy of concepts of curriculum. Of course these books have their problems too; since every taxonomy is based on its own criteria, the classification offered is only one of many possible ones that might be offered. In effect, the difficulty of answering people's questions is simply raised to another level. We avoid the classification-of-other-points-of-view problem by offering our own concept of curriculum. It is a concept that some might call dialectic. That is, it is a view in which all of the others may be seen if one wishes to do so.

3

What is the central idea of our view? It is simply that all teaching and learning questions—all curriculum matters—be looked at from the point of view of the involved persons. We believe that curriculum development and curriculum planning are fundamentally questions of teacher thinking and teacher doing. We believe that it is teachers' "personal knowledge" that determines all matters of significance relative to the planned conduct of classrooms. So "personal knowledge" is the key term. And this key term is one that lets us bring together, rather than categorize and separate, different answers and different points of view. To begin a discussion of matters that are explored more fully throughout the book, we observe that the two questions "what is curriculum?" and "how do I do it?" are brought together within the person. The "what is" and the "doing" are intimately connected through the personal knowledge of the individual teacher.

Later in this chapter we lay out a simple model: a kind of conception that will begin to put flesh on this idea and to which we will continually return in the book. But, first, let us do a little exercise of seeing just how different people have answered the question "what is curriculum?"

CURRICULUM: DIFFERENT THINGS TO DIFFERENT PEOPLE

The Latin root of the word "curriculum" means race course. Perhaps because of this linguistic origin the most common everyday definition of curriculum is a course of study. While this definition is not at all popular in the research literature, it is still probably the most common idea held in and around schools. Try asking a parent what he or she thinks it would mean to be assigned to the school's curriculum committee. Or ask a principal. Even if he or she attended a curriculum course that emphasized comparative curriculum definitions, she or he would likely answer by drawing attention to the school's calendar of courses.

When we turn to the written literature, this more or less straightforward, commonsense notion of curriculum is lost in a welter of different possibilities. A science teacher reading this book might imagine that writers who more or less agreed on a definition would state that definition in very similar words. The reason a science teacher might think this is that a scientific object, for example, an atom or a particular biological genus, is defined in pretty much the same way by different people working in a particular area. But in the curriculum literature the words often differ a great deal. Sometimes it is very difficult to decide whether two authors agree or disagree with one another, since their words may be different but the meaning may sound somewhat similar, or vice versa.

Skim through the following list taken from reasonably well-known writings in the field. This will give you some idea of our meaning.

A sequence of potential experiences is set up in the school for the purpose of disciplining children and youth in group ways of thinking and acting. This set of experiences is referred to as the curriculum (Smith et al., 1957).

All the experiences a learner has under the guidance of the school (Foshay, 1969).

A general over-all plan of the content or specific materials of instruction that the school should offer the student by way of qualifying him for graduation or certification or for entrance into a professional or vocational field (Good, 1959).

We hold that curriculum is a methodological inquiry exploring the range of ways in which the subject matter elements of teacher, student, subject and milieu can be seen (Westbury & Steimer, 1971).

Curriculum is the life and program of the school . . . an enterprise in guided living; the curriculum becomes the very stream of dynamic activities that constitute the life of your people and their elders (Rugg, 1947).

A curriculum is a plan for learning (Taba, 1962).

The planned and guided learning experiences and intended learning outcomes, formulated through the systematic reconstruction of knowledge and experience, under the auspices of the school, for the learner's continuous and wilful growth in person-social competence (Tanner & Tanner, 1975).

Curriculum must consist essentially of disciplined study in five great areas: (i) command of the mother tongue and the systematic study of grammar, literature, and writing; (ii) mathematics; (iii) sciences; (iv) history; (v) foreign language (Bestor, 1955).

The curriculum is considered to be the increasingly wide range of possible modes of thinking about men's experiences—not the conclusions, but the models from which conclusions derive, and in context of which these conclusions, so-called truths, are grounded and validated (Belth, 1965).

Try sorting this list on your own. Can you classify these definitions? What are their similarities? What are their differences? If you are an experienced teacher, you will undoubtedly have government, board, or school documents that state or imply a definition of curriculum. Add these to your list. You might also want to go to the textbook and/or research literature and add still others. Try to make some sense of the variation you find.

CURRICULUM AS EXPERIENCE: THE IDEA OF THE BOOK

One of the reasons there are so many different definitions of curriculum is that people focus their definition on one or another of the many different parts of the classroom and its processes. They may emphasize objectives, learning outcomes, materials, students, and so forth, as you have seen in the little exercise above. We, instead, want to focus on it all by stressing the very general terms "experience" and "situation." The general idea is that curriculum is something experienced in situations. People have experiences. Situations are made up of people and their surrounding environment. Let us see how this works out. Figure 1.1 brings the idea together, and we pull it apart in the five points that follow.

1. *A situation is composed of persons, in an immediate environment of things, interacting according to certain processes.*
In a classroom the key "persons" are the teacher and the students. The "things" are books, desks, lighting, and so forth. The "processes" are instructional and include such matters as lecturing, laboratory, reading,

Figure 1.1: Experience in the Classroom Situation

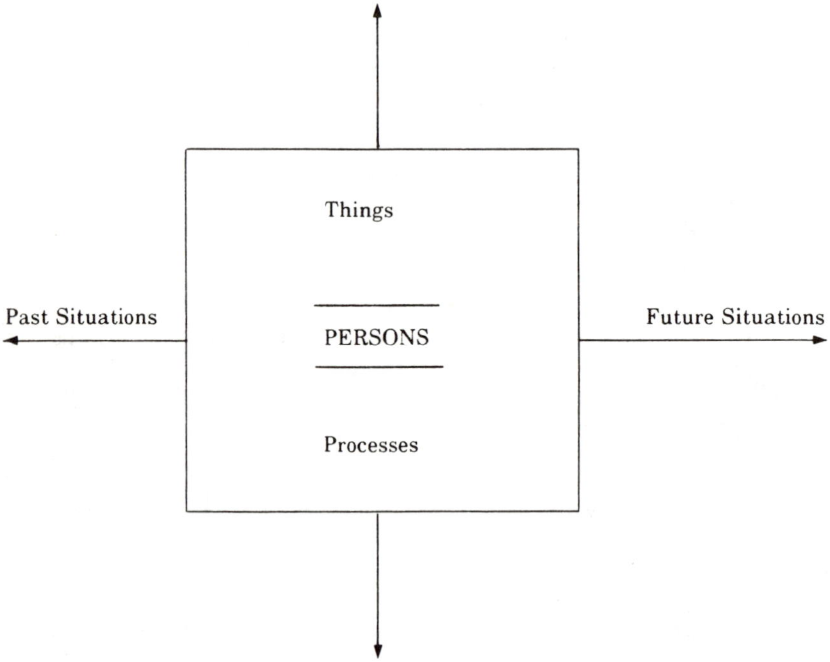

friendship, smiles, disputes, warmth, and the like. If we hold tightly to our notion, we see right off that while persons are foremost in the view, our definition of curriculum includes things and processes as well and is not any one of the three in isolation.

When we say the word "curriculum," then, we need to have a picture in mind in which all of these parts are in interaction. This is important enough that you should practice a little picturing. It is a very different thing to say the word "curriculum" and then have a textbook flash to mind or a teacher lecturing flash to mind or an evaluator measuring intended learning outcomes flash to mind than it is if the total picture of a classroom, preferably one with which you are familiar, flashes to mind. Read ahead to Chapter 4 where the process of "picturing" is discussed. Your picture is important to understanding this book. If a mental picture of a classroom situation does not automatically, and intuitively, flash before your mind when the word "curriculum" is used, you will have trouble following this book. If it does flash into your mind, you will probably wonder why we wrote the book because everything we say will seem so obvious. Your mental picture is crucial.

2. *At any point in time there is a dynamic interaction among persons, things, and processes.*
The parts of a situation are not static elements put in their proper place but are, instead, in a fluid state of interaction. This is an important addition to your picture. Even if your picture is a "quiet" one with students reading, heads bowed over text, and the teacher sitting at the front of the room, you must imagine the interactive tensions at work: students' minds at work on the text, or possibly at play in imagination entirely outside the classroom, the teacher responding to journals and thinking warmly of an experience recorded by a student, the underlying awareness that students have of each other and that they all have of the teacher, and vice versa. So, now, when the word "curriculum" is used, and the picture flashes before your mind, it should be shimmering with intensity. Your picture should bring with it feelings. After all, as Chapter 4 points out, pictures are not abstract diagrams inscribed on the mind. They are part of us and bring with them our emotions. Your picture of curriculum should be one in which you feel the dynamic forces at work in the classroom situation.

3. *Every classroom situation grows out of some preceding classroom situation.*
All situations are historical. It is important to be flexible in thinking about this historical dimension. Situations are historical on a moment-to-moment basis. That is, what happened in a classroom five minutes ago influences and

is part of the history of what is happening right now. But it is also true that what happened yesterday, and the week before, and in fact at any stage during any one participant's life also is part of the history, for that person, in that situation. Thus, your picture of the classroom situation must also be dynamic in an historical sense. You need to see participants in the situation as having a history and as reflecting that history. More than that, you need to think of them continually remaking that history as they deal with the particulars of the situation at hand. Read ahead to Chapter 5 where the notion of "telling your story" is discussed. This idea of people telling and retelling their histories will become a more powerful notion for you. When the word "curriculum" is used, the picture that flashes before your mind is one in which the persons are storytellers living out their past and remaking that past to deal with their current situation.

It is not only the people but the things and the processes that have a history. At a simple level, books get old and outdated and are redone and remade. Carpets wear out and new technologies come in and, more generally, the histories of other people in the situation make a difference to the situation. And so does the history of the school, and the community of which the school is a part, and so on. Both the things and the processes therefore must also be thought of as having a history. Try to make this part of your picture.

4. *Situations have a future.*

Every situation leads to another situation. Just as you need to be flexible in thinking of a situation's history, you need to be flexible in thinking of its future. Particular tensions of the classroom at any point in time will influence that classroom five minutes later. All of this has a bearing on situations tomorrow, next week, a month later, and throughout life. Now, someone might say that something so specific as a reprimand in a teenager's classroom will have little bearing on the kind of adult into which the teenager grows. It is true that these detailed kinds of causal connections are difficult to trace. But it is also the case that all of our experiences in situations become part of us in lesser or greater degree. It all contributes. It all makes a difference. Your picture of the situation must have this future dimension to it. There must be a sense of the situation moving forward and reaching into the future. When the word "curriculum" is used, your picture of the classroom situation should have a forward feel to it, a sense of pushing into the future.

These two sides to the time dimension of a situation, its history and its future, contribute, overall, a dynamic, temporal sense to the idea of a situation in our notion of curriculum. Just as the picture has a sense of tension associated with the interaction of persons and things in processes, so too the picture has a sense of temporal tension as it reflects the past and pushes into the future. You need an abstract visual model, which is shown in Figure 1.1. But you also need an emotional picture, and that is why we ask that you read Chapters 4 and 5 and think about picturing and storytelling. You need to *feel* your picture of curriculum if you are to develop a definition of curriculum of the sort this book describes.

5. *Situations are directional.*

Situations are pointed into the future towards certain ends. Almost no one lives his or her life at random. Instead, people are going somewhere. So a situation does not merely move into the future simply because time passes but is pulled into the future by the ends we all hold out before us. Some people tend to think of these ends as very specific things and to write about objectives or even behavioral objectives, intentions, goals, purposes, intended learning outcomes, and so forth. Curriculum courses are sometimes organized around this very idea. But other people think of directionality as more of a general guide. Some, for instance, talk about a philosophical outlook. This may appear as a rationale for a curriculum or possibly as a personal set of beliefs and values on life that shapes the way the person does things, thereby permitting the person to keep a sense of direction as life progresses. For our purpose here it is not necessary to settle just exactly how we want to talk about directionality in the curriculum. What is important is that your notion of a situation, and therefore your picture of curriculum, contain the idea of directionality.

Directionality acts upon situations in the way that the history of situations does. It shapes and reconstructs the situation. One may even say that a sense of direction is one of those things that reshapes the past in the telling of our stories (see Chapter 5). There is a very curious thing about situations, and therefore about our idea of curriculum. It is this: The past shapes the future through the medium of a situation, and the future shapes the past through the stories we tell to account for and explain our situation. Where we have been and where we are going interact to make meaning of the situations in which we find ourselves. Make sure you add this sense of a situation to your picture. Coming to grips with the directional/temporal character of curriculum will be important to the meaning you make of this field.

PUTTING THE IDEA TOGETHER

We know that the ideas advanced in this chapter are quite commonplace. There is nothing new in talk about the future, about the past, about processes, about people, and about things. Yet, the very familiarity with these notions can act as a barrier to understanding the idea of curriculum advanced. Zerubavel (1979) has said that things that are so much a part of us that they remain unnoticed are like "invisible glass walls." They are noticed only when we walk into them. The picturing process may help make these ideas a little more visible. But, following Zerubavel's metaphor, we urge you to bump into the glass walls as you read the book. The little intellectual bumps that result will help to crystallize the idea of curriculum into visibility. After all, as John Dewey said so well, thinking is inquiry, inquiry is life, and life is education. When we bump into the obvious, it becomes a puzzle or a problem, and we think about it. Living is thinking, and that, said Dewey, is what education is all about.

RECOMMENDED READINGS

For a discussion of a theory of experience you can do no better than to read John Dewey's *Experience and Education* (1938). This little book was written well into Dewey's career and is aimed at teachers. It was written to counter the progressivist trend in American education that had grown up around his ideas. In the book he argues that "progressivism" in its extreme form is as mis-educational as is "traditional" education in its extreme form. Two other essays of John Dewey's that you will find of interest are "The Child and the Curriculum" (1969) and "School and Society" (1969). Readers who wish to probe more deeply into the philosophic background of these works might read *Logic: The Theory of Inquiry* (1938) and *Art as Experience* (1934). A more recent writing on the theory of experience is Schutz and Luckmann's *The Structures of the Life-World* (1974). Schutz and Luckmann do not address the problem of curriculum, but you will be able to make the links once you grasp the theory of experience advanced.

Part II

UNDERSTANDING YOURSELF

For each of us, the more we understand ourselves and can articulate reasons why we are what we are, do what we do, and are headed where we have chosen, the more meaningful our curriculum will be. The process of making sense and meaning of our curriculum, that is, of the narratives of our experience, is both difficult and rewarding. It, too, has a curriculum in that narratives of experience may be studied, reflected on, and articulated in written form. Some of the tools for the study of our own curriculum are set forth in this section.

2

What Does It Mean
to be Personal?

So far we have said that to think of curriculum means to think with the terms "experience" and "situation." We have also said that the teacher is the most important agent, after the students of course, in a curriculum situation from the point of view of its planning and development. It is the teacher's personal knowledge that makes all the difference. But what does it mean to be personal? One might think that all we were offering was an excuse for a teacher to visit his or her idiosyncrasies on students. Critics of decentralized curriculum planning, in fact, often say that this is about all that decentralization amounts to. They think that emphasizing the local situation and in particular the teacher gives way to mere personality. Sometimes, in fact, "progressivism" has come to mean something like this, and that is one of the reasons John Dewey wrote his objection to it in *Experience and Education*, noted in the recommended readings of Chapter 1. We do not, of course, mean to license individual whim in the curriculum. What then do we mean?

In this chapter we propose to take the reader on a rather quick guided tour of a relatively recent research literature on this problem. We will show how that literature and the ideas of the personal contained therein are understandable in the light of the idea of curriculum advanced in Chapter 1. It may or may not surprise you to learn that the term *personal* also means different things to different people. Just as we made no attempt to cover the full array of definitions of curriculum in Chapter 1, we make no attempt to cover the full array of possible definitions of the personal here. Instead, we want to lay out a basis for understanding the range of possibilities so that you may be able both to read and hear new definitions meaningfully as they occur through your career, and to do this from the point of view of the curriculum.

ONE DOZEN RESEARCH STUDIES

We have chosen a series of studies from the late 1970s and early 1980s for your review. These studies are summarized in Table 2.1, "Studies of the personal: What each study asserts," and Table 2.2, "Studies of the personal: What each does and claims." Looking at the studies this way lets us see not only what the authors say they are up to but also how they go about doing what they set out to do.

Getting Inside the Head

In a review of this literature, Feiman-Nemser and Floden (1984) said that the intent of these studies was to "get inside teachers' heads to describe their knowledge, attitudes, beliefs and values." The first thing we see from looking at Tables 2.1 and 2.2 is that while most of the studies do seem to be aimed at getting inside the teacher's head, some of them appear to be more interested in doing what Goodlad and Klein (1970) suggested—getting behind the teacher's classroom door. Other studies seem interested not so much in the classroom or in the teacher's head as in the teacher's background and history. Perhaps you see what we are doing in these last few sentences. We are using the concepts of Chapter 1 to think about studies of the personal. The next section will make this clear.

(*text continues on p. 18*)

Table 2.1: Studies of the personal: What each asserts

Authors	Key Terms	Stipulated Definition	Origin of Ideas
Halkes & Deijkers	Teachers' teaching criteria	Personal subjective values a person tries to pursue or keep constant while teaching	Literature on innovation and curriculum implementation; teacher thought, judgements, decisions and behavior; and attitudes to education
Marland	Principles of practice	Principles that guide a teacher's interactive teaching behavior and that can be used to explain teacher interactive behavior.	Not stated
Pope & Scott	Personal constructs/theories/epistemologies	Teachers' view of knowledge and of pedagogic practice.	Kelly's personal construct theory
Olson	Construct	An underlying theory that teachers use in thinking about, evaluating, and classifying teacher and student behavior.	Kelly's personal construct theory

(continued)

Table 2.1: (continued)

Authors	Key Terms	Stipulated Definition	Origin of Ideas
Munby	Beliefs and principles (implicit theory)	Coherent structures that underlie a teacher's practices.	Kelly's personal construct theory
Bussis/Chittenden/ Amarel	Teachers' understanding	Teachers' beliefs about curriculum and students in terms of classroom activities (surface content) and teachers' learning priorities for children (organizing content) and the connections between the two.	Phenomenological inquiry
Janesick	Perspective	A reflective, socially derived interpretation of experience that serves as a basis for subsequent action. Combines beliefs, intentions, interpretations, and behavior. A frame of reference within which the teacher makes sense of and interprets experience rationally.	Symbolic interaction
Larsson	Teachers' conceptions	A conception describes the way teachers conceive of some phenomena. The conceptions are basic elements in the understanding of teachers' ways of looking at their work and in some cases, of understanding their acts.	Phenomenography
Lampert	Personal knowledge	Personal knowledge (PK) is knowledge of who a teacher is and what he/she cares about and knowledge of students beyond paper & pencil tests. PK is used by a teacher in accomplishing what she/he cares about, what students want and what curriculum requires.	Not supplied
Elbaz	Practical knowledge	A complex practically oriented set of understandings which teachers actively use to shape and direct the work of teaching.	Phenomenology (particularly Schutz and Luckmann)
Berk	Biographic narrative	A disciplined way of interpreting a person's thought and action in the light of his or her past.	Experiential theory; published biographies
Pinar	Currere	The study of educational experience	Existentialism, phenomenology, and psychoanalysis

Table 2.2: Studies of the personal: What each does and claims

Authors	Problem	Method	Outcomes
Halkes & Deijkers	To identify teacher criteria used in solving class disturbances.	Analyze literature to develop seven categories of teaching criteria; convert to sixty-five operational statements presented in a Likert-scaled instrument; have teachers respond.	A set of summary statistics of the teaching criteria used by teachers.
Marland	To identify teacher thoughts that guide teaching behavior and can explain teaching behavior.	Videotape teaching events; conduct stimulated recall interview describing "thoughts" while teaching; sort individual statements from interview into categories of statements called principles.	Five principles of practice that guide teaching behavior.
Pope & Scott	To explore pre- and in-service teachers' epistemologies; their views on teaching and learning and what interactions, if any, there are among these interactions with implications for teacher education.	Identified four theoretically derived epistemologies; conducted interviews and observations of pre- and in-service teachers in which teachers reflected on own views of knowledge and practice; researchers derived teacher's personal theory or epistemology. Administered REP test; personal constructs derived from teacher's response to Repertory Grid test; sorted data from REP tests and interviews and observations from individual teachers into the four theoretically derived categories.	Concludes that student teachers can become aware of their initial epistemologies.
Olson	Problem of implementing a new science curriculum; how teachers deal with a new curriculum	Identified different science teaching methods; prepared and presented statements of 20 science teaching events to 8 teachers; teachers sorted events; discussed and located basis of grouping; labelled basis of grouping.	Identified underlying constructs in implicit theories of teaching; identified main feature of new science curriculum; identified ways teachers changed curriculum project to make it compatible with personal constructs.
Munby	Problem of explaining how and why a nominally common curriculum is interpreted and implemented differently by each teacher.	14 teachers each generated 20 descriptive statements (elements) of what a visitor to his/her class would see; teachers sorted elements and discussed basis of grouping; terms and phrases used became constructs within teacher's implicit theory; constructs further analyzed through interviews which led to labels for groups and their relationships; produced statements called teachers' beliefs and principles.	Illustrated wide individual differences in beliefs and principles of teachers working at same school and within same subject matter specialization.

Table 2.2: (continued)

Authors	Problem	Method	Outcomes
Bussis/Chittenden /Amarel	To investigate the understandings and constructs of teachers implementing open or informal teaching.	Clinical interviews with teachers implementing open or informal teaching. Analyzed data to identify orientations for aspects of teachers' belief systems.	Identified four contrasting orientations for each of four aspects of teachers' belief systems: curriculum priorities; role of children's needs and feelings; children's interests and freedom of choice; importance of social interaction among children.
Janesick	To describe and explain the classroom perspective of a teacher.	Participant observer with teacher; interviews with teacher, other school staff and students; analyzed data base to offer interpretation of teacher's perspective.	Identified the teacher's classroom perspective and offered an account of how the teacher gave meaning to the day-to-day events in classroom and how he constructed curriculum.
Larsson	To describe teachers' assumptions about phenomena in their professional world.	Semi-structured interviews with 29 adult educators on phenomena of learning and knowledge in order to gain insight into conceptions of teachers. Analyzed data in order to identify conceptions and restrictions of teaching.	Identified two restrictions and two conceptions of teaching (two qualitatively different ways of conceptualizing what teaching ought to be).
Lampert	To examine teachers' thinking about the problems of practice.	Teacher-researchers gathered weekly over a two-year period to discuss everyday work dilemmas; during these discussions they were observed and interviewed. Conversations/ discussions considered as "text" to be interpreted and understood as an expression of the way they think about work dilemmas. "Text" analyzed to produce comparisons.	Noted comparisons among theories of teaching constructed by scholars, theories constructed by teachers themselves and teachers' concrete reflections on practical problems that arise daily in their classrooms.
Elbaz	To offer a conceptualization of the kind of knowledge teachers hold and use.	A series of semi-structured interviews with one teacher; analysis of transcript data base; researcher interpretation of teacher's practical knowledge.	Identified five content areas of practical knowledge; five orientations of practical knowledge; three ways in which practical knowledge is held.
Berk	To disclose the educational significance of events in another person's life.	Journal records of ongoing experience kept by person whose biography is being written; interviews with that person to discuss journals. Drafting themes, ideas, and plots to explain in educational terms the experience recorded.	An explanatory narrative of someone's educational experience.
Pinar	To understand a person's curriculum as revealed in recollections of past experience.	Free associative process to relive earlier experiences; self analysis.	An autobiographical account; knowledge of self with political consequences.

17

The studies and the idea of curriculum.   Figure 2.1, which is a straight-forward adaptation of Figure 1.1, presents these studies along the temporal continuum of situations. An inspection of this figure shows that some studies are primarily interested in the future as it unfolds in classrooms, most are interested in teachers' thinking directly (the present), and one is interested in teachers' personal history (the past). Notice that none of the studies is focussed purely on the "past" or purely on the "future." The reason for this is that all of these studies are concerned with teachers' thinking and so they are presented in the context of the person. There are many studies in the literature that would fall into our future category, with little or no emphasis on the personal. If you wish to sample this work, read on the topics of classroom processes and classroom interaction analysis. Many of these studies are descriptions of action but have little to say about thinking.

It may seem surprising to you that such radically different things are done in the name of teachers' thinking and the study of the personal. It is not until the simple concept of curriculum (Chapter 1) is used that these differences stand out. When you have finished reading this chapter, try to locate other studies of interest to you on Figure 2.1. Remember to think of the studies in terms of the idea of curriculum.

Studies of what is in the head.   Now that we have our dozen studies organized in terms of curriculum let us return to those that are concerned directly with teachers' thinking. At the time this book was written there was considerable interest in studying this matter, as reflected by the longer list of research studies on the "person." One of the first things we notice about these studies is that the researchers' ideas of what it is that teachers have "in their heads" differ from one researcher to another. Halkes and Deijkers think of teachers as having "criteria" in mind, while Marland thinks of teachers as having "principles" that are practical. Larsson thinks of teachers as holding mental "conceptions." Pope and Scott, Olson, and Munby are quite similar to one another because they have the same theoretical base, Kelly's personal construct theory. Even so, they use different words to

Figure 2.1: Teacher Thinking Studies and the Idea of Curriculum

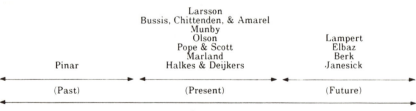

describe their idea of what teachers have in their heads—"personal constructs/theories/epistemologies," "constructs," "beliefs and principles." Bussis, Chittenden, and Amarel's notion is perhaps the simplest, with their idea of "teachers' understanding."

This is not the place to enter into a discussion of similarities and differences between these various notions of what it is that teachers have in their minds. What is important for teachers as consumers of this research is to be able to understand what kind of notions these are. From the point of view of curriculum, these research studies may assume that teachers' thoughts and ideas have a history, but the studies do not take that history into account. That is, we do not know why a teacher holds certain "criteria" or "constructs." We know nothing of the teachers' past experience and so know nothing about the origins of, say, the "criteria." What we do know is that, given the methodological conditions of the particular research study, a teacher has such and such an idea in mind.

Nor do we know what difference those ideas make to how the teacher moves into the future through his or her classroom work. Almost all of these studies use a rather straightforward logic on this point. Their authors believe, and often, although not always, state that what a teacher thinks will show up in what the teacher does. This logic has a commonsense ring of plausibility about it. "If we think this way, then we will do that." But you must be very cautious of interpreting such studies this way. Given our notion of curriculum, it is clear that the researchers in these studies know nothing about what happens in the particular teacher's future, since classrooms are not observed in the research. Nor do the researchers, or we as readers, know anything about how deeply grounded in the person's mind these concepts are, since there is no study of the person's prior experience. We say this not to be critical of the studies but as a kind of warning to teachers who read the research. One needs to be cautious about reading too much of curricular significance into studies of teachers' thinking that are effectively cut off, in their methodology, from the past and from the future.

Getting Inside the Future

The four listed studies on the future side of our curriculum conception also show a diversity of terms—"perspective," "personal knowledge," "practical knowledge," and "biographic narrative." The first thing to notice is that while these terms refer to ideas in the mind of the teacher, they are also, in an important sense, ideas in practice. They are ideas in the future as it unfolds. Janesick's notion of "perspective," for instance, is defined by her as including belief and interpretation that might be thought of as being "in the mind." But she also includes intentions and behavior, both of which are future oriented in the sense we have used the idea of the future. Thus, while her term is summed up as a "frame of reference," it is a frame of reference that includes behavior and intentions. Although the idea of teachers' thinking being both in the teacher's present thought and also in the future is clearest in Janesick's idea, the notion is also evident in the work of the remaining three. Lampert's and Elbaz's idea of knowledge is one that grows out of and is expressed in practice. Unlike the studies of the mind described earlier in this chapter, these authors give accounts of the mind at work in a classroom situation. Again, we may say that knowledge for these authors is both in the mind and in the future, defined as ongoing action.

Berk uses a quite different term, "biographic narrative," which, in some respects, is the best term of all to illustrate the emphasis discussed here. The idea of a biographic narrative is both personal in the sense of biography and developmental and process-oriented in the sense of a narrative. Thus, his notion is less one of fixed ideas that are expressed in practice and more one of developing ideas that are found and grow in classroom practice.

Getting Inside the Past

The only historical study listed in Figure 2.1 is Pinar's, although, of course, there are other people working in biography and autobiography. Of the three general emphases noted in this chapter—in the head (present), in the classroom (future), and in the biography (past)—the historical is probably least evident in the literature and so the chart is reasonably representative. Pinar's term "currere" is defined in such a way that many other studies could be said to use the same definition. What is special about the notion of currere is that it emphasizes a person's experiential history both in and out of schools. From the point of view of curriculum the idea is that the curriculum a person has experienced is found in that person's overall past record of experiences in private life as well as in professional life.

Notice also that the term "currere," in common with Berk's notion of "biographic narrative," points to processes of experience, in this case processes in the past; in Berk's case processes are in the future as actions unfold. The study of biography and autobiography has consequences for what is in the mind and for what is in the future. But in Pinar's notion the "data" are memory recollections unlike, for example, Berk's, which are records of ongoing action or, for those who study the mind, thoughts the teacher has about certain matters.

Just as we suggested that you be a cautious consumer of studies of the mind, we also suggest caution with respect to interpreting biographical and autobiographical studies of the past. The idea of narrative (Chapter 3) and of the curriculum in this book is one that emphasizes past, present, and future. Studies of the past alone may or may not tell us something of our current state of mind and of the future. The past is brought forward in many different ways depending on the circumstances in which we find ourselves. If the circumstance is an autobiographical inquiry session, that is, in which we are studying our past, then different aspects of our experiential history may be brought forward than if we are reflecting on our past to account for a particular teaching situation. If the studies do not investigate the future through inquiry into classrooms, then the implications of an autobiographical or biographical study for a future course of action can be said to be speculative at most. Our caution applies not only to reading the research but also to reflecting on your own history. Chapter 3 puts the ideas of the past, present, and future together with the notions of narrative and personal practical knowledge.

OBJECTIVITY AND SUBJECTIVITY:
VALUES, AESTHETICS, AND EMOTION

Traditionally we are taught to think of researchers and what they claim to know from their studies as being "objective." Studies of the personal that focus on what is in the mind tend to have this characteristic. That is, they tend not to deal with the subjective states of mind of teachers. It is true that these studies might obtain information on values held by teachers, but this tends to be done in an objective way. The research might say, for example, that teachers hold certain values about children (see Halkes & Deijkers, 1984). These values may be listed in summary form, the teachers classified according to the values held, and the teaching profession characterized as having a certain structure of values toward children.

But studies that focus on the future and the present, or the past, present, and future together may concern themselves with values as states of mind of specific teachers studied. Four studies are particularly informative in this respect (Janesick, Lampert, Elbaz, & Bussis/Chittenden/Amarel). These studies admit as evidence in their research "affective" states of mind of the teachers in the research. Elbaz's teacher, Sarah, for example, describes how she was unhappy in certain teaching situations. Elbaz tells how Sarah created other teaching situations in which she felt better about herself as a teacher. This information becomes part of Elbaz's notion of "practical knowledge." That is, Sarah's knowledge is not knowledge *of* value but *is* value. She does not say she holds certain values but that her knowledge of classrooms is, in part, a valuing.

This "subjective" idea of knowledge is quite foreign to the way most of us have been taught to think of knowledge. This notion of knowledge and knowing also characterizes Lampert's work. Janesick's "teacher group perspective" is laden with value. This use of value not only is cognitive and objective—as it would be if one were to study the teacher and the teacher were to assert (or the researcher were to assert on the teacher's behalf) that one of his or her values was a group perspective—but Janesick claims that the teacher holds a structure of, and belief in, group action and also a feeling of a certain intensity, altered by circumstance, of the worth of particular group teaching situations.

According to a narrative approach to curriculum, the notion of knowledge means something that not only has the temporal dimensions described above but also has these moral, emotional, and aesthetic dimensions as well. Chapter 3, which deals with narrative, will make this idea much clearer. It is central to the idea of curriculum advanced in this book.

SUMMARY AND A PEEK AT NARRATIVE

What have we learned so far about the personal? First of all, this is an active area of research. Perhaps the chapter will encourage you to dig into this fascinating literature. You will want to read far beyond the references listed in our summary tables.

We have also learned that it is possible to think of studies of the personal in terms of the concept of curriculum. That is, some studies conceptualize the personal as located primarily in a person's past, some place it primarily in the present, and some locate it primarily in the future. An interesting thing comes to light about the research in this respect: None of the researchers would say that the personal was in one of these places only. But while they would never say this, their research proceeds as if it were the case. People working in the mind collect data only on the present, although they would surely acknowledge the past and the future. The same is true for people working in the past and in the future. Thus, as is often the case when teachers read research studies, your ideas and concerns are broader and more comprehensive than are the researchers'. You need a more complex notion before the research ideas can be of use to you. The idea of curriculum in this book is one such idea, as are the notions of narrative and personal practical knowledge discussed in Chapter 3. You cannot read the research at face value; you need to read it from your curricular point of view. Chapters 8 and 9 are designed to help you think about the problem of reading research studies from a teacher's point of view.

RECOMMENDED READINGS

To begin with, you might read all of the articles suggested in this chapter. Perhaps one of the best places to start locating research literature on this topic is the 1986 *Handbook of Research on Teaching*. Although his book is not on curriculum, you will find Sullivan's *A Critical Psychology: Interpretation of the Personal World* interesting reading because he shows how psychologists are beginning to develop a notion of the personal in their research. This may seem surprising to you, since you may have thought that that is exactly what psychologists do. But Sullivan points out that psychology has actually suppressed the personal in its history.

3

Narrative:
Your Personal Curriculum
as a Metaphor
for Curriculum and Teaching

We asked "what is the personal?" in Chapter 2 and gave a fragmented answer. We said that, in general, the personal is something in the past, something in the present, something in the future. But as teachers, we know that the answer of Chapter 2 is only a partial answer. All of us who teach know that matters of lasting importance are somehow or other found in the whole. We need to know the parts, but it is in the whole that we find most meaning. The curricular whole, which serves as the intellectual context for this book, is a situation with a past, present, and future. And it is the person in the situation that holds our attention.

When we think of life as a whole, we tend to think narratively. We tell stories about ourselves that are historical, explanatory, and foretelling of the future. "Man," says the moral philosopher McIntyre (1981), is "essentially a story-telling animal." Stories, of course, are neither seen nor told when one part of life is focussed on in isolation from other parts. When this happens, we analyze and learn about the parts. But the unities, continuities, images, and rhythms in the whole are not seen. These ideas are dealt with in later chapters of this book. For now, we only want to stress that for the person in a curriculum situation, "narrative" is an idea that permits us to think of the whole. A narrative is a kind of life story, larger and more sweeping than the short stories that compose it (see Chapter 5 for a discussion of storytelling).

Narrative is the study of how humans make meaning of experience by endlessly telling and retelling stories about themselves that both refigure the past and create purpose in the future. Thus, to study narrative in the manner described in Chapter 2 in trying to understand the personal, one needs to ask questions not only about the past, or the present, or the future, but about all three. For any one teacher, therefore, clues to the personal are obtained from one's history, from how one thinks and feels, and from how one acts. These clues may be obtained in a variety of ways, both personally and in research using tools described in Chapters 4 and 5. One's educational history may, for example, be brought forward for inspection by interview and self-reflection; the same is true for one's present thinking style and concepts. How a teacher lives out the future may be inspected by observation and participant observation of classroom work.

Constructing a narrative account of oneself, or of someone else, is difficult, rewarding work. It is difficult because so many aspects of life need consideration and because people are so complex that they all have many life stories, not only one. It is rewarding because it is curricular and educational. It is a way of making educational meaning of our lives as we continue with the daily grind.

PERSONAL PRACTICAL KNOWLEDGE

We use the term "personal practical knowledge" to emphasize the teacher's knowing of a classroom. This term is closely tied to Lampert's notion of "personal knowledge" and Elbaz's notion of "practical knowledge" discussed in Chapter 2. Personal practical knowledge is a term designed to capture the idea of experience in a way that allows us to talk about teachers as knowledgeable and knowing persons. Beware! Do not take the word knowledge to mean something *only* objective, conceptual, or found in books. This is discussed further later in the chapter.

In answer to the question "where is personal practical knowledge?" narratologists such as ourselves say that it is in the person's past experience, in the person's present mind and body, and in the person's future plans and actions. Knowledge is not found only "in the mind." It is "in the body." And it is seen and found "in our practices." When we watch a classroom, we watch a set of minds and bodies at work.

When we ask "what is personal practical knowledge?" for any one person, the answer is that it is a particular way of reconstructing the past and the intentions for the future to deal with the exigencies of a present situation. This may be a bit of a mouthful for a reader at this stage. We will try to make more sense of this notion as we proceed through the book. It is important, though, for purposes of the book for readers to understand that a narrative, curricular understanding of the person is an understanding that is flexible and fluid, and that therefore recognizes that people say and do different things in different circumstances and, conversely, that different circumstances bring forward different aspects of their experience to bear on the situation. According to this view, a person's personal practical knowledge depends in important measure on the situation. In many ways we are different people, and may be said to know different things, when we talk to a child than when we talk to the principal, and again when we engage in recreation, and yet again when we act as parent, friend, or lover. A narrative understanding of who we are and what we know, therefore, is a study of our whole life, but it does not presume a kind of syrupy "Hollywood" unity. It acknowledges the tensions and differences within each of us. We are, in important ways, what the situation "pulls out" of us.

Objectivity and Subjectivity

In Chapter 2 some studies were discussed that began to nibble away at the idea that what a researcher can know must be said to be objective. The ideas of narrative and of personal practical knowledge take this a step further. Beginning with the narrative idea that we understand our lives by telling stories about them, we must admit to the rich affective quality of the experiences on which the stories are based and of the stories themselves. After all, what story is ever "objective" in the way that we have been taught to think of scientific knowledge?

If it is true that we know ourselves through our stories, then it is true that our knowledge of ourselves, which we have termed "personal practical knowledge," is an affective knowledge. All of our experiences take place with our total being. It is virtually impossible to imagine having an experience that does not carry with it emotional, moral, and aesthetic content. Experiences are felt. Experiences are valued. And experiences are appreciated. We are not saying that all experiences are positive in these respects. All manner of possibilities exist, including conflicts in which we may recognize beauty in something that we believe is morally wrong, in which our emotional content is low in a situation that we judge to be right, and so forth. The point we are making is that our experiences, and therefore our personal practical knowledge that makes up our narratives, are never devoid of these affective matters. To know something is to feel something. To know something is to value something. To know something is to respond aesthetically.

While this notion might seem somewhat at odds with the ideas of knowledge with which we grew up, it is not at odds with what our common sense tells us about experience and about life. It is a notion that makes a good deal of sense given the concept of curriculum developed in Chapter 1 and the idea of the personal used in this book. One almost never learns and/ or experiences anything "objectively," as one might say a computer does, but instead one always learns with the body. And so, when we say that we know something that is located in the past, present, and future, we are also saying something that is laden with the human qualities of emotionality, value, and aesthetics. These are some of the things that are meant when we ask, as we did in Chapter 2, "what does it mean to be personal?"

Schooling and Education

The idea of narrative as a story of life as a whole, combined with the notion of curriculum advanced in Chapter 1, means that we need to broaden our idea of education beyond that of schooling. Education, in this view, is a narrative of experience that grows and strengthens a person's capabilities to cope with life. It is true that some such experiences occur in school, but it is probably also true that many of the most important educational experiences in our narratives occur outside of school, for instance, in family relationships, births, deaths, and marriage. These, and many other matters, often make up the core of our narratives. These are the experiences that we say make most difference to us in life. Such experiences are educational.

We do not wish to suggest that the school should take on all of life's challenges. Even now many complain that the school is asked to take on tasks that are best reserved for the home, the church, and the community. What we do say, however, is that in understanding ourselves and our students educationally, we need an understanding of people with a narrative of life experience, of which the school is only a part. Life's narratives are the context for making meaning of school situations. It is no more possible to understand a child as *only* a student than it is to understand each of ourselves as *only* a teacher. We are that, but we are many other things as well. Indeed, the kind of teacher that we are reflects the kind of life that we lead. The same may be said of our students.

FOOLING AROUND:
AN ILLUSTRATIVE SCHOOL STORY

Chapter 5 describes storytelling as a way to help us reflect on the larger stories, the narratives, of our lives. The following is a story taken from our research in Bay Street School, an inner-city, multi-ethnic school where we have been participant observers for five years. While short stories such as these cannot capture the full range of a narrative, you will see in this story the drama of the affective side of experience. You will also see the force of the distinction between schooling and education. And we hope you will use your imagination, perhaps by projecting 20 years into the future of the students described, and consider how those students might tell this story as part of their own narrative in years to come. The story unfolds as a set of participant observation field notes recorded by Rita O'Brien (see Chapter 5 for a discussion of participant observation).

When we arrived at the school for a meeting we noticed that there was an ambulance and police car outside. On the way in we met Donal McCann and he told us that one of the students had gone through the glass partition in the door and had been quite badly hurt and had been taken to the hospital.

When we went in the side door there was quite a lot of blood. It was all over the walls and on the floor and doors. One of the care-takers was coming down the stairs with a mop, cleaning as he went. It looked as if somebody had gone along with a spray can and sprayed it. It seemed to be everywhere. Phil Bingham [the principal] was there and he looked really shaken. He told us that two of the kids had been fooling around during lunch hour and that a girl by the name of Anna had pushed a boy student by the name of Jose and he had gone through a glass partition. He had cut an artery in his arm and he had run from the third floor down to the office with the blood spurting out all over the place. We asked Phil if they had any word on how he was and he said no, that he had just been taken a short time ago by ambulance to the hospital. Phil said that there had been a student teacher in the office when Jose had come in and that she had taken care of the situation. When Phil came along he put his belt around the boy's arm so as to stop the blood. Phil said that Mrs. Jones [of the of-fice staff] had also been marvellous and that she had had to go home because she was just about covered in blood. Phil said that he didn't know how things would be this afternoon so he couldn't say definitely if there was going to be a meeting. We walked with him into the staff room and Anna, the girl who had pushed Jose through the glass, was there and was quite hysterical. Kathy Brown [a teacher] and Bev [a teacher aide] were trying to calm her down. Kathy had obviously been crying and her eyes were very red. Bev also looked very shaken and was doing her best to try and calm the girl down. Anna had her head in her hands and was just hysterical.

We made our way up to Room #34 and Dick and Dennis (teachers) were there. An announcement then came over the loudspeaker to say that Phys. Ed. was cancelled for the seventh and eighth grades this af-ternoon. Dick said that they were going to show a film to the class. The class all seemed very subdued as everyone by now had heard what had happened. Dick told the class that if there is an accident of any sort people should try and not panic. He said that's what happened with Jose, that he ran from the third floor down to the office and in the course of that time he lost three or four pints of blood. He said that that was the worst thing that he could have done. Dick told us later that they were having difficulty in contacting the boy's father and they needed his signature because they wanted to operate on the arm. They thought that there might still be some glass in there. He said Jose did have an 18-year-old brother but they hoped to be able to get in touch with the father fairly soon.

A short time after that there was an announcement over the loudspeaker to say that the whole senior school was to meet in the gym at 3:00 PM.

We assembled in the gym at 3:00 PM. Phil started by saying that they had received word that Jose would be okay. He complimented a lot of people on their quick action. He said that particularly the Grade 7 student teacher, had acted superbly. He said they owed her a lot for her quick action. Phil then talked about trust and how it is something that is built up. He said that he would trust every one of them as if nothing had happened unless they gave him cause not to trust them. He said that they should be proud of their community. He said that the school at the moment is their community and that they have a lot to be thankful for. He said that they have a good school and that they have good teachers. He then referred to the Bay Street code of behavior. He went down through each point separately. He then listed the points and enlarged on each on how they could adhere to them. He skipped over the first few, which were to do with school attendance and preparation of work for class. He went down to the point that says enter and leave the building by the doors suggested in order to reduce traffic and improve safety, as well as avoiding unnecessary interruption of other programs. He said that this isn't being done. He looked around the room and told the students that each of them knew who wasn't obeying this particular rule. He said that there are certain students that come into the school before class starts in the morning and before class starts in the afternoon and they're not supposed to be in there. He said that that was how this accident occurred. He made the point of saying that the students responsible for breaking this rule knew what he was talking about. He said that he sees the same students in the school when they're not supposed to be here. He also talked about respecting other people's space in the halls, stairs, classrooms, and playgrounds. While going through these points he returned continually to the theme of being proud of the community that they are part of. By this he was referring to the school. He also emphasized a few times the point about respecting each other. He then referred to an award that is given out at graduation each year to the top male and female students. He looked around the hall and said that everybody sitting here today was capable of obtaining that award. He said "we'll wipe the slate clean and start from today." He indicated that it was something to work towards and that he hoped that the students would respect each other and be responsible for their actions.

The overall theme of his discussion was to be proud of themselves, to respect themselves and others and the school property. And also to think before doing something and if it's not going to help not to do it. He then talked about the fact that the enrollment is on the decrease and they could do with some additional students. He told the students that if they know of anybody who is changing schools or is just start- ing school to recommend Bay Street. He said that it's a school to be proud of and that anyone who attends it should be very proud.

Each of the classes then went out in single file. (*Notes to file, April 11, 1985*)

We have chosen this story for this book because it is so dramatic. We want to highlight our points with a real-life story. No one could say that this story lacked emotion, especially for Jose and Anna but also for almost everyone in the school and for many of those whose lives touched the lives of participating teachers, students, and others in the school. No one could say the story lacked morality. Phil's lecture was a lecture in school ethics. No one could say the story lacked aesthetics as people reacted with horror to the blood. What is told in the extreme in this story is what happens in all of the experiences that make up the narratives of our lives.

No one could say that this incident was not educational for the people involved. Teachers will remember the incident; it will constantly return as they see threatening situations of a similar kind. The students directly involved will never forget the event, and it is likely that many years from now young students, even students in the primary school who were detoured through the halls away from the principal's office that afternoon, will recall that something of importance happened. "Fooling around" will never again be the same for any of these students and their teachers.

We may say, therefore, that these participants' personal practical knowledge of relationships to others, particularly physical relationships, will be marked by intersubjective affect.

And because the incident was so startling, it is clear that this story was doubtlessly told in many homes throughout the community that evening. Parents and friends would have talked about it and would have learned from it. It is not only Jose's father and family for whom we might say the experience was educational beyond schooling. More likely this experience touched the lives of adults, peers, and other teachers outside the school. And certainly we might expect that the involved students and teachers would carry the lessons learned into their lives as a whole.

In Chapter 2, we talked about getting inside the head, getting inside the future, and getting inside the past. Our story gives some idea of what it means to get inside the curriculum. It is getting inside the head (mind and body), the future, and the past. But it is doing so all at once and as a whole. Our narratives, and our knowing of classrooms, encompass this temporal dimension, and they do so with the passions that make us human. Our personal practical knowledge in narrative is intersubjective. It always occurs with substance, as in the story above, and so there is an element of objectivity. But it never occurs without the body, and so there is an element of subjectivity. In the end, we say that our narratives and our knowledge are intersubjective.

YOUR PERSONAL CURRICULUM AS A METAPHOR
FOR CURRICULUM AND TEACHING

Let us now return to the theme of this chapter. We have explained the idea of narrative and we have shown why it is important for an individual to think narratively. It is important to think of one's own curriculum in narrative terms. But what does this have to do with being a teacher? Isn't it true that what has been said may be said for all of us?

The answer, of course, is "yes." But as teachers, the idea has a double meaning for us. When we say that understanding our own narrative is a metaphor for understanding the curriculum of our students, we are saying that if you understand what makes up the curriculum of the person most important to you, namely, yourself, you will better understand the difficulties, whys, and wherefores of the curriculum of your students. There is no better way to study curriculum than to study ourselves. When we have a grasp of the difficulties, for example, of figuring out something simple such as how we think and feel as a component of the personal, we will understand the really serious difficulties of trying to figure out how someone else, our students, think and feel. After all, we are not privy to our students' overall lives, or to their history, or even to their intentional future. Once we recognize that understanding our students is an important task, we also recognize that no amount of test-giving will tell us the important things. This realization will come about as you ask yourself very hard narrative questions. Your curriculum is a metaphor for understanding your students' curriculum.

RECOMMENDED READINGS

We have been working on narrative and personal practical knowledge for some time and so think you might start with one or two of our own writings. Clandinin's book, *Classroom Practice: Teacher Images in Action*, tells the narrative of one teacher, Stephanie. If you are interested in narrative as a research tool, you might find our article, "On Narrative Method, Personal Philosophy, and Narrative Unities in the Story of Teaching," informative. An excellent but very theoretical book is Mitchell's *On Narrative*. While its contributors are not education authors, you will find the idea of narrative as discussed in theology, literature, psychotherapy, history, and so forth well worth your time. An article that we like very much is the theologian Crites's "The Narrative Quality of Experience." Bruner's book, *Actual Minds, Possible Worlds*, touches on this notion in its opening chapters. An outstanding book is McIntyre's *After Virtue*, in which he points out that the narrative unities in our lives ought to be the basis of ethical theory and not, as he says is common in ethics, abstract treatment of proper relations among people. For the idea of knowledge as intersubjective, readers will find Polanyi's *Personal Knowledge* and Buber's *The Knowledge of Man* useful reading.

4

Tools for Reflection: Working by Yourself

The process of coming to know ourselves as practicing teachers is difficult. So much of our personal practical knowledge is tacit, unnamed, and, because it is embodied in our practice, difficult for us to make explicit. Furthermore, teaching provides little opportunity for reflection. "Doing things" is such a significant part of our daily pressures that we have little occasion to sit back and ask ourselves "what am I doing?" We move forward but we find it hard to think back. We do. But do we reflect?

In our work with teachers over the past 10 years, we have developed some tools that you may find useful in "thinking back" and coming to understand yourself. We will describe each method and give some examples of teachers engaged in reflection on their personal practical knowledge using the method. Before we turn to that task in this chapter and the next, we want to connect these reflective tools to the idea of curriculum development presented in preceding chapters.

THE IDEA OF CURRICULUM
AND TOOLS FOR REFLECTION

As you read Chapters 4 and 5, you may wonder how the various tools for reflection relate to the idea of curriculum presented in this book. You may also wonder how the various tools differ from one another. It may be clear enough how they differ procedurally, but the important question to settle is "what different kinds of things can we learn about ourselves from the various tools?"

Figure 4.1 is designed to help sort this out. This figure is an adaptation of Figure 1.1 and so allows us to sort the various tools according to our idea of curriculum.

As you think this through, you must realize that the organization is "for the most part." For instance, autobiography and biography, while empha-

Figure 4.1: Organizing the Reflective Tools*

		Narrative		

Narrative

← Storytelling →   ← Biographic narrative →

Autobiography Biography	Interviewing Picturing	Letter Writing Journals Participant Observation

(Past)   (Present)   (Future)

Person

---

*Document analysis is useful in conjunction with any of the tools.

sizing a reconstruction of a person's past, are also telling of the person in the here and now and in the future. Conversely, letter writing, journals, and participant-observation are primarily records of events as we move into the future. But they also tell of the person in the here and now and in the past. So, as you think about these tools in terms of the idea of curriculum, do not be too rigid in your classification.

Notice that several of the methods are specifically designed to overlap two or three parts of the general scheme. Storytelling is the process of reconstructing events in the past and is designed to be useful in understanding ourselves in the present. Biographic narrative is a way of understanding a person through a record of biographic observations as time passes. Narrative is designed to be thought of as an overall life study. As such it encompasses a person's past, his or her current state of mind, and his or her personal knowledge, which shapes teaching work in the future. All of the various tools, therefore, contribute to an overall understanding of one's narrative.

The methods we present in this chapter are ones you can use when engaging in reflection alone. We discuss journal keeping, biography, picturing, and document analysis as methods appropriate to aiding your reflection when you do not have another teacher with whom to work. In Chapter 5, we discuss other methods, which you can use when you are able to work with someone else, either in your school or in a course.

JOURNAL KEEPING

One of the tools we have found useful is to keep an ongoing journal account of our daily actions and our thoughts about those actions. The journals are ongoing records of practices and reflections on those practices. They certainly do not have to be kept for years or even for a year, but they do need to be kept fairly consistently for a block of time. Before we discuss journal keeping further, it may help to see a sample of a journal. Here is part of a journal kept by Stewart, a beginning kindergarten teacher.

Journal Entry, October 7, 1985

Purple day today—so I am purple from finger to elbow from writing their stories on their paintings! That can be the most rewarding, the most boring, the most exciting, and the scariest thing with kids. I think they are so innocent (so naive, maybe) that they blurt out whatever they are thinking—the ones with a natural creativity are right with you when you write the story—they know their words complement their picture and that the combination makes something "real" in their lives and their parents' lives—they won't let you miss a part of the picture and they want to take the picture home NOW!
     Others are more wrapped up in the feel of the thing, if that's the right image—they dabble with the paint or splash it on or create the same picture four days in a row (and tell me the same story four days in a row!!). It's not as if they are painting something; it's more as if they are experimenting with something—really just "doing" something they like to do. I like to take a lot of time with them because although I don't know kids' art at all I think it's probably a stage they have to go through before they can make pictures that also tell a story.

     This is part of a journal entry that Stewart made on a day early in his teaching career. He is noting classroom activities, his behavior, his observations of specific students and groups of children, and recording the ongoing work. He is also noting what sense he is making of his practice: "It's not as if they are painting something; it's more as if they are experimenting with something." Later on in the entry he speculates on how what he is observing might fit with theory. "I think it's probably a stage they have to go through before they can make pictures that also tell a story."
     This ongoing reflection-on-action on a daily basis begins to provide insight into personal knowledge when you reread entries over several days and weeks. What connecting threads are apparent over time? Are there events or ideas that recur?
     For example, the following are some thoughts that Phyllis had after an examination of a journal she kept on her teaching for several weeks. She notes as one theme:

The element of "time" was to be a recurring theme in my data: time to plan, time to reflect, time to experiment and try out answers without putting pressure on oneself and others. . . . Another connection between ineffective verbalizing and time pressure came one day when this same boy blurted out in frustration as he was attempting to explain something: "I know what it is, but I just can't say it." That expression of exasperation sometimes comes to me as a student in my university courses and my diary entry for February 10 reads: "The thoughts jumble up in your head in the great effort to answer correctly, convincingly, and clearly. Why not relax about it." Why not indeed! How often I had been in the same situation in my teaching where intuitively I knew something, but was not able to verbalize it because either I didn't have the correct words with which to express the pedagogical point I was trying to make, or was feeling the pressure of time in a staff meeting where there were still many items left on the agenda and colleagues were looking at their watches. These insights into how I as a teacher and learner had feelings similar to Matthew made me better empathize with him. Remembering that my journal entry to the first week referred to him as having a "perpetual look of boredom" and that I would really "have to work hard at getting to like him," I now realize the value of having consciously looked at what I was doing, for it helped me in relating to him.

Questions and Suggestions

When teachers and students first begin to keep journals, they have a number of questions, and we have given some thought to ways in which journal keeping can be most useful in reflecting on teaching. There are not hard and fast rules, but there are some general guidelines that we think are useful.

What should I use to keep the journal in? First of all, get a book or notebook. You want to have a book that is bound in some way rather than one with loose pages.

What should I write? Write as much as you can in the journal. Be descriptive of action, children, events, and reactions that you have both while teaching and after you are finished teaching. Record the feelings you have about your practices and the various events that happen. Be alert to past experiences that come to mind as you react emotionally and morally. If you decide to keep a journal while you are a student, focus your journal on the experience of being a student.

How often should I write? Write regularly. Make an entry every few days or more frequently if you have time or if something particular occurs to you. To be useful to you as a reflective tool, the journal needs to be an ongoing record of thought.

Do I go back and reread it? As you can see from Phyllis's analysis of her journal, it is helpful to reread your journal entries from time to time and try to make sense of the kinds of things that are important to you. We will have much more to say about this in Chapter 6, Understanding Your Personal Practical Knowledge. Briefly, however, we can suggest some preliminary actions to take as you read over several weeks of journal entries. As you read the entries, look for things that suggest ideas and patterns to you. Make notes in the margins about those ideas. In research we call these notes "theoretical memos," but they are really just thoughts that you have about the text. Read carefully to see if you can pick up any threads or themes, things that seem to recur. Perhaps it will be something such as "time," which seemed to be a useful theme for Phyllis, or "control" or "responsibility." Keep an open mind and try to see what patterns emerge. Keep comparing the ideas with what went before. As we begin to outline the other tools, you will want to examine emerging patterns from the document analysis, from the stories, and perhaps from the letters. We will have more to say about this when we discuss images, metaphors, rhythms, and personal philosophy in Chapter 6.

BIOGRAPHY

Another tool we have found useful in reflecting on our personal practical knowledge is biography and autobiography. These two methods need to be differentiated somewhat. Autobiography is the telling of our own history, while biography is someone else reconstructing an individual's past.

Our interest here is mostly in the reconstructing and telling of our own past, although we often find reading the biography of another person useful in helping us to understand ourselves differently. We find Lou Smith and Paul Kleine's life story work with the teachers from the Kensington School project (Smith et al., 1986) useful in helping teachers reflect on their own experience.

But our main focus here is to outline a biographic method for trying, alone or with a colleague, to understand our own autobiographies. Let us look first at a fragment from an autobiography written by Laura, a teacher in one of our classes.

After high school (in 1968/69), I went to Toronto Teacher's College. I
then studied at Trent University (1970/73), as a full-time student. It
was a relaxed experience. . . . I treasured the protected environment
and individualized attention of the seminar system.

My first teaching position was at the Huronia Regional Center, in
the school. I worked there for half a year. I was doing some innovative teaching in the industrial arts area and they did not want me to
go, but I was actually glad to move on and try some regular classroom
teaching.

The situation was, in fact, quite stressful. I witnessed a 13-year-old
boy, who wore diapers, put his fist through a window in anger. I had
a 14-year-old girl throw a hammer across the room at me. She was
terribly disturbed because she couldn't get my attention in class. I
didn't see the hammer coming; someone yelled just in time for me to
duck.

I was rehired and completed the year teaching French and music,
with Grade 5–6 homeroom. I then left teaching for a while. I felt disil-
lusioned; I was very idealistic. It seemed to me that teachers did not
really care. York County was on strike at the time. Actually, my class
had been a difficult group to handle; there were some drugs floating
around and it was a bit scary. The Superintendent sat in on one of my
classes, and afterwards, asked me to please just take a leave of ab-
sence. I had done a super job but, looking back, I think I feared that I
could never have kept it up with those kids.

I got a job in term deposits in a bank in Toronto; I stayed for a
year. It was a comfortable position in the T.D. Center and I was considered management material. It was flattering and there was challenge
in learning something about business, but I came to realize that I need
to have a job that has more substance in a long-term sort of way . . .
not just the status (which had appeal initially) but an inherent worth. I
have a talent for teaching and I missed the children. I suppose, although I was "safer" in the commercial milieu, I was ready to take on
more.

Later in the autobiography we learn that she goes back to teaching. In
the next fragment she tells about her childhood experience.

A major educational influence in my life was the fact that I was raised
in the country. The peaceful nature of the pastoral environment was
like a magnet; I took solace in long walks by the river and to the hill-
top overlooking the village. It was a slow-paced life. A lot of things
were taken for granted. It was commonplace to "accept" in that local-

ity. It was extremely difficult for me to see beyond, to break out. I was very shy, quiet, and passive. . . .

I went to teachers' college right after high school because my Dad said that was a good thing for a girl to do (then after she raised her family she could always go back to work). All my friends were going to University. We didn't have much money. When I did decide to go to Trent the following year (because I had such a longing to do so), my father still didn't approve but I said well, soon all teachers were going to need a degree. I looked after the financing myself.

My family background has been the most significant influence on my education. I am the eldest of eight kids and was always a caretaker.

In this we can see a particular construction of Laura's experience. She highlights the place of education in her life experience. It is a particular reconstruction of her narrative, and there could be other reconstructions. We can see, however, how this particular autobiographic reconstruction is telling of her in the here and now and in the future as she continues to teach.

Because most of us have not tried any biographic retelling of our lives, we feel it is a most helpful starting point to exploring our personal practical knowledge. We often begin our classes with having participants share brief autobiographic statements. It is helpful to follow up this brief oral presentation with longer written versions. We also ask our graduate students to begin their theses and dissertations with their own autobiographies. Following are some of the questions we are frequently asked.

Questions and Suggestions

How long should my autobiography be? If you had enough time, you could write a book of your autobiography. However, given the time and skill constraints most of us have, we advise that you write between five and ten pages. Less than that is not enough to really capture the details of your life.

Where do I write my autobiography? Once again we suggest you put it in a bound book of some sort. Include it in a section of your journal or letter writing book, for example. We do suggest, however that you do at least one rough draft. Do the autobiography once in rough draft, leave it for a couple of days, reread it, and perhaps add details or events. At that point you can make your entry into the bound book.

What do I do with it when I am finished writing it? As you reread your autobiography, look for things that suggest patterns or themes. Earlier we discussed making notes called theoretical memos on those points that become apparent to you. In Chapter 6 we will discuss further analysis you may wish to undertake.

PICTURING

Another reflective tool described briefly in Chapter 1 is picturing. There we wrote about picturing the concept of curriculum. As you read in Chapter 1 (and perhaps tried out), the pictures we create in our minds are part of us and have emotional dimensions.

We have adapted the process of picturing from work ongoing in psychology, where picturing is used as a tool in counselling and for helping individuals understand their personal constructs.

David Hunt (1976, 1987) uses a similar technique in his work with teachers in helping them to become their own best theorists. He begins by asking participants to close their eyes and feel comfortable. He then moves them through a sequence of instructions directing them to create mental pictures of themselves in various spaces and participating in various events, such as teaching or talking with children or colleagues. He asks them to allow their senses to make the pictures "come alive" and to experience the feelings they have associated with the pictures.

We have found this process of picturing to be useful in helping teachers understand the meaning they hold of various concepts. We have, for example, worked with teachers and others using this technique to help them to begin to reflect on the meaning they attach to concepts as diverse as curriculum, work, collaborative research, and problem children. This tool can be used at any time during the process of reflecting on your personal practical knowledge. At several points in the book we may ask you to stop and picture a particular concept or term to which you are being introduced.

Questions and Suggestions

The following are some common questions with our responses.

When do I use picturing as a reflective tool? We have found the process of picturing to be helpful when you begin to reflect on particular terms or concepts. It is often a very useful starting point when you are trying to get in touch with what particular terms or ideas bring to your mind. It is also useful in ongoing reflection when you want clarification of your ideas and you are unable to find appropriate words to express your personal understanding.

How do I engage in the process of picturing? We have found David Hunt's process, outlined above, to be particularly effective. It is important to relax and allow a picture of your understanding to emerge. Allow your emotions to come with the picture.

Do I keep a record of the pictures? We feel it is important to keep a record of the picture that comes to mind when you engage in the picturing process. Your journal notebook is a good place to record the concept or idea you pictured, with brief notes on what came to mind. Try to record the time you engaged in picturing, the context, and some of the details of the picture. Also capture the emotions that went with the picture. If the picture changes or if the emotion changes as you engage in picturing, note these changes as well.

DOCUMENT ANALYSIS

We have only recently begun to explore using our school and classroom documents such as school newsletters, classroom plan books, course outlines, and timetables as useful tools for reflection. Rob Walker in *Doing Research: A Handbook for Teachers* (1985) notes the possible use of such documents as research data in a section on "intraviews." We see the possibility of using the analysis of such documents as ways to reflect on our personal practical knowledge. The power of using these documents for reflection comes from their use in conjunction with other reflective tools, such as letters, journals, or story writing. Let us look briefly at one use of such materials for reflection.

In the following analysis, Lori used a course outline from an earlier year to reflect on her practice and to plan her new course. The process Lori followed was an analysis of the old outline with comments and theoretical memos about what worked and what did not work, what changed over the course of the year, and what she was uncertain about, as well as notes on the books and resources used. She then thought through her new theoretical understandings, which she had been recording in a journal, and from this organized a new course outline. The following is a brief summary statement of her new understandings.

> Many of the areas that I felt were important still remain so. The big difference is that now I have a framework that I can use when making decisions about curriculum. Before, when I lacked the background, I would do activities that were extremely successful, but would not know why they worked so well. Now I can look back and see more clearly why certain areas were weak and why others were so much better.

The most important aspect to me now is that students see language arts as an integrated whole and begin to realize the importance of communicating effectively. Along with this goes the philosophy that reading and writing are active processes of meaning making and that the skills that aid in comprehension can be taught. These skills take a great deal of time to acquire and must be taught as an ongoing process.

Writing will continue to be a main priority in my class for I feel that through writing, students internalize concepts. The writing conference will be an important vehicle to get students to focus on content so that their voices can come through.

I want students to have more responsibility in their learning by teaching them strategies to aid in comprehension and critical thinking. This can only be accomplished by relinquishing my control. I must create the nonthreatening environment that will allow students to question me, but at the same time give guidelines and structure until students are ready for more independence. This is not an easy task, but I feel my course outline now gives direction to my teaching. Because so much thought has gone into my course outline, and it reflects my personal beliefs about teaching, ones I had not thought about or voiced before, I am excited about what the next year holds for me.

We have not used this approach extensively, although from our brief experience with it we sense its potential as an aid to reflection. There are, we imagine, many questions participants will ask. Here are three of them.

Questions and Suggestions

What documents can I use? We do not know what kind of documents you have as records of your teaching. We think that long-range plans, course outlines, and books of short-range plans such as the daily plan book, unit or center plans, or monthly plans would all be useful. You may also have regular newsletters that go home from your class to parents, and these would also be useful documents for analysis.

What other reflective tools would fit well with document analysis? We think many of the other tools would work well with document analysis. Participant observation combined with document analysis would be very powerful. We could also imagine that journals, such as Lori's reflection on her document analysis, or letter writing with biography and document analysis would also be very effective. See Figure 4.1 and try to imagine ways in which you could use a variety of data sources to help create a narrative account.

How do I use the documents? Lori's process, described above, seems to be a particularly powerful one. We will later describe in more detail a process to help you come to understand your personal practical knowledge.

RECOMMENDED READINGS

We have provided a brief overview in this chapter of the methods you can use to aid your reflections on your personal practical knowledge. The methods described in this chapter can be used in situations in which you are engaged in reflection without the involvement of other colleagues.

Most of the tools described in this chapter are adapted from various research and counseling methodologies. You may wish to read more about these tools as they are used in research settings.

There are two excellent handbooks that encourage teachers to become classroom researchers. One, *A Teacher's Guide to Classroom Research*, is by David Hopkins, and the other is *Doing Research: A Handbook for Teachers* by Rob Walker. These both provide an overview of the use of some of the tools we have described for research purposes.

For further reading on journal keeping, we refer readers to Ira Progoff's book, *At a Journal Workshop*, and to M. L. Holly's book, *Keeping a Personal-Professional Journal*. Sylvia Ashton-Warner's book, *Teacher*, is a fine example of a teacher's journal. You may find it useful to read as you begin to keep your journal.

There are beginning to be some good works out in the area of teacher biography, and we refer you to the work of Len Berk, "Education in Lives: Biographic Narrative in the Study of Educational Outcomes," published in *The Journal of Curriculum Theorizing*, and Richard Butt and Danielle Raymond's recent work, "Individual and Collective Interpretations of Teacher Biographies."

David Hunt's work entitled *Beginning with Ourselves* is good reading for a more intensive treatment of what we have called picturing.

There is little work in the area of document analysis that would be useful to you in your reflections other than to read the section of Rob Walker's book, noted above, dealing with this area.

5

Tools for Reflection: Working with Others

In Chapter 4 we outlined four methods for engaging in reflection when you are working alone. In this chapter we outline four methods—storytelling, letter writing, teacher interviews, and participant observation—that you can use when you are able to work with a colleague or group of colleagues. As you read keep Figure 4.1 in mind so that the idea of curriculum is kept alive.

STORYTELLING

A tool that we have found useful in reflecting on our own personal practical knowledge and in helping teachers reflect on theirs is storytelling. We ask teachers to write three stories of themselves as teachers, recording as much detail as they can. Who were the characters? What was the setting? When was it—early in your career, a few years ago, last year, or last week? The story, of course, always involves you as the teacher. This is a story and stories have plots. In many of the stories, however, the plot may not be immediately apparent to the teller, you the teacher.

Teachers we have worked with find this both an easy task and a difficult one, difficult because they are rarely asked to tell stories about themselves as teachers and easy because they have so many that immediately come to mind.

We will share three stories from three different teachers so you can see what we mean by stories.

JUSTICE DONE

My first year of teaching was in a fairly remote northern town. I was all of 20 years old and full of the weight and importance of what I saw as my role. Rules and regulations had played a large role in my own socialization both in the two-room school I attended for Grades 1 to 7 and in the one-room school where I took my eighth grade. In the latter, I had my older sister for a teacher and her expectations for me were very high. After all, I was the "teacher's sister" and what would people say if I were not a shining example of decorum and academic excellence.

So you see, I had come by my ideas of the "right and wrong" and "desirable and undesirable" quite honestly. I also wanted to be as wise, fair, and respected in my job as my sister had been in hers.

About the third month into the school year, I ran into a problem—a real dilemma for me. The rules against swearing carried the punishment of a strapping. One of my more mischievous and active boys had been caught out saying "the F-word" by the teacher on supervision.

I liked this boy, even though he was often naughty. His naughtiness was only the reflection of having come from a large family of boys where such actions were the norm. He and I were beginning to develop a bond through the extra reading we were doing together after school every day. He demonstrated a quickness of mind and a spirit that was fanciful.

However when the report of his infraction reached me, I took it personally. I felt that he had let me down. But part of me rationalized that, given his home environment, such language was the norm and that surely such punishment did not fit the crime.

A tearful boy stood in front of me as the accusing supervisor continued her tirade. "He was always fighting—picking on those younger" and on and on and on.

I knew it was my responsibility to see "justice done." The supervisor was a threat to me too. She was older, experienced, and in her own words "knew how to teach circles around" the novices straight out of Teachers College and "wet behind the ears." I felt the weight of her presence and knew I had to do this, but it was so distasteful to me. Failure to do it would have meant a visit to the principal who firmly believed in keeping such actions as cussing and fighting under control. "We must set the standards in this uncivilized northern mining town," he was often heard to remark.

I made my way to the desk, gaining more courage with each step I took away from Madame Morality. This courage rapidly failed as I reached for the dreaded, ugly piece of rubber and leather, and I felt the tears come. Not wanting to appear as weak as I felt, I squared my shoulders and bade the boy come to me. As we faced each other, matching tremble for tremble, tear for tear with an accompanying rising sense of frustration, I said the fateful words to him, "You know

what I have to do will hurt me more than it will hurt you." With his
inimical charm, in spite of the impending danger, he cried out, "Well,
what are ya doin' it for then!"

A very good question—one which has remained with me for 23
years and has served me well as a teacher, then as a mother, and now
as a teacher again.

Yes, "justice" was served, I guess, in that situation. I used the strap
once on each hand for the first and, thankfully, for the last time in my
life. From time to time in my life at work and home, I stop and ask
myself, "What are ya doin' it for?"

BUDDY AT LUNCH BOX

Shortly after joining the staff at my present junior high school, I decided that the students needed more exposure to the outside world. In
my second year there I took two classes of Grade 9 students (about 60
students) to Lunch Box Theatre to see "Carmilla," a female vampire
play. Despite the fear and trepidation among my accompanying colleagues, who were skeptical and feared that we would be embarrassed
by terrible displays of "east end behavior," all went well. As we were
leaving the theatre the worst loudmouth among my Grade 9 boys (and
the most negative language arts student) said, "Mrs. Smith, that was
great! Why didn't you tell me it would be like this?" I asked what he
meant because I thought I had prepared them well. "I thought it
would be like a play in the gym," he told me. Buddy had never seen
live theatre performed by professionals before.

ELFROS, SASKATCHEWAN GRADE 7/8

There were about 15 students in all. Some big farm kids were bussed
in and others came from the small town. Two in particular were my
concern, Dwayne and David. All they wanted was to be able to turn
16 and get a driver's licence.

We were doing a novel study on Jean Valjean, and their attention
and participation was excellent. They would often be reluctant to stop
the lesson and go to another subject. I remembered feeling very gratified that something at school was involving their interest. They enjoyed discussing the novel.

Ten years later these two visited me here in Calgary, one a mechanic
(David) and the other in construction (Dwayne) and both married.
Why was I so concerned about what would become of them?

These three stories, written by very different individuals, are just a sample of stories told by teachers about their teaching. We have not completed any analysis of these stories, for we feel the analysis needs to involve the teacher-author. However, we do feel these stories have a great deal to say to each teacher about how she thinks about, and acts within, her classroom.

After their stories are written, we ask the teacher-authors to share them with another teacher whom they trust. After they have shared their stories, we ask them to ask questions of their stories to gain some distance from the pieces. Some questions we suggest they pose are: What view of students do I have? Of subject matter? Of teaching? Of the teaching/learning relationship? Of the context in which education happens? Of course there are other questions that you may want to ask of your stories. These may be unique and personal to you, and all the more important in helping you think about your teaching and classrooms. We cannot suggest these questions. They must be your own. Some sample questions teachers have asked are: Have I changed in my teaching since I began teaching? What view of discipline do I have? What view of science (reading, social studies) do I have?

When you have had an opportunity to ask as many questions as you can of your pieces and have had a chance to respond to another teacher's questions, we ask you to look across your three stories to see if there are themes, patterns, and/or similar ideas expressed in them. As with journal writing, we will eventually try to understand the stories from the perspective of personal practical knowledge. We will say much more about that in Chapter 6.

Questions and Suggestions

The following are common questions teachers ask about story writing, along with our suggested answers to their questions.

What should I write my stories in? It would be possible to write your stories in another part of the book that you have designated for your journal writing. However, you may choose to keep the stories on loose-leaf pages. Each story should start on a different page. Each one becomes, to some extent, a separate document. We think this helps in the analytic process described above.

What stories should I tell? There are several matters to be considered here. The first concerns with whom you plan to share the stories. Do not write stories that you would be uncomfortable sharing with someone in the class. The writing and sharing of some stories may constitute too great a personal risk. Do write stories that are important to you. Think back over your teaching experience. Often, teachers with whom we have worked tell stories that happened in their first years of teaching. Try to write stories that seem to be "telling" of your teaching.

How many stories should I write? We ask teachers with whom we work to write at least three stories. Three seems to be a minimum number to examine for themes, threads, or patterns. You can, of course, choose to write more stories, but three seems to be a minimum.

Do I go back and reread them? As noted above, we encourage you to go back and read the stories, read them with a colleague, and then alone, and together ask questions of the stories. As noted in our discussion of journals, eventually we ask you to look at the stories in the light of an examination and telling of your personal practical knowledge, as described in more detail in Chapter 6.

LETTER WRITING: DIALOGUE BETWEEN PROFESSIONALS

Another tool that we have found to be valuable in aiding reflection is ongoing dialogue between two teachers. In our course settings, we see the dialogue as occurring between our students and ourselves. In settings outside the course, this dialogue can occur between you and another teacher.

In our research we began to develop this technique into teachers' personal practical knowledge. We have since adapted the research technique into a reflective tool useful both in our teaching and outside of our courses as a way for teachers to engage in reflective dialogue.

In the letters, we ask teachers to reflect on how the ongoing experiences in the course, in the classroom, and outside of the classroom help them to think differently about their practice. We ask you to be descriptive of action and events and reactions that you have. In this way letter writing is similar to journal writing except here you are engaged in a written dialogue with another practitioner. You have control of the dialogue. You choose the topic, decide whether to respond to questions and comments made by the other person, and refocus the discussion when you want. The entries can be as long or as short as you like, but you must remember that it is an ongoing dialogue, a written conversation.

We have taken an excerpt from a letter-writing exchange between one of us and a beginning teacher registered in a course.

The teacher entry: In the initial reading of Donald Holdaway I became very excited about his theories on developmental learning of reading and writing. I do feel, however, that he shouldn't try to justify his approach by citing learned scripture because at times his arguments don't hold together. I think he has a very valid point in saying that the other methods of teaching reading just don't seem to work. Not only do they not work for the students, often they do not work for the teacher. I for one am very uncomfortable with graphemes, phonemes, morphemes, etc., and feel they would make great characters in a video game. The gap between understanding the theories of linguistics and teaching Johnny to read and hoping above all that he will be lucky enough to develop the same love for literature that you have is too wide.

Holdaway makes a clear case for the natural development of reading through constant approximations of reading. I found the whole business of children approximating reading behaviour fascinating. The whole process suddenly seemed so normal, natural, and, dare I say, "easy."

The response: His analysis is fascinating. There is some interesting work going on in children's oral language development, and researchers Gordon Wells and David Olson are both working in the area. You might like to check some of that work as well.

The teacher entry: The next chapters that deal with the mechanics of the program were very easy and exciting to read. The only question I have here is "When do you begin? Is kindergarten too soon?" I have now observed several children in an ECS class that I volunteer in once a week exhibiting these emergent reading characteristics. Is it too soon to implement a program like this because as I was reading my mind was flooded with ideas of activities and drama and books to share with them using the model.

The response: Why would you be so hesitant to try this out with kindergarten children? I would like to explore your hesitation a bit further.

The teacher entry: The Friday class which dealt with children's books was a great one. I've always loved reading and seeing some of my old favorites was like visiting the house I grew up in. It kind of wraps me up in a warm feeling. I'm sure most of the other people in the class feel the same way. I found the process of analysing a book kind of difficult. To be objective about an old favorite, e.g., *Curious George*, is hard. In the end I have to go with my instinct in thinking that I am still very much a kid at heart, and if I like a book I'm sure many of my students will like it too. *Winnie-the-Pooh*, Beatrix Potter, the Grimms' fairy tales—I loved them all and I think they have a power that transcends generations.

The response: That is an interesting problem. How do we distance ourselves from something that has good memories? I hope we can talk more about that. Usually when a teacher does love a book, it helps to make the children appreciate it more. The ones you mention do seem to have the power to transcend time. I wonder if you have read Bruno Bettleheim on this topic?

In the ongoing dialogue we see the teacher trying to make sense of a new theory from the perspective of her own beliefs about teaching. She also asks questions about what the theory would mean for children and for the classrooms she is just now getting to know. In the final exchange she is reflecting on her own childhood experiences and is trying to see how that fits with ongoing classwork. Throughout, the exchange is full of emotion, morality, and a sense of what constitutes her aesthetic sense of knowing teaching and learning as she reflects on her experience.

This ongoing dialogue in letters is often initially approached with some concern and with questions such as the following. The questions are presented here with responses that we have formulated.

Questions and Suggestions

What should I keep my letter writing in? The letters need to go back and forth between two people so it is a good idea to keep the letters in a bound book of some sort. Usually a scribbler or keytab book is enough, but some people like to use a hard-cover diary. Beause it can often get quite lengthy depending on the time over which the exchange runs, make sure you have a book with enough pages. Divide each page in half vertically and write on the right-hand side of the dividing line. The left side is then free for the other person in the dialogue to write comments and questions. It can also be used by you to record "theoretical memos" as you reread the dialogue.

How long will each letter entry be? Once again, there are no hard and fast rules, but you do want to say enough to stimulate some dialogue. It is better, however, not to write anything than to write something that you have not really thought about. Such comments may send the dialogue off in a less than useful (to you) direction.

How often do we write? In our experience with students, we have found that once a week for each participant is enough. More than that becomes a burden. Less often and it becomes too disjointed because the time between entries tends to fragment the conversation.

Do I go back and reread the dialogue? Rereading is often a good way to pick up themes and patterns that begin to emerge from the exchange. For example, you may find that most of your entries have to do with evaluation or with one or two other topics, and you may wish to reflect on that. Go back and reread the section under journals to see how you can use letter writing to gain an understanding of your personal practical knowledge. There are many similarities except that in letter writing there is ongoing reflection-in-action between the two participants.

TEACHER INTERVIEWS

We have borrowed the next tool from Margaret Yonemura who refers to what we call teacher interviews as "teacher–teacher conversations."

Yonemura (1982) describes teacher–teacher conversations as "serious examinations of and reflections upon the practices and underlying theories of one teacher to which another gives undivided and supportive attention at times set apart for this." Teachers are given the following opportunities in their conversations: to reflect on and appreciate teaching as a practical art; to gain some release from the isolation and tensions of teaching; and to attain a higher level of congruence between espoused theories and beliefs about teaching and actual practice. Yonemura notes that "out of these reflective, supportive conversations a clearer identification of the practical principles guiding teachers can be formulated."

While Yonemura outlined five stages in the conversation, we see the interview process as somewhat less structured. The interview questions focus on central curricular concerns such as settings, teaching styles, materials, teacher beliefs about children, the teaching and learning process, and so forth. We have found questions such as asking the teacher to describe a teaching day to be appropriate opening questions. The interview questions are open-ended, personal, and concrete, and the data from the interviews are rich in the details of practice.

Here is a small sample of a transcript from a teacher interview.

Jean: When you are thinking about what it is you are going to plan, is it the children you are thinking of?

Stewart: Yes, I would say so because that is what I think I have to plan for. I don't know whether that makes sense or not, but I find if I have not planned for the children, then just experience has taught me that everything will go wrong. You know what I mean? Like if your day isn't planned out and that is what I find I get more and more worried about—not being planned out.

Jean: And planned out. Say more about what you mean by planned out.

Stewart: If I don't know what I am doing, then the kids will end up doing something that I don't want.

Jean: And how do you go about planning for them then?

Stewart: I try to interpret what is going to happen in a day and plan for that. Does that make sense?

Jean: Say something else about it. Tell me how you are going to plan for tomorrow.

Stewart: Okay. What I will do is I will sit down tonight and, in between probably 7 and 9, sometime in there, I will just start to think about what is going to happen in the morning. I know the kids are going to come back with their books, so I have to be ready for that. So it's almost verbally talking to myself about what I think is going to happen from the time that they come in the door, even to what I am going to say to them. Usually I think about, I will go through the big front doors where they line up, and I feel good if I know what I am going to say to them. It is not always off the cuff, you know, even if it sounds, you go out there and you say, good morning boys and girls, everybody got a smile on? Or something like that or I will make a joke and say, oh well pull one out of your pocket then, or I will say, I will give you a smile sort of thing. Something like that I like to have planned so that they are already tuned into me, and they know I am tuned into them. That is the kind of planning I like to do and I just like to step myself down through the day. Okay, so I bring them in. Did you want me to just go through a whole day?

Jean: Yeah. Tell me, well this is what you are doing, I mean you are doing it now almost mentally when . . .

Stewart: Yes, exactly. And I think that is what you have to do, I think. At night, before you actually experience it, you have to have thought about it. I find anyway.

This is just a fragment from the first part of an initial interview. Other interview fragments look much different, but the concrete, rich details of practice are there in each segment.

We see the teacher considering his practice in detail, and those considerations reflect the emotional ("I get more and more worried"), the moral ("I feel good if I know"), and the aesthetic ("It is not always off the cuff") dimensions of personal practical knowledge.

Questions and Suggestions

Once again we provide some of the questions we are commonly asked and our general guidelines for interviews.

How do I get started in an interview? Remember that you are interested in the day-to-day work of teaching. You do not want the interview to become either a session of complaining about the hard work of teaching or a discussion of various theories of education. You do want it to become a discussion about the teacher's work in education, her thoughts, her feelings, and how she has come to engage in the work of teaching. These ground rules should be discussed initially so you are both clear about the purpose and intent of the interview.

How do I keep a record of the interview? There are two ways to keep a record. One way is to tape-record the interview and prepare a written transcript. This involves a great deal of work, and, while you would probably find it useful, you need to carefully consider the amount of time it will involve to prepare the transcript. A one-hour interview takes about ten hours to transcribe. Another way to record the interview is to take written notes during the interview. Keep a record of the questions you ask and keep quick notes on the responses. Try to get some of the responses as direct quotations. When the interview is over and as soon as possible after, prepare a summary account of the interview, providing the questions with a summary of each response. Often when you choose to work in this way it helps to have an interviewing team so that there are two people who can ask the questions, listen, and take the notes. When one interviewer is engaged in asking questions, the other person should be trying hard to get as complete a record of the conversation as possible. This team approach to interviewing allows for both more detailed records and also more thorough questioning.

What kind of questions do I ask? The questions should probe all aspects of the teaching process from planning to teaching to reflecting on the teaching to the context in which the teaching takes place. Ask questions about children, books, materials, planning, organizing, questioning, and so forth. Listen carefully to the responses. Let the teacher take the lead and allow the conversation to follow that lead. Try to probe responses with comments such as "tell me more about . . . ," "why," "have you thought about that further?" and so forth. Ask if the teacher has ever experienced similar events that have influenced his or her practice in this situation. Ask what led to that practice. Listen carefully for the emotional and moral side, that is, the feeling and the "should" side to the responses. Remember that it is the teacher who is talking and that you should try to listen and follow where the teacher is leading and not where you would like to go.

What do I do when I have the transcript or notes prepared? Share the notes with the person you interviewed. Both of you should read the interview record and decide first of all if it is an accurate record of the interview. There may be places where you or the teacher would like clarification; a further interview to clarify those points may be helpful. When you are satisfied that you have a good account, then you are ready to use that data from the interview in the further work of preparing an account of your personal practical knowledge (see Chapter 6).

PARTICIPANT OBSERVATION

One of the most useful tools for reflection that we have found is participant observation. Participant observation can be loosely defined as participating in the ongoing work in someone else's classroom while engaging in making observations on the student and teacher activities, conversations, materials, events, and so on, as well as on your own activities. The observations are usually recorded as field notes, a sample of which is given below.

We see a number of possibilities for ways in which teachers can engage in reflection on their practice using participant observation. An important rider on each of these methods, however, is the focus on participation. It is not enough to observe. One must participate in the ongoing action in order for participant observation to be useful for reflection. It is, perhaps, most useful to have another teacher come to your classroom for several days to act as a participant observer. It is also possible to learn a great deal about your own practices by acting as a participant observer in someone else's classroom, perhaps claiming the same spare period over several weeks. It may also be possible to have someone who is not now teaching but who has taught, such as an administrator, a consultant, or a university researcher, take the role of participant observer in your classroom.

Before we go on to discuss the process further, read the following partial set of field note records of participant observation in a Grade 1 teacher's classroom.

Marie had already started to talk about the pumpkin but she stopped doing that and went immediately to do the calendar. She said again that she wasn't very good at remembering these kinds of things. They worked on counting the number of days to Hallowe'en after they had put up the days that were missing—Friday, Saturday, Sunday, and Monday.

Marie then went back and by this point one of the students had picked up the pumpkin. Marie described the pumpkin as being heavy. She then allowed each of the students to have a turn holding the pumpkin. She talked about the pumpkin briefly and drew their attention to the hard, smooth surface of the pumpkin.

She then went over to the table with them to cut it up. They talked about what they needed to draw on the pumpkin's face. She asked what they wanted the pumpkin to look like and they said "scary." She asked what shape they should use for the eyes and most of the students said "triangle" but one student said "circle." Marie drew triangles for the eyes and then asked the shape for the nose. Most of the students said a "square" but the one student who had said circle for the eyes said "circle" for the nose and Marie made a circle shaped nose. She then asked how they wanted the mouth made and they described that they wanted teeth coming down and teeth going up and described it as bumpy. Marie drew that shape on. She then drew the line on the top for where she would cut the top off the pumpkin. Marie then started to cut the lid off.

Marie asked what they thought was inside the pumpkin. The students said "seeds" and Marie asked what else. One of the students said that it was all mushy inside and another said that there were things hanging down like spider webs. Marie went along cutting out the shapes and for the most part the children watched. She kept talking with them, at times talking about her difficulty in cutting out a pumpkin and how she hadn't done this before and engaging the children in talking about whether they had done this at home. During this time I stood at the table with the children and from time to time commented on what Marie was doing and talked with the children trying to encourage them to talk about what they would find inside the pumpkin. (*Notes to file, Monday, October 28, 1985*)

It is possible to learn a great deal about two teachers' personal practical knowledge from participant observation conducted over a period of time. For example, in this fragment of field notes we can begin to ask questions about the two teachers' practices that could be explored in further participant observation settings. As we read the notes there are a number of "foreshadowed questions," to borrow one of Bob Stake's (1978) terms, questions such as why the teacher is involved in the cultural tradition of making a jack-o'-lantern. We can speculate on the ways in which she talks with and questions the students. We see her encouraging children to express their ideas verbally as well as to experience things using their senses. We sense her uncertainty in the value in keeping a class calendar. We can learn about the participant observer as well. We see a parallel interest in encouraging the children to talk about their experience and in the importance of naming action. In future sessions and indeed in the remainder of the field notes from this one day, we can begin to speculate on the two participants' personal practical knowledge.

There are perhaps more questions about participant observation than about other of our reflective tools. It is a role with which teachers have little experience. Participant observation would be an easy extension of team teaching, and yet the team teachers with whom we have worked have rarely tried participant observation. They have not considered the value in using it for reflection. We hope the following questions and answers about participant observation will give these teachers the incentive to try it.

Questions and Suggestions

The following are some of the questions we have been asked about participant observation with our responses.

How do I find someone with whom I can work in participant observation? As noted above, there are a number of possible people that can be asked to work with you in a participant observation role. Perhaps the easiest way is to try to make an arrangement for you and a teacher with whom you feel comfortable and who is willing to work together in a team teaching situation to do so for a short period of time. If this is not possible, and it may not be possible in some school situations, then pursue the other options noted above. There may even be a graduate student who would be willing to negotiate research possibilities with you. We did this very successfully in a research study that we undertook. The teachers who were involved in the study were able to pursue their interest in reflecting on their practice, while we were able to serve our research purposes.

Is there a role for video- or audiotaping in participant observation? There is not really a need for such analytic tools in a participant observation relationship. However, such records may add to the richness of the insights into your practice, when they are used in conjunction with participant observation. Bodily actions and facial expressions will stand out more in a videotape than in your notes.

What should I record in my notes? As noted above, keep notes on as many activities, events, exchanges, materials, conversations, instructions, bodily movements, facial expressions, and uses of time, space, materials as possible. Remember that your focus is the teacher working in the classroom. Make sure you keep track of your activities and the ways in which your participation influences the ongoing work in the classroom. Keep a record as well of the joint planning sessions with the teacher. Keep notes on discussions about plans and proposed activities. Particularly note those points where you sense uncertainty about what one of you is doing and what the other is proposing. Those emotional feelings of uncertainty or disharmony often mark important insights into our personal practical knowledge.

Make a detailed sketch of the classroom, noting the arrangement of furniture, materials, and resources. Keep a record of how the space is used in the activities in which you are participating. Remember that your interest is in recording as many of the details of practice as possible. The more details captured, the richer will be the data source for reflection. Try not to record interpretive or judgmental comments in the field notes. You need to clearly separate your interpretations from the field note data.

How should I record my notes? As soon as possible after you finish the period of participant observation, try to reconstruct the day. Divide each page in half vertically and write your detailed notes on the right-hand side of the page. Leave the other half of the page free for your interpretive analysis.

What should I do with my notes? After you have recorded your set of notes, share them with the teacher. Discuss those points of interest that come up in discussion. Make sure that you keep a record of the discussion in the margin on the left-hand side of the page, noting carefully the notes that triggered the discussion. After you have shared the notes and discussed them with the other teacher, reread the notes and go through the process of theoretical memoing described above. Look for themes and patterns in the material. Note those things that stand out and seem particularly important. Often these points are marked by emotion or a sense of disharmony. We will discuss the further analysis of the field note material in the next chapter on analyzing our personal practical knowledge.

RECOMMENDED READINGS

We have provided a brief overview in this chapter of the various methods you can use in reflecting with a colleague to help you understand your personal practical knowledge of curriculum. Most of these tools are adaptations of various research and counseling methodologies. You may wish to read more about these tools as they are used in research settings.

As noted at the end of Chapter 4, there are two excellent handbooks that encourage teachers to become classroom researchers. One, *A Teacher's Guide to Classroom Research*, is by David Hopkins, and the other is *Doing Research: A Handbook for Teachers* by Rob Walker. These both provide an overview of some of the tools we have described.

You would do well to read Glaser and Strauss's book, *The Discovery of Grounded Theory*, for an excellent treatment of the process of theoretical memos. Spradley's book, *Participant Observation*, is a fine account of participant observation work. We recommend Michael Armstrong's *Closely Observed Children: Diary of a Primary Classroom* for an excellent example of participant observation work.

Spradley has also written an excellent book on interviewing, *The Ethnographic Interview*. You would do well to read that as well as Margaret Yonemura's work published in *Curriculum Inquiry*, "Teacher Conversations: A Potential Source of Their Own Professional Growth." Freema Elbaz's book entitled *Teacher Thinking: A Study of Practical Knowledge* is an excellent example of teacher–teacher interviews.

In the area of storytelling, we suggest that you read the work of Madeleine Gumet, whose work on storytelling was an important starting point to our own work.

There has been little work written directly on the topic of letter writing as we have dealt with it. We suggest you read a book by Nystrand entitled *Language as a Way of Knowing* for another brief treatment of the topic.

6

Understanding Your Personal Practical Knowledge

In the preceding chapters we described a way to understand curriculum as a situation with a past, present, and future. Our particular interest was on the person, you, in that situation. In Chapter 3, we introduced narrative as a notion that provided a way of understanding how we as teachers, and as people, make meaning of our lives. We also introduced the idea of personal practical knowledge, which we see embodied in each of us as we participate in educational situations. Personal practical knowledge is a moral, affective, and aesthetic way of knowing life's educational situations. In the conclusion to Chapter 3 we talked about how understanding our own narratives may be a metaphor for understanding the curriculum of our students. As teachers, it is important to learn to read our own "text," our own narrative, or, as we said earlier, our own curriculum as a way of gaining some understanding of our students' curriculum.

Chapters 4 and 5 outlined various tools of reflection, which you could use when engaged in reflection alone or with colleagues. Each of these tools is helpful in learning something of our own personal practical knowledge. As each reflective tool was discussed, we briefly described some preliminary analyses that you could undertake.

These tools, however, do not provide you with more than some data, some stories, parts of the whole. How can we give an account of the narrative as a whole? We said in Chapter 3 that it was both difficult and rewarding to understand one's own narrative. We said it was difficult because so many aspects of life need consideration and because people are complex. It is also difficult because we need to find new ways of talking about educational experience. We need a language that will permit us to talk about ourselves in situations and that will also let us tell stories of our experience. What language will let us do this? The language we, and others, have developed is a language close to experience, a language of affect, morality, and aesthetics. It is a language of images, personal philosophy, rules, practical principles, rhythms, metaphors, and narrative unity.

One of the confusions we often experience when we discuss language is that people interpret us to mean language only at the level of words, sentences, and symbols. But we mean an embodied language. It is also the syntax and semantics of our bodily movement, manipulation, and activity. It is a language of practice. A language of practice is in words, of course, but it is also in our bodies. It is in our practices and in our experiences. The language is, then, what we use to narrate our stories. It is a language of educational experience and thus is temporal, located in our past, present, and future.

In this chapter we describe this language of educational practice. We show how it is part of our experience and how it may be used to help tell our narratives.

IMAGE

Image is one term in our language of practice. What do we mean by image? We use the word image in a different way than do many authors whose idea of image is similar to picturing (see Chapter 4 for a description of picturing). By image we mean something within our experience, embodied in us as persons and expressed and enacted in our practices and actions. Situations call forth our images from our narratives of experience, and these images are available to us as guides to future action. An image reaches into the past, gathering up experiential threads meaningfully connected to the present. And it reaches intentionally into the future and creates new meaningfully connected threads as situations are experienced and new situations anticipated from the perspective of the image. Thus, images are part of our past, called forth by situations in which we act in the present, and are guides to our future. Images as they are embodied in us entail emotion, morality, and aesthetics.

Stephanie's Image of Home

It may be helpful to read about an image held by a Grade 1 teacher, Stephanie. For Stephanie the classroom is "a home." Her classroom is her "idea of how a home should be . . . a group of people interacting and cooperating together." Stephanie holds an image of the classroom as home. We did not give her that image nor did we ask what image she held of the classroom. The image was expressed in her practices and in the way she talked about her classroom in interviews (see participant observation and teaching interviews in Chapter 5). The image subsumed various elements of the content of her personal practical knowledge. Knowledge of the instructional process, of herself as a teacher and person, and of appropriate subject matter for primary school were all captured by the image.

The origin of the image is in four areas of Stephanie's experience: in her professional experience, her professional training, her own school experience, and her private life. The professional and personal origins are linked in Stephanie's classroom practices by the image of the "classroom as home." We saw many narrative fragments that could be understood as the embodiment and enactment of Stephanie's "classroom as home" image. Three we have written about are Stephanie's practices around an administrative move to reduce the number of children in her classroom; a unit on plants that she undertook in her room; and the celebration of Hallowe'en in her classroom. We will describe one: the narrative fragment on the planting unit.

When Stephanie first asked me to work on the unit, I did not understand it as anything more than a science unit in the program. At the time I saw it more or less as a random choice and thought it could have been any other unit. However, I now see Stephanie's request as minded, in part, by the "classroom as home" image. The link between her personal private life and her educational life is especially important in providing an understanding of how the image functions within her personal practical knowledge.

To many people and particularly to Stephanie, a home should have a garden or at least have growing things as part of it. Her emphasis on a "living" component of the home image suggests that importance, as does her choice of her personal home, an old house she is renovating in an inner-city neighborhood. To be able to grow things is important to Stephanie. Her interest in the planting and growing activities serves functions in both her personal and professional life.

On one side, the planting activities contribute to the "home in the classroom." The bean plants, the garden, the avocado, the geranium (all part of our classroom activities in the planting unit) contributed to the homelike classroom environment. On the other side, the planting activities at school were a way for her to try out something for her personal life. With the success of our activities at school, Stephanie took her newfound skills home. She planted her front yard bathtub with geraniums and, in her backyard, grew a garden complete with vegetables and pumpkins for the classroom Hallowe'en party. The classroom "home" became a testing ground for her personal home.

In this we see how the unity of the personal and professional in Stephanie's personal practical knowledge is expressed in both the personal and professional spheres of her life. Furthermore, we see how the personal and the professional interact reflexively within the image of "classroom as home." The effect on both home and school of the image expressed in action is dramatic. Elements in both are transformed. On the school side, school subject matter is selected and organized in a particular way; the classroom atmosphere is changed; inner-city students are given new experiences; Stephanie sees herself as a resource to other teachers interested in planting; and she seeks out staff members who are interested in similar activities. On the personal side, her home life is enriched as new hobbies develop and the physical appearance of her personal environment is enhanced.

In this account of Stephanie's image of the classroom as home we see the ways in which data gathered from her biography, participant observation, and interview are woven together into a narrative of her personal practical knowledge.

Aileen's Image of a Child

We have written about other images: some of our own, others of Stephanie's and those held by other teachers. For example, we wrote about another primary teacher's, Aileen's, image of a particular child. In an interview she spoke of the image in this way.

> And then E. and I in a couple of situations when we were really hassled about time and getting things done and trying to see this kid and that kid and this poor little tyke would come up and just want to share his plasticene or something . . . we'd say we don't have time now . . . put it down on the table over here where I can see it and when I'm free I'll come and find you. And really that's so bad because we should have said to hell with everything else and stopped and gone to that kid. Now that's an image that I use everyday when I feel like saying to a child, no, I'm really busy right now but I'll come and see you. Incidents keep coming up in my head and I say no, you know, just stop, nothing is too important to listen. And I know for a fact E. goes through the same thing and we talk about that same instance . . . many times. . . . It was the look on the child's face when we did that to him . . . that's going to haunt me, probably for years. So in that way it's positive cause it's making me try and be better with kids . . . but it's a negative image.

Aileen now views her experience with this particular child as a turning point in her teaching, frequently calling his face to mind when confronted with other children's problems. This child's face and Aileen's relationship to the child form the core experience around which the image has developed.

Self-Reflection

Images have a number of dimensions that may help you understand images in your own narratives. Image is one kind of glue that melds together a person's diverse experiences, both personal and professional. Images are not only part of school knowledge but are part of our knowledge as people, our personal practical knowledge. An image has emotional and moral dimensions. As you reflect on the data you have now collected about yourself and your teaching, look for places particularly marked by emotion, places of strong feeling. This may point to an underlying image. Notice also whether the way you talk or feel about the practice or child or thought has a sense of morality, a sense of rightness or wrongness, better or worse. These may provide clues to your images.

Make notes or theoretical memos as you read your personal records (Chapters 4 and 5) and think about possible images. Once you feel you have identified one, read back over your other material and ask yourself, "Can I understand this practice or event or reaction as an expression of an image that I hold?"

In the next two sections we briefly discuss practical rules, or maxims, and principles, both concepts developed by Freema Elbaz. Rules and principles are basically distillations of experience. Think of them as abstract, shorthand ways of summarizing your experience of how to get things done.

RULES OR MAXIMS

Rules are one of the terms in our language of practice. A rule of practice, according to Elbaz, is "simply what the term suggests—a brief, clearly formulated statement of what to do or how to do it in a particular situation frequently encountered in practice. A rule of practice may be highly specific . . . or may apply to somewhat broader situations" (Elbaz, 1983, pp. 132–133). A highly specific rule that Elbaz uses to illustrate her point is a high school teacher's, Sarah's, rule for dealing with a learning disabled student. Sarah tries to show the student that: "He has my full attention after I finish all the instructions." (Elbaz, 1983, p. 133).

More general rules may relate to such matters as organization of materials or the giving of assignments. Elbaz indicates, however, that "the rule makes reference to the details of the situation to which it relates, to means; the ends or purposes of action are taken for granted" (1983, p. 133).

Rules can take diverse forms: sometimes a brief statement and sometimes an extended description of practice from which a number of closely related rules may be inferred. Elbaz (1983, p. 136) writes of Sarah that another statement of her rules of practice is the following:

> I certainly try very hard to listen very actively to the kids, to paraphrase, to encourage them to paraphrase, and at most times to allow them to express their concerns and to discuss their concerns without judging them.

Elbaz (1983) describes how in this comment Sarah states a number of distinct rules: listen actively, paraphrase, encourage students to paraphrase, don't judge. These rules taken together constitute an approach to communication in the classroom which can be expressed in the statement of a principle. It is clear from the comment, however, that Sarah distinguishes a number of separate practices which she follows regularly and almost systematically in her teaching. (p. 136)

Two examples of Aileen's rules of practice are:

> I'm trying to encourage them to always try not to put up their hands but just to speak when no one's speaking; You never ask the kids to do anything that you wouldn't expect of yourself to have to do.

Clandinin points out that these are both rules which apply to broad situations. We call them rules because they make reference to the what and how of the situation with the purpose being taken for granted (1986, p. 46).

It may be helpful as you try to understand your own rules to read over your interview notes and your descriptions of your practices (see journals, letter writing, or participant observation in Chapters 4 and 5 as places to start) and note those spots where you say "I always . . ." or "I never. . . ." Often we find our spoken expression of rules is in terms of absolutes.

You also want to stay alert to other expressions of rules. Rules are sometimes embodied in our classroom routines and not stated verbally. Examine your teaching practices, instructional and management practices in particular, to see if you can find embodied expressions of your rules. You may be surprised to find that you work by certain rules that you have never articulated.

PRACTICAL PRINCIPLES

A practical principle is a "more inclusive and less explicit formulation in which the teacher's purposes, implied in the statement of a rule, are clearly evident" (Elbaz, 1983, p. 132). A practical principle, thus, embodies purposes in a deliberate and reflective way. The statement of a principle contains a rationale that emerges at the end of a process of deliberation on a problem.

Elbaz (1983, p. 137) gives the following example of one of Sarah's principles concerning the evaluation of teaching and learning. Sarah pointed out that:

> whatever I expected from the kids, I had to give them first; we have to teach the kids some things before we mark the kids on them.

This principle, formed by Sarah in the Learning Course work, directed all of her subsequent teaching.

Elbaz (1983, p. 137) notes another of Sarah's principles in that, with respect to remedial teaching or reading or skills, Sarah held to the principle of beginning with the student's emotional state:

> by giving "unqualified positive regard" and by "trying to make the kid happy to walk into that class."

This principle is related to a variety of different practices ranging from unstructured talk to working closely with a student to help him pass an upcoming chemistry exam.

As you try to understand your own practical principles, look for what you have marked as possible rules and images. Practical principles are often related to rules, as noted above, or can be seen to be ways of saying in words various practical expressions of our images.

RELATING IMAGES, RULES, AND PRINCIPLES

These different terms in the language of practice, rule, principle, and image are terms in an embodied language. The terms interrelate at the level of words and symbols, but they also are part of the experience, the embodied action, of a teacher in the classroom.

An example is given by Clandinin, as follows:

> Another powerful image for Aileen (whom we introduced earlier in the chapter) is her view of the instructional process: an *image* she states of "planting the little seed to see if the children are interested." It seems she derives practical *principles* such as the principle of allowing students to choose their own activities from such an image. "I wasn't afraid to let them go because I knew that they would learn in a more interesting way." *Rules* that derive from this image may be "I might just put something

down that they don't know what it is and let them try and figure it out." or "so you plant the seed in their heads but you don't make them feel they have to do it." (1986, p. 47).

In this example, we see how the language of practice is also a language embodied in her actions, in her practices, and in her relationships with children. It is not only a language of words.

The language is helpful in telling our educational narratives, the stories of our lives as teachers. It is a language close to, in fact part of, our experience. It captures and pulls experience out of the past as it describes present practices and gives a sense of direction to the future. Images, practical principles, and rules are embodied in teachers' practices such as Sarah's, Stephanie's, and Aileen's. We "see" images, rules, and principles when we observe a classroom. We can understand how the meanings of these terms in our language of practice capture the history of an individual as situated in a particular place in a particular institution and how this points the direction for the future. For each of us the language is filled with different experience and different meaning, for, as you have seen, the narrative experience of each person is different from that of others. But the language terms remain the same, and it is with them that we can give an account of the narrative, unique as it is for each of us.

Still, we cannot yet speak clearly about our narratives, for we need other terms with which to give a more complete account. We have found that the concept of personal philosophy allows us added insight into our narratives.

PERSONAL PHILOSOPHY

Personal philosophy is a way one thinks about oneself in teaching situations. Personal philosophy has within it a notion of beliefs and values. We mean by this the way in which we, as teachers, are often asked to describe or give an account of our beliefs and values by completing various verbal or written questions, like the ones we are often asked in job interviews and the like. Sample questions we have all responded to at one time or another are "what beliefs do you hold about children?" or "what do you value most in your teaching?"

Personal philosophy goes beneath the surface manifestations of values and beliefs to their experiential narrative origins. Studies of beliefs and values usually refer to a coherent account of a teacher's stated beliefs, values, and action preferences, whereas personal philosophy refers to a reconstruction of meaning contained in a teacher's actions and his or her explorations of them expressed in the form of a narrative of experience. Explanations contain beliefs, values, and action preferences, but within a narrative they are grounded and contextualized in terms of classroom events. They are submerged within the narrative that contains the personal, situational meaning of events. We mean much more than just an "explanation" and/or a statement of what we believe.

Bruce's Personal Philosophy

In the following section we examine how we came to understand one teacher's personal philosophy. We draw heavily on the work of Siaka Kroma (1983) in the following account of Bruce, a Grade 7 science teacher. We use two narrative fragments based on data from participant observation, interview, and letter writing (see Chapter 5) to illustrate the idea of personal philosophy.

The first fragment is drawn from a letter (or, as we call it in our research, a "narrative account") from Kroma to Bruce several months into their work together.

> In May I observed a pattern of note-taking in biology lessons that was different from the geography and history units. We talked about this in our conversation of June 19, 1982. The following transcript section covers your explanation of this practice.
>
> *Siaka*: What purpose do you see their note-taking serving in this case?
> *Bruce*: The note-taking . . . I see it as more in preparation for Grade 9, where they'll have to do large copious notes rather than. . . .
> *Siaka*: I'm talking about their copying notes rather than making the notes for themselves, you know. . . .
> *Bruce*: Oh, in . . . are you talking about science? or social studies? or whatever?
> *Siaka*: Are there differences?
> *Bruce*: Yes, because in science I specifically have them copy down the questions to the work that they're doing as well as the answers because sometimes the answers are so vague.
> *Siaka*: Let me go over what I have observed (sure). Sometimes you dictated notes (oh yeah, yeah) that the students had to copy. Sometimes they received handouts that they copied, (right) sometimes they read with you. . . . You went through questions that they then wrote the answers to.
> *Bruce*: Alright. Got it. You're still talking about science. The reason I would go with copying notes is I was running out of time and I

wanted them to have a note. And if they do an individual note it means that I will have to look them over. I did not have time. We didn't have the time to look at 28 individual notes. Therefore it was a matter of convenience that we did the same notes together. Just like me dictating. We need 14 months during the school year. We can't do it. So that was the whole reason behind that.

In this fragment Bruce does not talk about the nature of science nor about what his purposes were. He simply says that neither he ("I did not have the time") nor the class as a whole ("We need 14 months") has the time to prepare biology notes in an individualistic way. Our first hint as to how Bruce thinks about science teaching, then, is that it reflects his own energies and capabilities, on the one hand, and, on the other, the overall program that he intends to offer for the Grade 7 year. Note-taking in science becomes meaningful when it is understood as embedded within Bruce's sense of how history, geography, writing, and reading have progressed to this point in the year.

Let us look at another narrative fragment for more insight into how we might understand Bruce's personal philosophy. Once again this is written from Kroma to Bruce.

I first became aware of your treatment of subject matter language in the biology lessons in April of 1982. In one of the lessons, for example, you spoke of plant seeds as "their kids," and cotyledons as "their lunch pack." On one occasion a student's question and your response to it went like this:

Student: What type of roots does a potato have?
Bruce: It's called a tuber. It's a fancy word but we won't worry about that now.

I assume that these observations were clues to a certain understanding of language in relation to subject matter. I explored this assumption in an interview as follows.

Siaka: One thing I observed during the biology lessons, okay, is how you introduced some of the ideas in biology. For example, I remember when the kids copied the flower. There was a word, er, what? "receptacle" and you said it's an old-fashioned word, they shouldn't worry with it. . . . They didn't need to copy it. And then. . . .
Bruce: They used the word "sepal" and I felt that it would be getting too finicky for Grade 7. . . . We're looking at things they're going to

get much more in-depth once they get in high school. I want them to get used to what to expect and to work in a science book some enjoy. Some don't enjoy it but at least next year in Grade 8 when I do it again, they will have even more experience. And then when they finally move on to 9, they will have had it twice.

Here we see that Bruce is almost indifferent to technical terminology. He personifies the parts of seeds; he tells students that "tuber" is a "fancy" word and that "receptacle" is "an old-fashioned" word; and he further tells students that "they shouldn't worry" about either term.

Understanding Personal Philosophy

How can we understand these narrative fragments of Bruce's practices in terms of his personal philosophy of teaching? We see in the first fragment that note-taking becomes meaningful in terms of the overall curriculum in Grade 7 and as preparation for Grades 8 and 9 where they will have to do copious notes. In the second segment his downplaying of scientific terminology is also seen as meaningful in terms of the next two years of the students' schooling.

From a personal philosophy point of view, we see that the teaching of science in Bruce's class takes on meaning when it is seen as embedded within the science curriculum and the overall junior and senior high school curriculum as they are played out in his narrative. This personal coherence is a kind of unity and is what we call "personal philosophy."

We can also see in the narrative fragments that the teaching of science represents another part of Bruce's personal philosophy, that of his view of his students. Bruce's emphasis on preparing students for high school is not so much a concern for biology content and for high school requirements as it is a preparation of students for a later phase in life. He does not say that "such and such is important and should therefore be understood," but rather he says that "because students will have to do something later I want to make sure they are ready for it." We ultimately see this as an expression of Bruce's way of thinking about the fact that his are inner-city students, that their community consists of urban high-rise, low-income housing, and that most of them come from, and will enter, working-class occupations. We see that science is a carrier for other matters Bruce considers to be more important for his students. Other subjects would serve as well, but, in a replay of the note-taking fragment, he reminds us that time has run out. He is obligated by provincial government policy to cover certain science units; thus, a combination of this requirement, his sense of what is important for his students, and the progression of the overall curriculum in Grade 7 to this point in the year accounts for how science is taught.

Our intent here is not to provide all of what we see as Bruce's personal philosophy, but to give some idea of what we mean by the term "personal philosophy" in our language of practice. As you can probably see by now, personal philosophy is what we respond with when someone asks us as teachers what we believe about children, about teaching and learning, or about curriculum. But it is not just our espoused theory, as Argyris and Schon (1974) would have it, but our beliefs and values contextualized in our experience. We see our personal philosophy in our actions, and that is why we want you to examine closely not only your words in the interview data (see Chapter 5), but also your stories, your autobiography, your journals (see Chapter 4), and other data collected on yourself. It is in these data that you can understand your personal philosophy. They will allow you to write about your beliefs and values as experienced biographically, as practiced in your classrooms, and as thought about in your reflections and statements.

METAPHOR

Another term in our language of practice is "metaphor." We use this term in a somewhat different way than you may remember from your high school English classes. For us it is an experiential term. Lakoff and Johnson's notion of metaphor is close to our own. Here is how they introduce their book, *Metaphors We Live By*:

We have found . . . that metaphor is pervasive in everyday life, not just in language but in thought and action. Our ordinary conceptual system, in terms of which we both think and act, is fundamentally metaphorical in nature. The concepts that govern our thought are not just matters of the intellect. They also govern our everyday functioning, down to the most mundane details. Our concepts structure what we perceive, how we get around in the world, and how we relate to other people. Our conceptual system thus plays a central role in defining our everyday realities. If we are right in suggesting that our conceptual system is largely metaphorical, then the way we think, what we experience, and what we do everyday is very much a matter of metaphor. (Lakoff & Johnson, 1980, p. 3)

Lakoff and Johnson direct our attention to the way in which our concepts, derived from our personal, historical, and cultural narratives, structure the way we act in the present and guide our future practices. These authors argue that concepts are largely metaphorical in nature. One such example is the "argument as war" metaphor that structures the way we think and act in arguments. Read their fascinating book for a more detailed account of their research.

Following Lakoff and Johnson, we view metaphors as important parts of our personal practical knowledge and as a central form in our language of practice. We understand teachers' actions and practices as embodied expressions of their metaphors of teaching and of living. It makes a great deal of difference to our practices, for example, if we think of teaching as gardening, coaching, or cooking. It makes a difference if we think of children as clay to be molded or as players on a team or as travellers on a journey. Metaphors structure a range of curriculum practices. Let us modify Lakoff and Johnson's title to read "Metaphors We Teach By."

How can metaphors be identified? Perhaps the most direct way is to listen to speech. How do you talk about your teaching? But metaphors found in speech are often not the best indication of "metaphors we teach by." Speech metaphors are often used for communication or as a way of exploration rather than as a way of action. It is quite different to explain oneself by saying "I think of school as something like a factory producing educated citizens" than it is to live out, day by day, the idea of schools as factories and children as products.

We think it is more telling for you to examine your practices, interview material, stories, and journals to capture your metaphorical concepts of teaching. To do this we suggest you need (in a way similar to our earlier comments on personal philosophy) to contextualize your metaphors within your experiences and to see them played out in your practices. Our intent is not to have you see this way of understanding practice only as a way of talking about practice, but also as *part of* your practice.

Gayle's Mountaineering Metaphor

We want to share with you one metaphor written in a class one of us teaches. The metaphor is "teaching as mountaineering." Reflecting on the metaphor has helped this teacher examine her curricular practices, because it is part of her particular language of practice. It is part of her experience. The metaphor emerges from her prior experience and directs her practices into the future. The author is Gayle Fields, a junior high special education teacher in Calgary, Alberta.

If you look west to the mountains, you know that they are never the same—each year, each season, each moment they change. It is like my classroom always changing, whether it be the curriculum, the "other" curriculum, or the students. Nothing remains constant and nothing is ever duplicated. The mountain's terrain tantalizes the explorer with its variety, its moods, and its divergency from the gentle alpine meadows to the towering icefields and pinnacles. My students and I are like a mountaineering team; at times I lead, at times they lead, but whatever the case, we climb together as a team, depending upon the past experiences, the wants, the abilities, and the interests of others.

Like learning experiences, when we first enter into the climbing experience, we start with a venture that is nonthreatening; safe, yet rewarding—here the basics are learned and practiced and the first challenge is issued. We share moments of insecurity, encouragement, and laughter. Gradually the bonding process grows and we feel safe and secure with our partners in adventure. As we become more confident in each other, we attempt new mountains and new routes on previously climbed mountains.

As in planning for classes, it is always important to know the route we want to climb—what the difficulty rating is, what the dangers are, and then the ascent plans are prepared with each member having input. What equipment will we need? How long will it take us? What physical and mental preparations must be made? When will we attempt it? It is vitally important that these decisions be made together if the climb is to have a chance at success.

Climbing, as in teaching, involves total trust and commitment amongst the team members—this is not a desire but a necessity. The route you decide to climb must be within the capabilities of the weakest member, yet it must still remain challenging. Along the way, some members might falter for lack of confidence or fear, but there will always be the fellow team members who will offer support and encouragement.

Climbers, like teachers and students, are constantly using aids to reach their goal; the safety rope linking the climbers together like the bond of acceptance and understanding between teacher and students; pitons for security and safety; chockblocks for artificial footing; rope ladders to get above the overhangs; crampons for firmer footing on ice—all necessary for the success of the climb and the safety of the team.

The excitement, the joy, the adventure never stops but continues; changing and challenging as each step is taken and so it is in the classroom. Each section of the climb is a mini-adventure and challenge in itself, requiring different techniques, different skills, and different aids. Sometimes there is silence as one of the climbers focusses all his energies and thoughts on a difficult section, but still there is continuous communication through the belay of the safety rope and the thoughts of the fellow climbers.

Sometimes we find ourselves on a route too difficult for our abilities and/or equipment, and we must backtrack. As in education, this must never be considered failure, for backtracking on a mountain is an art unto itself, and any disappointment that might be felt is taken away through the freedom and enchantment of abseiling. It is never perceived as failure, because that section of the climb will remain there and we will be back at a later time.

The climbing party, like the class, is made up of people that are as different as the mountains. One may have great physical strength, but lack experience; one may be eager and cooperative, but need to develop his physical conditioning; and another may be quite intelligent, easily able to see the easiest route, but climb slowly because of his stature. The climbing party brings together a combination and variety of strengths and weaknesses; everyone using their strengths to help the others develop and grow in ways unique to themselves.

The size of the mountains we climb never matters, for there is always another in the future, and sometimes a small mountain can issue a very difficult challenge. Each climber, like each student, sets his own challenge, according to his own abilities, and each should be proud of the accomplishments made, for each is a precious and valued member of the team.

Through my experiences with my fellow climbers and my students, I too have grown, for mountaineering and teaching is the coming together of all resources so that all may reach the summit. The emotions that a person experiences when standing on the summit with climbing companions is something which I do not have the expertise to express in words. Each individual has faced a personal challenge, and has struggled in his/her own way to overcome the difficulties that faced him/her. We have become better persons for knowing each other, sharing our feelings, and working together to reach a common goal.

Postscript: There are dangers and losses in mountaineering. When you hear that first crack of an avalanche, the first thunder of a rockfall, the first scream of a falling mountaineer, time stops—for a split second—then everything goes into action. Eyes on the climber; prayers to God; you pull on the safety rope. You put forth every ounce of energy, every ounce of concentration, and pray. You feel the tug on the belay and hang on with everything you possess—mentally, physically, spiritually—and you wait. When the "yea oll" comes, the spirit soars and thanks are given.

But sometimes, it doesn't come . . . and there is silence.

When the first shock has passed, all climbers converge on the fallen climber; prayers in heart, and questions in mind.

To lose a fellow climber is to lose part of yourself. You question.

What went wrong? What could have been done differently? Why? You begin to self-doubt; begin to analyze why you climb. You begin to question your motives, your abilities, your dependability. Your confidence is shaken and you take an in-depth look at yourself. Can they depend on me? Can they trust me? How you answer these questions is very important to yourself and your climbing companions.

I gave up mountaineering in 1975—I still teach.

We can see in Gayle's written expression of her metaphor the deep feeling that is part of her understanding of teaching. It allows us to understand much about Gayle's curriculum practices. It is not merely an abstract expression of how Gayle might conceive of teaching, but it is an expression of the way in which her concepts of teaching, metaphorical in character, emerge from her narrative of experience.

Identifying Metaphors

As you read over the data you have now collected about yourself, pay close attention to metaphor. Some will be readily apparent as when a teacher states, as did Sarah, that she sees herself as "opening the window" for students to learn. Others may be less apparent as when a teacher says she is tired of "calling the plays" in her classroom.

You may not come up with only one metaphor. You will probably find several, some in conflict one with another. Write about as many as you can, but for each try to spin out the "entailments"; the way in which the metaphor structures various practices. This will probably lead you back to your images, principles, and rules and may give you new insight into your personal philosophy.

NARRATIVE UNITY

There are two other terms in our language of practice, narrative unity and rhythm. These terms are more at the level of syntax, while the others are more at the level of "parts of speech." Syntax is concerned with the interrelationships of words and word groups within the sentence structure of language. Narrative unity and rhythm are, therefore, terms that help connect the other terms with each other within narratives of experience. Narrative unity and rhythm provide a way of looking across the temporal span of our narratives.

We turn first to narrative unity. Narrative unity is a continuum within a person's experience and renders life experiences meaningful through the unity they achieve for the person. What we mean by unity is the union in each of us in a particular place and time of all we have been and undergone in the past and in the tradition (the history and culture) that helped to shape us. It is a meaning-giving account, an interpretation, of our history and, as such, provides a way of understanding our experiential knowledge. Within each of us there are a number of narrative unities. Ongoing life experience creates the narrative unity out of which images are crystallized and formed when called on by practical situations.

So far this may seem quite abstract and removed from experience. You may well be asking "what would a narrative unity be in my life?" Try to understand a narrative unity as a thread or theme that runs through the narrative of experience and that provides a way to see how the rules, principles, images, and metaphors relate one to the other as they are called out by the practical situations in which we find ourselves. This thread becomes apparent, then, when we act in our classrooms. Remember our talk about past, present, and future. Here it is again, for narrative unities emerge from our past, bring about certain practices in the present, and guide us toward certain practices in our future.

Self-Reflection

To start to understand the narrative unities within your own narrative, we suggest you turn to your narrative data. Reread your stories, your autobiography, your journals, and so on. It helps to begin this task after you have given content to some of the parts, for example, your specific images, rules, personal philosophy, and so on. Once you begin to understand these parts, you can start to look for experiential threads and to reflect on how those threads relate to your past, present, and future directions.

In the following, we share with you a narrative unity from our work with Phil Bingham, a Toronto elementary school principal with whom we have worked closely for several years.

A Narrative Unity
in Phil Bingham's Life as Principal

We began our exploration into a narrative unity in Phil's experience by closely observing his school administration practices, by interviews with him about his work, and by analysis of documents such as staff meeting agendas, school newsletters, and school philosophy statements produced by Phil. Based on our analysis of this material and subsequent discussions with Phil, we came to understand him as having an image of "community" in which the school is itself a community as well as part of the larger community with which it is in dynamic relationship. This image of "community" is an expression of a narrative unity in Phil's life. The image is not the narrative unity. The narrative unity is composed of the threads that connect Phil's image of "community" to his ongoing narrative. The threads are found in Phil's childhood and school experiences in inner-city Toronto, in his experiences on the Toronto islands as a child and as an adult, in his first teaching experience in the Island school (which serves the community that lives on the Toronto Islands), and in his later experience at two innovative community schools. Phil's personal narrative is embedded within the cultural and historical narratives of his immigration to Toronto as the son of Irish parents, the Toronto School Board, inner-city Toronto schools, and more generally Ontario education. It is these threads that both contribute to the image and illustrate how it is based on a narrative unity in Phil's life. In this way we can understand Phil's practices in his present school as expressions of an image of community.

Understanding Phil's image of community as an expression of a narrative unity in his life provides a way to understand Phil's practices: his responses to parents, the activities and relationships he develops for and with his staff, the programs he wants to encourage in his school. The narrative unities in his life give a way of understanding the relationships among other components of Phil's personal practical knowledge, his images, practical principles, rules, personal philosophy, and metaphors.

RHYTHM

Rhythm is another way of understanding the syntax of our language of practice. Teaching rhythms form part of our personal practical knowledge. Rhythm is an expression of some part of the narrative unity arising out of our past and embedded in our cultural and historical narratives and the institutions of which we are a part.

Rhythm captures the way in which we, as teachers, "know" the cycles of schooling and come to "know" when certain cyclical patterns in our narratives of school life will draw out certain images. For instance, a teacher may know the school year as a cycle of three reporting periods, with the final one marked by pass/fail decisions on students. Suppose the teacher failed a student in the past who subsequently committed suicide, leaving a note saying it was because she felt herself a failure in life. As that teacher rhythmically knows his teaching, the approach of the final marking period may fill him with a sense of dread and depression. His image of the student emerges as a beat in his rhythm of the year. Most of us have times of the year, for instance, when pronounced mood shifts can be connected to certain things that happened to us at that time of year in the past.

Stephanie's Rhythm of the Year

Stephanie, whom you met earlier, knows the school year as a series of school celebrations punctuated by downtimes with an accompanying sense of expectation, and uptimes with an accompanying sense of ending. Her rhythmic sense of knowing the classroom involves a sequence of events in which the celebration of one holiday involves knowing there is another holiday to follow. Therefore, even as Hallowe'en is celebrated in her classroom, she begins to draw out a sense of expectation by gently turning the children's thoughts from the excitement of Hallowe'en to the happenings of Christmas. Three events are particularly important in this respect: the transformation of the classroom through displays and decorations; counting the days to the next holiday; and organizing the curriculum around the celebration. In our narrative study of classrooms we have come to understand teaching rhythms in terms of our lives more generally, and so it is with Stephanie. In her class she is able to establish a rhythm that takes account of her own cultural rhythms and those of the children in the class that she teaches.

The rhythms that each of us establishes in our teaching are, of course, unique to each of us. They are similar to the rhythms of other teachers to the extent that they are conditioned by the institution of schooling and its cyclic temporal structure. But we each bring our own specific rhythms to our knowing of the school context. Furthermore, there are, for each of us, any number of rhythms.

NARRATIVE ACCOUNTS:
ACCOUNTS OF THE WHOLE

In this chapter we have presented a language of practice that allows you to construct your own narrative account. The language provides a structure or means of talking about your experience and a way of seeing your practice in different ways.

We do not want you to think, however, that you can reduce your narrative to a logical, coherent, sequential story. Experience is not like that, although perhaps it is less fragmented than many of us think. Narratives are too complex to summarize neatly. Still, the effort of searching for unity and rhythm, and the understanding so attained, are worth the effort. One of the main benefits, after all is said and done, may be the wonder that comes from realizing how complex our personal curriculum is. Using the language of practice, you will, hopefully, be able to tell your story with new insights, perhaps with a spirit of "re-vision."

RECOMMENDED READINGS

Several people have written on teachers' personal practical knowledge. We suggest you read Freema Elbaz's book, *Teacher Thinking: A Study of Practical Knowledge*, and her *Curriculum Inquiry* article entitled "The Teacher's 'Practical Knowledge': Report of Case Study" for a more detailed account of rules and practical principles.

Siaka Kroma in his doctoral dissertation, *Personal Practical Knowledge in Teaching: An Ethnographic Study*, did an intensive study of the personal philosophy of two teachers. Esther Enns-Connolly in her doctoral dissertation, *Translation as Interpretive Act: A Narrative Study of Translation in University-Level Foreign Language Teaching*, treats the notion of image and narrative.

Of our own work, we refer you to Jean Clandinin's book, *Classroom Practice: Teacher Images in Action*, and her *Curriculum Inquiry* article entitled "Personal Practical Knowledge: A Study of Teachers' Classroom Images" for an in-depth analysis of the notion of image. We also suggest you read our articles entitled "On Narrative Method, Personal Philosophy, and Narrative Unities in the Story of Teaching" and "Personal Practical Knowledge and the Modes of Knowing: Relevance for Teaching and Learning" for more on the ideas of personal philosophy, narrative unity, and rhythm. The former article also deals with the notion of personal philosophy.

We recommend Lakoff and Johnson's *Metaphors We Live By* for further reading on the topic of metaphor. Our own ideas on metaphor derive from the ideas presented in that book.

Part III

UNDERSTANDING INFLUENCES
ON THE CURRICULUM

Everyone exists in a situation, and situations, as seen in Chapter 1, are defined, in part, by individuals in interaction with an environment. We can no more understand ourselves in isolation than we can understand society devoid of individuals. The study of personal narratives of experiences can never, therefore, be a single-minded egocentric study of the individual. It is, instead, a study of the individual in context. This part of the book addresses key contextual matters for teachers in their classrooms.

7

Recovery of
Curriculum Meaning

The central theme of this book might be stated as "the reconstruction of curriculum meaning from a study of personal experience." Our attempt in Chapters 1 to 6 has been to give life to the idea that one's own narrative may be reflectively reconstructed for curricular reasons. By "reconstruction" we mean the sort of thing John Dewey had in mind when he wrote that "there is no intellectual growth without some reconstruction, some remaking, of impulses and desires in the form in which they first show themselves" (1938, p. 64). Through reflection it is possible to reconstruct, to rebuild a narrative that "remakes" the taken-for-granted, habitual ways we all have of responding to our curriculum situations. We use the word "reconstruction" to describe this process. It is not a process of discovery nor a process of recovery, although these play their role in reconstruction. It is a rebuilding to meet the demands of particular curriculum situations.

But in "reconstruction" there is also a sense of "recovery." When we tell a story (Chapter 5) as descriptively as we can, we are recovering an important event in our experience. It is when we ask ourselves the meaning of a story, and tell it in a narrative, that we reconstruct the meaning recovered in the story.

The same process holds for the reading of curriculum texts more generally. Remember that for curriculum, a text to be read may be our experience, in the past, present, and future as it unfolds, or it may be what it usually means, printed pages. So we may think of experience, as well as printed texts, in terms of the recovery and reconstruction of meaning.

The distinction between recovery and reconstruction, of course, is not hard and fast in the practice of reading, although we may separate the notions quite rigorously at the level of idea. Let us see how this works out "in practice."

In recovery of meaning, we read while demanding that our own biases, prejudices, perspectives, outlooks, wants, and wishes be held at bay. Two key questions we ask are: "what is the author saying?" and "what does he/she mean?"

Furthermore, recovery of meaning implies that we do not bring outside frameworks to the text to "explain" it. We often hear people saying of a text, "It's not surprising that such and such was said since the author wrote in the last century" or "What can you expect? The author is a cognitive psychologist." In these kinds of remarks the author's message is demeaned by attempts to explain it away historically and psychologically. When the purpose is to read a text *in its own terms*, other perspectives obscure the author's meaning. Thus, for recovery of meaning, it is important not to historicize, psychologize, politicize, sociologize, or other -ize a text.

The very opposite of this process often occurs in our thinking and writing when we are looking for something very specific *in our terms*. Our purpose may be to read the text historically or psychologically. We do not care what the author "meant" to say. Instead, we want to see how we can use the text to help us say or do something we mean. For instance, I may be interested in the role of motivation in the design of curriculum materials. If so, I will read the motivation literature and relevant philosophical literature with a very specific biased eye. I will pick and choose those things that bear directly on my problem.

Now, recovery of meaning, to find out what a text is saying, and reconstruction, for the purpose of saying what we as readers want to say, are two extremes. They are extremes at the level of idea. But in practice every sensitive reader knows the impossibility of doing either of the extremes, although we may shift the balance of reading attention one way or the other. If I try to suppress my own likes and dislikes and read a text in its own terms, I quickly discover myself responding to the text, struggling with the interpretation of terms, wondering what the author meant as I recall examples from my own experience, and so forth. In short, it is impossible not to put ourselves into the text. But it is also impossible not to be influenced by a text, even when we are reading from a very specific point of view. It makes a difference whether we read literature set A versus literature set B, even when we are not interested in either A or B but only in our own purposes.

We lay out this simple idea of reading texts for two reasons. First, when reconstruction and recovery are taken to their theoretical extreme, we are able to more clearly see the different kinds of things possible in reading. Both of these two kinds of things are at the heart of this book. In this particular chapter we wish to stress the recovery of meaning side. But we do so in aid of the book's central theme of reconstruction of meaning. The second reason for setting forth this reading structure is to make sure we understand that what is torn asunder in theory may be integrated in practice. All text reading, whether of personal experience or of textbooks, is an integrated balance of recovery and reconstruction. No one can tell you what that balance should be. You must decide for yourself every time you "read" a curriculum text.

Now that we have this simple idea of what it means to read curriculum texts in mind, let us turn to a discussion of tools useful for the recovery of meaning of curriculum texts. In this chapter we describe two sets of terms, one a set of commonplaces and the second the terms "theory and practice." Chapters 8 to 11 discuss in more depth influences on the curriculum whose "curricular meaning" may be recovered using the tools described.

THE COMMONPLACES OF CURRICULUM

John Dewey has a line in the introduction to his *Experience and Education* (1938) that reads "all social movements involve conflicts which are reflected intellectually in controversies." He goes on to say that these conflicts and controversies set a problem for theory. There are many things that might be said about this. The point we wish to make is that it reflects the state of thinking in the curriculum field, which is filled with conflicts, controversies, problems, theories, and, yes, quasi and half-baked ideas. The confusion that one often sees at the level of public policy or school board decision is reflected again in the academic and scholarly literature of education. When we are in the middle of a practical battle, we often say "how in the world can we sort this out?" But things are no better in the world of theory. Remember the Dr. Seuss story of Yertle the Turtle? Turtles kept climbing on top of turtles' backs to get a better view of the world. All the while the bottom turtle became buried deeper and deeper in the mud, and could see less and less as the pile got higher and higher. Theory has been something like this in education. The more theory we have—and we have a great deal—the more complex, rather than simpler, becomes the already complex world of practice. So the practitioner's question, "How do we sort this out?" makes as much sense when we are referring to Dewey's conflicts and controversies as it does when we are referring to competing theories. Chapters 8, 9, and 10 deal specifically with this problem.

Indeed, what should we do? Do we close our eyes and ignore theory? Do we pick a theory and say "hang it all, I'm going with that?" We hope not. Ignoring theory is an invitation to ignorance. Adopting only one theory simply raises prejudice to another level.

It is interesting, we think, that one answer to this dilemma was given by Aristotle at the time of classical Greek philosophy. Aristotle wrote about "topics" in his *Topica*. The idea is that when there appears to be a babble of voices about something that we all agree is significant, then what we need to help sort things out is a set of topics that help define the subject as experienced, while ruling no one's views out of order. We call these topics "commonplaces of curriculum." One of the first uses of the idea of commonplaces in the educational literature is found in a little-known lecture by Joseph Schwab (1962). If you check the Schwab reference, look for "desiderata" since he did not call the topics "commonplaces."

The commonplaces are a set of factors or determinants that occur in statements about the aims, content, and methods of the curiculum. Taken as a whole they serve to bound the set of statements identified as being curricular. They comprise the simplest model for looking at curricular problems. The commonplaces are:

> subject matter
> milieu
> learner
> teacher

Characteristics of the Commonplaces

Six statements on the characteristics and uses of the commonplaces follow.

1. They are commonplace in the usual sense of the word, i.e., they appear and reappear in curricular statements. We cannot escape them. An adequate curriculum statement must say something about each of them.

2. Many arguments tend to focus on a single commonplace. If so the role played by the others will be, in part, determined by the focal commonplace. For example, if "organized knowledge" is the focus, then the learner may be treated largely as a receptacle; the "teacher" as a dispenser; and "milieu" as the housing for the old knowledge and the accumulator of the new.

3. There are a number of different possible foci within a single commonplace. For example, three possible foci in the learner are: the learner as an inquirer, the learner as a social organism, the learner as a recording machine. The fact that there are several foci within a commonplace increases the complexity suggested in statement 2.

4. The commonplaces are useful analytic tools. Materials that may be analyzed in terms of the commonplaces are: philosophic, psychologic, sociologic, and other writings from which a curricular stance may be inferred; educational writings that take a curricular stance; lectures; panel discussions; policies; positions of curriculum committee members; and personal narratives and their components, such as images and personal philosophy.

5. The commonplaces are useful in examining historical curricular trends and in coming to understand the forces giving rise to changes in curricular foci. For example, in this century, we have seen a focus on the "learner" change to a focus on "subject matter" during the 1950s, back to learner in the intervening decades, and now to subject matter and milieu in public discussion and the back-to-the-basics debate. We can identify the "milieu" in the form of international competition as one of the forces accounting for this change in focus. Within the "subject matter" focus, we are witnessing a subtle change from knowledge to inquiry.

6. The commonplaces are useful in examining public "conflicts" and "controversies." Chapter 10 gives an example of conflict analysis using the commonplaces. The problem in that chapter is the banning of books and the different opinions that people have about this. One might also use the commonplaces to analyze "controversies" such as would be found in the printed literature surrounding a curriculum program with diverse points of view. A comparative analysis of two or three written curriculum proposals is an example.

Using the Commonplaces

The commonplaces are as empty of meaning as possible. Meaning is filled in as texts are read. The assumption is that a comprehensive curriculum argument is one that has something to say about the learner, the teacher, the subject matter, and the milieu. What the author has to say about those matters is the way in which the commonplaces are "filled with meaning."

How do we use them then? Very simply. Always ask: "What does the author *make of* the (learner or teacher or subject matter or milieu)?" Now, let us break this question down.

Write "L," "T," "SM," or "M" in the margin as you come across statements referring to one of the commonplaces. You need to read statements identified by a commonplace very carefully, since your everyday notion of the commonplace may not apply. For instance, a careful reading of Dewey's *Experience and Education* will show that for him subject matter is defined as activities and that activities, in terms of commonplaces, may be an interactive mix of learner and milieu in which subject matter as we normally think of it is part of the milieu. Likewise, many people, and certainly the authors of this book, take the view that in any curriculum situation the teacher is also a learner. This is the whole idea of narrative. Anyone to whom the notion is applied is thought to be a learner in the narrative sense.

The only real difficulty you may have with this process may come with the milieu. It helps to think of the idea of curriculum presented in Chapter 1.

If our interest is with a student in a curriculum situation, then everyone else and everything else in that situation may be said to be part of the student's milieu. But we might be interested in the curriculum situation as a whole, in which case the school might be the milieu. Likewise, the community might be considered the milieu for the school, and so on. A pagoda of milieus!

Since, as Chapter 10 makes clear, all curriculum writings have a prescriptive sense about them, we need to reconstruct the author's "argument." Helpful questions are:

Which commonplace is the author's argumentative starting point?
Which commonplace is the author's end-in-view?
Which commonplace is emphasized in the text?

For instance, an author may start his or her argument with a concept of the learner and use most of the pages discussing the nature of subject matter appropriate to the learner as conceived and as a means to a new view of social purpose (milieu). Thus, "L," "SM," and "M" end up playing different roles in the argument presented. If you are not a careful reader, you will think the argument is about subject matter, because of its emphasis, when in fact it is about the way in which subject matter links to learner in the creation of a view of society.

We think you will find the commonplaces both easy to use and revealing of meaning. Remember to use them on a wide variety of texts. Often, debates at staff meetings, or panel discussions on professional development days, can easily be sorted out using the commonplaces. We may gain insight into ourselves by applying them to our stories and interviews.

Finally, while we have described possible uses of the commonplaces in the recovery of meaning of an already existing text, you may use them to create a text. Suppose you are writing a rationale for a curriculum. The commonplaces have the same usefulness in reminding you of what it takes to create comprehensive arguments as they do in helping to analyze them. The next time you find yourself needing to argue something curricular, either verbally or in print, try using the commonplaces to help shape your views.

Let us now turn to our second recovery of meaning tool, the distinction between theory and practice.

THEORY AND PRACTICE

If there are two terms that plague our curriculum thought, they must be "theory" and "practice." We even divide our field this way, referring to "practitioners" as those doing a school job and "theoreticians" as those whiling away the hours in the universities. Those in between are sometimes in a difficult position: Practitioners often think of administrators, consultants, and policy makers as "quasi-theoretical," and theoreticians think of the same people as "quasi-practical." Theory/practice labels have a great deal to do with the way each of us chooses to walk our school curriculum paths.

There are tensions in the very existence of the classes of people defined by the terms "theory" and "practice." We often hear teachers and others scoff at someone's ideas, putting them down to "that's only theory." And, in the halls of academe, we hear the opposite, as professors often say of remarks by their teacher/students, "that's just a war story." Somehow these fundamental and all-embracing terms have come to be divisive in our curriculum world. We should be searching for ways to work collaboratively on the problems of curriculum situations. Instead, we frequently find ways of dismissing one another. Some writers, for example, argue that education professors with a school background do little other than maintain the status quo (Pinar, 1975). Using arguments such as these, some universities hire education professors who have no school experience. Yet, given the idea of curriculum in this book, we cannot believe that these are helpful responses to the problem of theory and practice. We need instead to "recover" the texts of life as a practitioner and life as a theoretician and then to "reconstruct" new, more productive relationships between them. One way of doing this is seen in the dialectic relation of theory and practice, described later in this chapter.

To effect the necessary "recovery" and "reconstruction," it is important to consider the *domains* to which the terms "theory" and "practice" apply. It is also necessary to consider the various *ways* in which theory and practice may be related to one another. Let us take up these matters in turn.

Separate Domains

In a straightforward sense the terms refer to the worlds specified by "theoretician" and "practitioner." A practitioner does curriculum; a theoretician thinks about it. The practitioner acts; the theoretician theorizes. As Aristotle made so clear in his writings on the nature of human thought, the ends of the theoretical mode of thinking are ideas and theories, while the ends of the practical mode of thinking are actions. So we see that the distinction between theory and practice is deeper than we might have imagined. It is not only that we have different levels of thought about the same thing, one practical and one theoretical, but also that the thing itself is different, one taking the form of ideas and the other the form of actions.

Partly, this distinction between idea and action is at the heart of the difficulties and tensions that exist in the curriculum world, noted earlier. If we follow Aristotle, the theoretician and practitioner not only do things differently, they value different things. What is valuable and important in the long run for the teacher/practitioner is good action. For this book, it is good curriculum. For the theoretician, what is important and valuable in the long run is good ideas. This may seem subtle, but try listening carefully to what it is that people say is valuable and important when a discussion of theory and practice erupts. The university professors might not even do their thinking in a practical context. That is, they may do controlled experiments, implement a program of test results, and do any number of things that are not "naturally" practical. The reason that the researchers do this is that their interest is in the ideas, not in the practice. When things do not work out quite the way as expected by the ideas, it is simply chalked up to experimental error or something similar. The proof is in the pudding, and it is a theoretical pudding.

But practitioners ultimately have no interest in this pudding, nor should they. Their pudding is the curriculum as a process operating over time. If things go awry in the classroom, it does not much matter what the theory was. The teacher is concerned because children have been hurt, their curricula have been sidetracked, lives have been disrupted. So, according to the Aristotelian notion, these fundamental differences between theory and practice are deeply rooted and require subtle and sensitive ways of bringing them together. Later we describe what we think are useful ways of thinking about how to bring these apparently very different worlds of theory and practice together in such a way as to serve common curriculum ends. As a teaser to carry in mind until we come to that discussion, we suggest you ask yourself these questions: "If the worlds of theory and practice are two different worlds, how is it possible for theory to find its way into practice and for practice to inform theory?" "How can we learn anything from the universities?" "How can the universities learn anything from us?"

So far, we have used theory and practice to refer to their common everyday domain. But let us think about the idea of curriculum and the notions of personal practical knowledge and narrative presented in this book. What do the terms "theory" and "practice" have to say to us as individuals?

There are two answers, one closer to the domain described above and one closer to our experience. Let us look at the former first.

Theory Application

As a teacher, one of your questions is "how do I use the results of research and theory?" When teachers stand at the boundaries of their curriculum situation and view their environment, when they stand at the doors of their classrooms and look out on the community, they see and feel a prescriptive world. As Chapter 10 points out, the teacher sees a number of stakeholders, all of whom think that she should be doing one or another thing in her classroom. All of these stakeholders have an idea of what should be done, and so it is possible to think of their prescriptions in terms of theory and practice. Sometimes, we suppose, it is possible to find a stakeholder, possibly a principal, who simply says, "Do things this way," and does not say why. The idea is missing. But almost always in this prescriptive environment of curriculum situations, there is a mix of "reasons why" as well as the "doings prescribed." It can be very helpful for a teacher to think in terms of theory and practice when asked to do something, because this provides two fundamental questions to sort out the prescription. You should always ask:

What does this stakeholder want me to *do*?
What is the reason (the idea) that this stakeholder gives for asking me to do this?

Asking these two questions will help to sort out the prescriptive claims on your classroom. If you always think of prescriptive claims as having a theoretical and a practical component, you will be better able to sort out reasons from actions, and ideas from practices, and, therefore, to put yourself in the driver's seat. It is easiest to think this way when listening to a university professor describe his or her latest research results and why it is thought that you should do such and such. But the point applies as well to anyone else, even those who sound downright practical, who wants you to do something. You must adjudicate among the theoretical and practical demands on your classroom.

What is said here applies equally well to curriculum materials (Chapter 11). New materials may describe new content and new activities. But this content and these activities will be based on an idea of some sort. Again, ask yourself the same two questions of all curriculum materials. It will help you sort out the theory/practice problem.

Theory and Practice in My Personal Knowledge

We may think of our own education through curriculum situations in terms of theory and practice. We learn something new and that may be said to be theory. It becomes practical when it seeps into our personal knowledge and becomes part of us so that we act in ways that reflect the new ideas. Our personal education may be thought of this way. Polanyi (1962) has a marvellous term for helping to make this point. He thinks of concept learning as an extension of skill learning and says that a skilled user "dwells in" the tool and is only subsidiarily aware of it as his or her attention is focussed on its use. This "dwelling in" is a notion similar to personal practical knowledge in that it is the knowledge in which we live and that lives in us. When things learned, ideas or skills, have this "dwelling in" state in our personal practical knowledge, we may say that the idea has become part of us and is no longer an idea per se but is an idea in practice, our practice.

Everyone has had the experience of learning something conceptually. That is, we learn something as an idea. We can repeat it on tests and may have perfect recall. But the ideas so learned and recalled for tests may feel very foreign. And we may soon forget the idea. We may say that such ideas always remain theoretical for us. They never become part of our personal practical knowledge. They never dwelled in us nor we in them.

Sometimes, however, almost the opposite occurs. We learn something and it makes so much sense that we do not learn it in all the precise detail needed for perfect recall on an examination. It often happens that for the things most important to us, we do not pay this kind of detailed analytic attention. Instead, what we do is "work the idea into us." We gnaw it around. We think about what it means in things that we do. We relate it to our private life. We drum up examples. We play with the idea. We may say that such ideas are beginning to dwell in us and us in them. For these ideas the "forgetting curve" on tests may be just as steep, but now we may say that the forgetting curve is not that at all, but is instead a curve of the integration of theory and practice. The more we forget and are unable to recall for a test, the more the idea has seeped into our being. It is, as Polanyi says, lost from sight. Just as sugar sweetens the tea but is lost from view, so a new idea may "sweeten" our personal practical knowledge and yet be lost from view and be unable to be recalled.

A beautiful illustration of this relation of theory and practice in our personal knowledge is seen in one of Juanita's stories told in a course on curriculum. This story is related to another, which tells of a traumatic teaching experience 17 years earlier when she began teaching and felt she had failed an inner-city class.

ESCAPING CHILDHOOD: GROWING UP

Towards the second week in September 1985, I was told by my principal, Mr. S, that the small number of pupils registered for junior kindergarten would necessitate reorganization of classes and my having to travel to another school during my luncheon period. Although this meant a reduction in my "free" time, I was elated to be offered the chance to break out of the comfortable nest I had built for myself over the years at T school. I viewed the half day as a gradual transition process in which I would be able to have the comfort of the known while learning the intricacies of the new.

It was with high hopes and an exhilarated spirit that I drove over the bridge on Maycroft Avenue on that first day, in September 1985. I felt so pleased, so excited to be breaking away at last. Alas! If I only knew what awaited me! That bridge was to become for me the crossing over or the link between giving up and finding the courage to face yet another day.

The first encounter with chaos after my trauma of 17 years ago came when the long awaited bell signalled that it was time to start the afternoon. I tried vainly to get these three- and four-year-old bodies to remain still while I ran after one or the other. I don't remember how we got into that classroom. What I do remember, however, is a bright-eyed little boy sitting in front of me. As I seated myself sedately and tried to look my most demure, he looked up innocently and with quick fingers lifted my skirt and asked loudly, "What's under there?" With the other hand he indicated under my skirt. I was horrified and immediately forgot that my actions and my bearing should reflect the notion of acceptance and tolerance. I don't remember exactly how I dealt with the situation; only the feeling of defeat remains. I now wonder if my reaction on that otherwise unforgettable day may have contributed to the misery I experienced over this past year.

Since most of that first afternoon seems to be now lost in my subconscious, I have decided to consult my daybook notes, which I recorded at the end of the day. I am surprised that the notes do not indicate the alarm that seems to come over me whenever I think of that September afternoon. This is indeed a mystery to me, although I think the inability to retrieve this memory may be related to the trauma of my first assignment 17 years ago. The visible scars are camouflaged very sweetly with the brave front and the donning of the "happy face," but the humiliation remains.

My Peace River dream was just that . . . A Dream! The beautiful bubble did not fill me with excitement as I travelled over that Maycroft hill every afternoon. The dread and hopelessness that filled my heart can only be understood if you have yourself failed.

This story is dramatic in its emotional trauma. A kindergarten teacher, joyously looking forward to a new assignment, responds in an unaccountable way to an innocent four-year-old's action. But the story is dramatic educationally when the incident is seen in biographic context.

Juanita was brought up in a fundamentalist religion and experienced rigid home discipline, including strapping. She saw much of her life in terms of escape from the physical and intellectual controls of her childhood. There is much talk in her journals of various movements forward, and falterings, as she strove to escape her childhood bonds. When the incident with the four-year-old took place, she had reached a point in life where she saw herself as a liberated woman and as a feminist. She also saw herself as a good teacher who created what she called a "mothering" environment for her preschoolers.

As Juanita tells the narrative of which the story is a part, the incident is doubly meaningful to her because she understands her reaction as a response from her childhood, compounded by a difficult first teaching assignment 17 years earlier. As she later wrote in the narrative that gave meaning to this story, she was still the "china doll" her religion and her family had made her as a child. She had only put on new clothes. The boy's action threatened the fragile doll and brought out long forgotten, deeply embedded values and responses.

Since this reconstruction, Juanita has struggled to tell a positive rather than a negative narrative. The negative narrative is one in which she gives up. After all these years of struggle and after having seen herself as liberated, a tiny four-year-old is able to show that it is all a cloth veneer and that she is still the little girl she wants to outgrow. This is a narrative of educational failure. But there is another narrative. It is the narrative of a life-long curriculum. It is a narrative that recognizes how difficult it is for ideas to seep down into our personal knowledge so that our ideas and our actions are one in our personal knowing of the world. But it is also a story that realizes that this process goes on over life and that incidents such as these are educationally positive because they reveal the tensions in a life narrative that still require pushing and molding. It is an educational experience that permits Juanita's continued growth.

For readers of Juanita's story, there are two fundamental lessons. One has to do with the relationships of theory and practice in our personal knowledge. The second has to do with the power of narrative telling. How she chooses to tell the story makes all the difference as to whether she gives up and considers her life's quest a failure or, as she chooses to do, views the incident as a positive tension in the process of resolving theory and practice in an educational narrative. This is an unfinished narrative. Theory and practice remain in tension.

Ways of Relating Theory and Practice

The most common way of thinking about the relationship of theory and practice in education is to think of practice as applied theory. Looked at from the point of view of theory, the problem is to implement it. It is a problem of developing tactics and strategies for applying theory to the appropriate practical situations. We may call this the "squeeze" idea of theory and practice. It is an idea where practice is squeezed into theory. Practice is made to take the shape of theory. But this is not the only possible relationship of theory to practice. Juanita's story, and the narrative of which it is a part, illustrates a much different idea of the relationship. Here, we see theory and practice blending in the actions of the person. Theory disappears as such and cannot be said to be applied. Likewise, practice is not directed by theory but somehow grows and changes through the narrative of experience, some of which occurs in pre-school classrooms with four-year-old boys.

The philosopher McKeon (1952) characterizes four possible relationships that have, through history, characterized the ways theory and practice have been related. He calls these four ways the logistic, operational, problematic, and dialectic. The squeeze theory is McKeon's logistic, and Juanita's story fits the dialectic. Let us sketch these four possibilities out in brief since we believe that thinking of these four forms of relationship between theory and practice will be immensely useful. We are so accustomed to thinking of only one possible form, the logistic, that we do not even realize that other possibilities exist. Theory and practice is one of those "glass walls" discussed in Chapter 1.

Logistic: According to the logistic conception, the worlds of theory and practice are seen as distinct. Practice is treated as applied theory, and it is assumed that the motives of action differ from the principles of knowledge. Action is seen as fundamentally irrational and, since there is no certainty in action, a science of action, which in education has become named "implementation and change theory," is needed to guide the uses of theory in practice. The research emphasis tends to be on the development of knowledge aimed at controlling the uses of theory in practice. This feature marks the attempts of educational reformers to build system analysis theories, implementation strategies, models of planned change, and the like.

The fundamental assumption in the "logistic" is that practice is essentially irrational. Rationality, therefore, consists of the various tactics and strategies by which the vagaries of practical action are ordered and made coherent. This view is fundamentally at odds with our own view, which is that practical reasoning is a sometimes deliberate, sometimes intuitive, intentional process governed by the reflection that takes place in curriculum situations. The difference between these notions, therefore, involves more than the mere idea of a relationship. It involves a different conception of the nature of human action, something that is valued and central to the view of curriculum presented in this book, but that is treated as irrational in the logistic.

Operational: Closely related, in the field of education, is McKeon's operational view of the relationship of theory and practice. Here, practice is seen as determining the relevant theory through the actions taken. Again, practice is seen as essentially nonrational and, as a result, truth is sought in opinion and in criteria of usefulness. Knowledge is viewed as mere activity and process. Characteristically, ideas are converted to processes, and one searches for operational procedures for persuading practitioners to operate in certain ways. Unlike the logistic then, where research is aimed at the development of rational, logical methods for translating theory into practice, the operational tends to "fly by the seat of the pants." It lays its trust in such matters as needs assessment and user opinion to get a fix on the attitudes and predispositions of practitioners. These are then used to manipulate and persuade practitioners through the use of proper rewards in the intervention process. The "change agent" modifying user attitudes, beliefs, and values is a familiar figure in the operational literature.

According to the operational relationship of theory and practice, practitioners are, as Schon (1983) says, "supposed to furnish researchers with problems for study and with tests of the utility of research results" (p. 26). The operational, therefore, is not a notion that is friendly to the idea of teacher-based "action research" discussed in Chapter 11. According to the operational, the needs assessment and user opinion strategies are often used to obtain attitudes and predispositions of practitioners for the purpose of using them as cues by which the researcher/theoretician may circumvent and work against the ongoing evolution of the practical situation. We do not say that obtaining information on attitudes is undesirable. We do say that it is often used in undesirable ways by people who operationalize a relationship between theory and practice.

Problematic: McKeon's problematic conception of the relationship between theory and practice has a limited expression in the educational reform literature. Here, the practical is essentially viewed as a form of inquiry, but differing from inquiry in the natural sciences. That is, the methods of knowledge production are viewed as different from the methods of practical problem solving. Nevertheless, knowledge is viewed as entering practice, and emerging from it, through problem-definition and problem-solving methods. According to this conception, knowledge is modified, adjusted, and used selectively according to the dictates of the particular problem confronted in practical situations. Problems are treated as they occur in ongoing experience. Notions such as action research and "mutual adaptation" acknowledge the problematic method (Berman & McLaughlin, 1979; Parlett & Hamilton, 1977; Shipman, 1974).

The problematic notion is seen in the 1983 book by Schon entitled *The Reflective Practitioner*. Schon is concerned with practitioners of all kinds and, in fact, does not draw special attention to education. He argues that practice is essentially a sequence of problem-solving episodes. Given that idea, he then shows how practitioners solve problems in practice. They may use theory, but they have no direct interest in it. Their purpose is to solve the problem that confronts them. In this problematic view, it is the situations and not the theory that is important. Furthermore, there are no general, theoretical solutions. There are only solutions to particular local problems as they emerge. This notion has a much more familiar ring of truth to it for those of us who think in terms of practice than do the more commonly used notions of the logistic and the operational. The dialectic, to be described next, represents our own notion.

Dialectic: McKeon's dialectic views theory and practice as inseparable. Problems of theory are seen in practice, and vice versa. Indeed, practice *is* theory in action. There is no essential dichotomy. According to this view, the practical constitutes a kind of proof, so that if theoretical notions and practice are incompatible, it is theory rather than practice that is seen to be at fault. This contrasts sharply with the attitudes of most policy makers and developers, whose fundamental assumption is that ever increasingly sophisticated ways of intervening need to be developed as evidence accumulates that practice is not affected in the direction of the intentions set by reformers. Theory, according to the dialectic, is much less fixed than it is in either the logistic or the operational, and it is assumed to change and be modified according to the shifting exigencies of the practical world. The essential task of the dialectic is to resolve oppositions.

Following the dialectic view of the relationship of theory and practice, we may imagine that researchers and practitioners would be co-participants in inquiry. A reflexive relationship is established in which the research becomes part of the situation, thereby reflexively altering its character as inquiry proceeds. The situation under study, while primarily defined by the givenness of the practical situation, is nevertheless the modified one, consisting of the researcher's intentions, purposes, predispositions, and practices within the situation.

In this view, the dialectic inquirer, both the practitioner in the school and the researcher in the university, government, or board of education, no longer watches situations, but rather participates in them. Here we see the basic notion of intersubjectivity described in Chapter 3. It is a view that is essentially at odds with the idea of objective knowledge, at least as that idea is commonly understood. It is a view in which the inquirers—researchers and teachers—care about the situation. Their caring influences the conduct of inquiry, and the results may be said to be intersubjective. Polanyi put the matter very well when he wrote, "I regard knowing as an act of comprehension of the things known, an action that requires skill. . . . Such is the personal participation of the knower in acts of understanding" (1958, p. vii). According to this view, knowledge is neither objective nor subjective. Rather, knowledge is made personal. And here is another way, with different terms, "theory" and "practice," that the narrative curricular theme of the book stands out.

SUMMARY

This chapter sets the stage for the remaining chapters in this part of the book. The first six chapters were concerned with developing a view of curriculum in terms of the concept of the personal. Once that notion was established, our emphasis turned to reflective tools that could be used to reconstruct personal meaning in narrative form. But as the concept of curriculum in Chapter 1 makes clear, all curriculum situations exist in a context and exert influences on the curriculum. Basically, we have organized those influences into ideas (Chapters 8 and 9), people (Chapter 10), and materials (Chapter 11). As soon as we think of these influences, we are immediately aware that it is necessary to understand them. It is necessary to recover the meaning in the influencing ideas, people, and materials. Accordingly, Chapter 7 provided analytic tools useful in the recovery of meaning process. From our introduction and discussion of these tools, it should have become clear to you that their use goes beyond influences on the curriculum and that they may be used to recover meaning from your own personal experience. This notion is discussed by using the idea of a curriculum text and then pointing out that a curriculum text may be personal experience as well as the printed page. Recovery of meaning and reconstruction of meaning were shown to go hand in hand in the reading process.

Two sets of recovery of meaning tools were described, the commonplaces of curriculum, and the terms "theory" and "practice." Four commonplaces—learner, teacher, subject matter, and milieu—were described and their uses in recovery of meaning illustrated. Theory and practice were shown to be fundamental to how we organize and think about our intellectual and practical world. The chapter described three domains to which the terms theory and practice refer: the everyday domains of the practitioners' and the theoreticians' worlds, the domain of theory use by practitioners, and the domain of personal experience. We then showed how most of us have only one notion of the relationship of theory and practice, that of application. Using the philosopher McKeon's ideas, this notion of the relationship of theory to practice was expanded to a set of four: logistic, operational, problematic, and dialectic. Each of these was described in terms of its significance for practice and practitioners. Our own view, embodied in the conception of this book, was seen to be dialectic.

RECOMMENDED READINGS

Readers who want to delve deeply into the idea of the commonplaces should go back to Aristotle's *Topica* and read any edition of it. Robin Enns's thesis, *Crisis Research in Curriculum Policy Making: A Conceptualization*, is a gold mine of references on the idea of commonplaces as interpreted in various intellectual fields. Readers will also want to review Schwab's uses of it in his *The Teaching of Science as Inquiry*. For a discussion of the division of human thought into theoretical, practical, and productive domains, see McKeon's *Introduction to Aristotle*, which contains large sections of translated Aristotelian text. For difficult but rewarding reading on the problem of theory and practice, see McKeon's article, "Philosophy and Action." Our essay, "The Reflective Practitioner and Practitioners' Narrative Unities," explores McKeon's ideas for purposes of understanding teaching. Schon's *The Reflective Practitioner* is a superb example of the problematic relationship of theory and practice.

8

Using Research Findings

If you have taught a year or more, you probably have heard the statement: "We can find support in research for any position and direction in education, even conflicting ones." For some of us, the apparent correctness of this statement has led logically to a conclusion like that reached by mathematicians studying the problem of dividing by zero: We have decided that something that has any possible meaning might as well be regarded as having no meaning. Others among us have allowed the statement to excuse us from consistently making research findings an important part of our curriculum work.

Educational research, it is true, does not yield a consistent and clear body of knowledge and, as a result, is often contradictory. Nevertheless, teachers who ignore research increase the risks of being overruled in their work by others. Good teachers are expected to make reasoned curriculum decisions and to be able to defend their actions. Without some knowledge of the directions and relative strengths of forces influencing their profession, they cannot expect to achieve professional autonomy. Their lack of specific knowledge creates a vacuum that others—trustees, researchers, administrators, parents, consultants, publishers, and students—eagerly fill, having been promoted by default on the part of the teacher to the rank of experts. Lack of knowledge on the part of the teacher also inflates the relative value and "clout" of whatever knowledge others possess or seem to possess. Too often, teachers are cowed by "research findings" reported in the popular media; as a result, poorly done research sometimes has the same impact on schools as that which is solidly conceived and painstakingly carried out. It is clearly part of our job as professionals to reduce the chances of this happening.

Teachers tend to react deferentially to researchers. Awed by the mystique of research, we are often influenced by the authority of researchers' positions rather than the authority of their reasoning or the credibility of their findings. We are often similarly guilty of accepting the expertise supposedly implied by titles such as "Professor," "Ministry Official," "consultant," "administrator," or "trustee," without critically examining the statements made in each case.

Blind acceptance of research findings is not the only expression of undue awe. Outright rejection of research (in such attitudes as "that's only theory" or "when was the last time he was in the classroom?") can also express the feeling of awe, accompanied by the juvenile's sense of rebellion against authority. If we cannot judge between conflicting sets of assumptions because of our lack of knowledge, the relative political power of the holders of the various positions will determine which position will prevail.

We hope that this chapter will help you make curriculum decisions according to the authority of knowledge rather than the authority of high-status persons.

CHARACTERISTICS OF EDUCATIONAL RESEARCH

For most of us, research in education is the offshoot of traditional psychological research, dealing with the comparison of groups as they perform a task, and using statistical analysis of the differences in performances. The "controlled experiment" and "objectivity" are distinctive features of this kind of research. But while much educational research is of this kind, a great deal of important research does not fit such a format. We need to develop a wider view of research.

We need to look at research from a teacher's point of view, and ask how research can be used in our curriculum planning and doing. Consider these characteristics of research.

1. *A researcher's authority refers to the researcher's own area of expertise and not to some other.*
This is so plain that it is easily overlooked. We have probably all listened to a "great man" begin a lecture with words like these: "The topic you've asked me to speak on today is not precisely in my own field. Nevertheless, I have had an interest in this problem for some time and . . . ." The lecture is then delivered as if the speaker were an authority on the topic and, further, as if this authority carried the weight of numerous research studies by him and his colleagues. The implication is that you should listen hard and do something about it when you return to your curriculum setting. Maybe you should, maybe not. Ask yourself, "What is the nature of his authority? Does he know what he is talking about or is he summarizing someone else's field? Is he trading on his good reputation in another field to give him credibility? Is his presentation rhetorical? Theoretical? Entertaining? And if so, can I separate the presentation from the substance of what he said?"

2. *A speaker's authority may come from experience as well as from research knowledge.*
Remember that someone who has "been through it"—that is, has successfully worked through a problem that you face—has gained wisdom based on experience that may not be part of a researcher's background. In practice, most speakers and proponents of positions have a mixture of experience and research. At one extreme is the 21-year-old Ph.D. with one study under his or her belt and no teaching experience; at the other is the veteran teacher who has not read a book since college. In between are the experienced researchers and research-trained practitioners. How do you sort out the sources of their authority and decide how much credibility they warrant? Ask yourself how much practical experience with the topic the speaker has, and how much and how long he or she has studied in the area involved. Do the strengths on one side balance the limitations on the other?

3. *Research answers questions in the terms in which they are asked.*
Let us suppose the topic is instruction, and you want to know what research has to say about the best methods. The first thing you will find is that different lines of research give different answers. The next thing you will find (which may be surprising) is that the different answers are not really in opposition. A careful look at how the various researchers have asked their questions will usually show that the antagonists are speaking different languages. They actually ask their questions with different words and, not surprisingly, get different answers.

Here is an example. Line of research (or professor) A says that the best forms of instruction are those in which the ratio of teacher-talk to student-talk is low, and the number of student–student interactions is high compared with the number of teacher–student interactions. The research goes on to point out that student-initiated interactions are preferable to teacher-initiated ones. You study the literature (or ask another professor) and find line of research B, which states that thought-provoking questions are characteristic of good instruction. Good instruction, says this research, stimulates higher levels of cognitive ability and is characterized by mental processes such as synthesis and analysis, rather than recall and application. Not satisfied, you keep reading (or ask still another professor) and find line of research C, which says that good discussion stimulates student inquiry: Such discussion involves the use of logic and leads to productive thinking—for example, the identification of facts on which to base a claim, the making of bright interpretations and defensible conclusions. More reading might turn up still another view, D, stating that good instruction is that which sticks fairly faithfully to the content being taught. A measure of good instruction, according to this view, is the extent to which it deals with concepts, terms, theories, and facts of the field.

So we have four lines of research giving us what appear to be four different answers to our question about the best method of instruction. Along the way, we picked up some bickering—Professor X objecting to Professor Y's notion of instruction, some critical commentary in the "background" section of research papers, and the like. Should we take this as an indication that someone is right and someone wrong? Probably not. Assume, instead, that they are all right in their own terms. They just asked their questions differently and got different answers. The first line of research framed its questions in terms of classroom interaction, the second in terms of individual cognitive processes, the third in terms of productive thinking, and the fourth in terms of subject matter. And so they are all right, provided, of course, that each was internally consistent and made no errors in experimental or discursive logic. Your question has been answered in four correct ways by the research. Some help! What will you do with these answers? It is up to you. Consider the next item.

4. *Research findings may need adaptation to be useful for your decision making.*
One of the lessons from the instruction example is that research asks its questions and you ask yours. While the questions may be related, they are not the same. In short, research does *not* answer your questions. To make use of research, you may have to change the questions a bit. Instead of asking "what is the best method of instruction?" ask "what do I want to do and what forms of instruction will be most useful in doing it?" You will then be able to decide more easily whether research on "inquiry instruction" or on "classroom interaction" is more appropriate for your purposes. You may decide you want to do several different things with your curriculum, and that all four lines of research will be of use for different parts of the curriculum. Figure 8.1 charts the relationship between your questions and those of research. Note that the lines of research describe what "is." As a teacher, you need to decide what "ought" to be done. Your function is therefore said to be "prescriptive." You have to make decisions ahead of time that will enable the instruction you provide to accomplish the goals you intend. The time, the place, the content of instruction, the people involved, and the action should be tentatively planned by you—they shouldn't just "happen."

5. *Research is always partial, but your situation is whole.*
Think of it this way. A statue stands in the middle of a dark room. Around the edges of the room are four people shining flashlights on the statue. Each

Figure 8.1: Lines of Research and Your Decision Making*

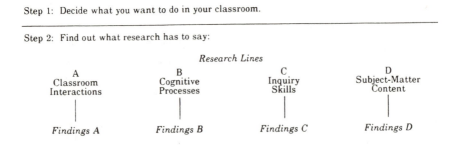

Step 1: Decide what you want to do in your classroom.

Step 2: Find out what research has to say:

Research Lines

A Classroom Interactions	B Cognitive Processes	C Inquiry Skills	D Subject-Matter Content
Findings A	*Findings B*	*Findings C*	*Findings D*

Step 3: Decide which of the lines of research might help you do the things you want to do in your classroom.

*From Connelly, Dukacz, Quinlan, (1980, p. 29)

records what he or she sees—and, of course, each sees something different in the statue. Lines of research may be thought of in this way. Each has its own terms (even its own assumptions, premises, propositions, arguments, and theories), and when these are trained on a problem during research, they answer questions "according to their light."

Mistaking the research "part" for the "whole" of the school situation partially explains education's weakness for fads. An idea appears with highly desirable features, perhaps with support from school research. But as the idea is applied to real school situations in a variety of places, its limitations begin to show up. It may not, for example, be appropriate for all children, only those with certain learning styles. This is where researchers, probably through naiveté, are most likely to mislead practitioners. The researcher is committed to an idea (as he or she must be, to spend the hours of research needed to get useful results). The researcher's success depends in part on an ability to see the problem in one way and to work out all the ramifications of that point of view. The researcher is then likely to be a strong proponent of that view and impatient with alternatives—already worrying about implementation of the idea in school. Beware of implementors! Ask yourself: "What part of the problem does this view represent? How closely does it represent the whole as I know it? Are there important things left out? How can I make use of the idea without destroying the good things I am already doing? How can I make use of the good things in the idea without throwing out my current work?"

6. *Research is general, but your situation is specific.*
When research is done, the results are generalized to apply to more cases than were actually studied. Experimental researchers talk about a "representative sample," the idea being that the results of a study of, say, 100 classrooms out of a group of 1000 can be said to apply to all 1000, with a little room for error, usually from 0.01 to 15 percent. The sampling technique is valid and makes the researcher's job easier. Still, you should not be quick to accept the generalized results. Remember that your purposes are different. The researchers want to say something "in general." But you want the opposite—you need to plan to do something "in particular," with this curriculum, with these children, in this school.

Indeed, what constitutes experimental error for the researcher—an exception to the general rule—may actually represent your situation. Note too that by the very nature of generalizing, detail is lost. "Controls" are used in a research study to control variables that in normal circumstances vary (for example, things like IQ, sex, age, parental background). But "normal circumstances" are your circumstances. Therefore, after reading the generalized results of a study, you need to look back to the actual research data to find out what was controlled, and what were the characteristics of the test situation. Then you can decide just how closely your own situation corresponds to that in the study, and whether the study's findings apply to your situation.

SIX RESEARCH PERSPECTIVES

We have also found it useful in understanding what various research is all about to examine the research perspective that is being adopted in the work. Each research study that you read adopts a particular conception of schooling, a particular method of inquiry, and a particular phenomenon or aspect of schooling. In Figure 8.2 we indicate six such research perspectives that we have identified in the literature. For each we show the conception of schooling used in the study, the main research question, the method, the character of the phenomenon being studied, and the kind of data generated.

Before we describe each perspective in detail, we provide a preliminary sense of how a researcher approaches his or her task within each perspective. A researcher adopting an analytic perspective seeks to analyze schooling into its component parts. At the outset, the researcher "sees" a kind of working mechanism and is interested in the way its parts interact. A re-

	Analytic	Portrait	Intentional	Structural	Societal	Narrative
Conception of Schooling	Schooling as a Complex Set of Interacting Variables	Complex Whole with Characteristic Ethos	Schooling as Accomplishments	Schooling as a Structural/ Functional Whole	Schooling as a Reflection of Society	Schooling as Personal and Social Narrative History
Characteristics of Method	Identification of Variables and their Covariance	Illumination of Essential Character of School Setting: An Insiders' View	Gaps Identified Impediments Discovered Solutions Offered	Structures Imply Functions and Vice Versa	Illumination of Societal Features in Schooling	Diverse Data Collected over Time on School Practices: An Insiders' View
Telling Data	Relationship Between Variables	Elements of the Whole	Performance Measures Judged Against Standards	Records which Clarify a Process or Reveal a Structure	Records of Differential Treatment of a Social Variable	Records which Reveal Narrative Origins and Embodied Meanings
Exemplary Study	Travers et al.: *Second International Mathematics Study*, in press	Lightfoot: *The Good High School: Portraits of Character and Culture*, 1983	Boyer: *High School: A Report on Secondary Education in America*, 1983	Cusick: *The Egalitarian Ideal and the American High School: Studies of Three Schools*, 1983	Ramsay: *Fresh Perspectives on the School Transformation/ Reproduction Debate*, 1983	Connelly and Clandinin: *Studies in Personal Practical Knowledge*, 1986

Figure 8.2: Perspectives on Inquiry into Schooling

searcher adopting the portrait perspective wishes to characterize schooling as an entity, for example, a classroom or a school. This researcher "sees" a working whole and attempts to describe it fully. A researcher adopting the intentional perspective is concerned with the purposes of schooling and with gaps between school intentions and their outcomes. At first glance, he or she sees a system marked by discrepancies and seeks to identify and account for the differences between goals and accomplishments. A researcher adopting the structural perspective is concerned with the structures and functions of schooling. He or she sees a set of structures common to schools and attempts to describe their corresponding processes and services performed for the whole. A researcher adopting the societal perspective focusses on the relationship of schooling to society. "Seeing" schooling as a microcosm of society, he or she seeks to identify correspondences and to explain schooling in societal terms. A researcher adopting the narrative perspective is concerned with the social and personal history of schooling and its participants. This researcher sees the school as a temporal entity, and his or her purpose is to identify the personal, social, and historical narratives at work. Each researcher, then, actually "sees" something different about schooling.

In the next section we provide a more detailed account and give one example of each study. As you read the research literature, make sure you understand what research perspective the researcher has adopted. This will help you to know if what he or she has to say is useful to you in dealing with your practical situation.

The Analytic Perspective

This perspective embodies a conception of schooling as a complex set of interacting variables. Schooling is viewed as a composite of these variables and the relationships among them. The principal characteristic of methods within this perspective is that variables are identified and their behavior in school systems is traced in natural, quasi-experimental or experimental settings. Variables may be identified in advance of inquiry or, given appropriate statistical and interpretive procedures, may be generated from the data.

The kinds of questions asked by those who hold this perspective tend to be specific rather than general, and to be posed either in terms of effect or correlation. For example, the question, "What is the relationship of parental economic level to student achievement in Grade 9?" is specific to Grade 9 achievement and is posed in terms of effect.

The phenomena of schooling are, accordingly, treated as sets of interacting variables in which telling data consist of predictable variations in the relationship between two or more variables. For example, data on student achievement become telling with respect to the influence of parental economic level when collected under covariant conditions through the question posed above.

The achievement studies of the International Association for the Evaluation of Educational Achievement (IEA) are examples of studies conducted from this research perspective. Other examples of such studies would be the studies of achievement and time-on-task when schooling is understood as the relationship between time spent on tasks and learning outcomes. Such studies are often referred to as process-product studies of interaction and achievement.

The Portrait Perspective

This perspective conceives of schooling as a whole, with a certain form, richness of detail, and a particular ethos that can be expressed in a written account. The principal characteristic of methods within this perspective is that the activities undertaken allow the researcher to illuminate the school's character so that the insider's view of what is important is represented. What constitutes the next appropriate steps in the inquiry is determined by the evolving observation, or even questionnaires to find clues to facets of the portrait.

The questions asked by those who hold the portrait perspective are, at bottom, generic questions aimed at discovering the essence of the setting. A question such as "what characterizes a good secondary school?" is illustrative.

The phenomena of schooling are treated as integral elements of a whole in which telling data consist of observations and other records through which a part of the whole may be constructed. Unlike an observation that might, in a study from an analytic perspective, be used for purposes of correlation, here an observation is used to create the portrait's form.

The portraits of good high schools done by Sarah Lawrence Lightfoot in *The Good High School* (1983) are examples of studies conducted using this research perspective. Other examples of studies from this perspective would be the connoisseurship studies of Elliot Eisner (1979) and Tom Barone (1983).

The Intentional Perspective

The intentional perspective conceives of schooling in terms of accomplishments: teacher accomplishments, student accomplishments, and social accomplishments. Schooling is essentially a quest for the realization of the intentions of parents, society, and reformers. The principal characteristic of methods within this perspective is that gaps between goals and achievements are identified, the intervening impediments and conditioning factors discovered, and solutions proffered. Inquiries within an intentional perspective may adopt different forms. For example, implementation studies often begin with intentions and search for gaps through the measurement of achievements. Alternatively, gaps may be indicated, for example, in policy studies such as *A Nation at Risk* (1983), and inquiry focusses on the identification of impediments. Impediments may already have been determined by major studies, such as Coleman's *Equality of Educational Opportunity* study (1966), and in these cases inquiry proceeds into methods of reducing their influence.

The kinds of questions asked by those who hold this perspective are structured in terms of intentions, achievements, and impediments. An illustrative question is "what are the trends in reading levels and what accounts for these trends?" Questions such as this are asked in a way that implies the possibility of improvement.

The phenomena of schooling are treated as more or less productive performances in which telling data consist of measures of performance judged against standards set by intentions. For example, meaningful data for the question on reading levels are judgments on the adequacy of current reading scores in terms of a historical benchmark. Government policy may be seen to account for the trend and, accordingly, its modification becomes the source of improving reading levels.

This method relies heavily on the identification of factors, trends, and insights found in the literature of schooling. It provides a framework of "issues" and questions that structure the study.

Boyer's (1983) study, reported in *High School: A Report on Secondary Education in America*, is an example of a study conducted from the intentional perspective. The implementation studies conducted by researchers such as Leithwood (1982) and Fullan (1982) also are within the intentional perspective.

The Structural Perspective

This perspective embodies a conception in which schooling is seen as the reflection of structural characteristics common to all schools. These structures enable specific functions, which serve the purposes of schooling, to be carried out in schools. The structural and portrait perspectives share a conception in which the whole predominates. In the structural perspective, however, the structural form is abstracted from a number of schools rather than being specific to one. The form is a genus identified through its concrete expressions in different settings, an account of what is common to existing schools or classrooms. It does not imply an ideal school, as is the case in the intentional perspective. It does, however, imply that individual wholes, for example, individual schools, are most appropriately described and understood in terms of their general structural characteristics.

The principal characteristic of methods within this perspective is that structures imply functions, and vice versa. If a process is identified, a search ensues for the structure; likewise, if a structure is assumed, certain school processes are sought. Several specific methodologies are appropriate to this process, for example, interviews, surveys, participant observation, question-naires, and document analysis.

The kinds of questions asked by those who hold the structural perspec-tive are either descriptive, structural questions or functional, process ones. A question such as "what are the decision-making structures in secondary school?" is illustrative. Ordinarily, of course, such a question is followed by its functional counterpart, for instance, "How is computer time assigned to English classrooms?" The phenomena of schooling are evidence of struc-tures and functions in which telling data consist of observations and other records that support an account of structure or process. These data, cast in structural and functional terms, contribute to an understanding of the whole, for example, the maintenance of school order.

A recent example of research from this perspective is Phillip Cusick's study (1983), reported in *The Egalitarian Ideal and the American High School: Studies of Three High Schools*. Other studies from this perspective would be work such as Doyle and Carter's (1984) work on academic tasks. They understood classrooms as structured by academic tasks with certain functions.

The Societal Perspective

This perspective conceives of schooling as a reflection of society. The school has certain values, structures, purposes, and patterns of action that are societal reproductions. The principal characteristic of methods within this perspective is that the activities undertaken allow the researcher to illuminate societal features as they are expressed in the school. The focus of data col-lection is on the correspondence between school and society in the treatment of race, gender, and class differences. Once again, several methods—interview, participant observation, critical analysis, and so on—are all appropriate.

The kinds of questions asked by those who hold the societal perspective deal with the relationship between school and society. A question such as "how do inner-city schools reproduce class structure?" is illustrative.

The phenomena of schooling are treated as versions of more pervasive societal structures. Meaningful data consist of observations and other records of differential treatment of a social variable such as gender. For example, in a study of school knowledge, such data might be information on the relative distribution of knowledge along gender and class lines.

Peter Ramsay's (1983) study, "Fresh Perspectives on the School Transformation–Reproduction Debate" is illustrative. Other research work that adopts this perspective is the work of Michael Apple (1979) and Jean Anyon (1981).

The Narrative Perspective

This perspective conceives of schooling as an expression of personal and social narrative history. A school at any point in time is viewed as a story in which inquiry focusses on the developing text in a way that the present and future are seen in terms of experiential reconstructions of the past. The principal characteristic of methods within this perspective is that a wide range of diverse data is collected over time on specific school practices. These data are then arranged in such a way that an account of practice is given in the form of a narrative. What is appropriate at any point in time and what constitutes the next appropriate steps in the inquiry are determined by the evolving narrative. One may need interviews, participant observation, questionnaires, or document analysis to complete a step in the narrative.

The questions asked by those who hold a narrative perspective focus on the meaning that specific actions hold in terms of participants' personal and social history. Questions such as "what is the meaning of the after-Christmas semester examination for students?" and "what experiential imagery accounts for the way this teacher's class is taught?" are illustrative.

The phenomena of schooling are treated as personally and socially meaningful acts. Telling data consist of observations and other records in which the narrative origins and, therefore, the embodied meaning of an act are revealed.

Our own research work is illustrative of such a research perspective. Other research work that adopts a similar approach is Valerie Janesick's "Of Snakes and Circles" (1982).

FORMS OF KNOWLEDGE
ABOUT A CHILD'S EDUCATION

Understanding research findings in terms of the perspective adopted by the researcher in the study tells us a great deal about how we can use the research to reflect on our practical situations. As an example let us consider the question "what kinds of things would we learn and know about a child's education from the six perspectives on inquiry?" (see also Figure 8.2).

Different forms of knowledge are generated by each perspective, and we may discover different kinds of things about schooling, or some aspect of it, from each one. Each offers useful knowledge about schooling. To understand schooling in all its complexity we need to understand it from these, and perhaps other, perspectives. For now we focus our attention on the education of a single child. We might have focussed our illustration on a classroom, a school, the learning of mathematics, and so on. We hope that as you think about using the perspectives to understand the research you read, you will try to understand other aspects of schooling from each of the perspectives.

From the analytic perspective, we understand the child's education in terms of interacting variables in his or her learning. Such matters as the child's age, sex, learning style, intelligence level, and age of entry into school are all important. Teacher factors such as teaching style, sex, age, preparation, years of experience, and teacher performance variables are also important. A similar analysis of matters such as classroom environment, school program, and parental characteristics is relevant. A comprehensive account of the child's education, according to this perspective, would consist of a listing of these variables and their correlations.

From the portrait perspective, a picture of the child's education would be built up through an holistic account of the child, the classroom, the school, or even the school board. The child's education is seen in the context of a portrait of this complex and pervasive "whole," and would be described in terms of the quality of the experiences provided by it.

From the intentional perspective, the child's education is seen as one of achievement in relation to educational goals that may be specified by others or even by the child. Measures of progress are available for comparison with either oneself or others. Using this perspective, we understand the extent to which the child is attaining standards and fulfilling expectations for his or her education.

With the structural perspective, we understand the child's education in terms of general structures common to schools and of the processes that result from these structures. We would understand the child's education in the context of such structural matters as curriculum levels, the adaptations of curriculum content, and processes of student choice—all within a child's education in terms of social services performed by school structures and functions.

With the societal perspective, we understand the child's education in terms of the predominant forms of treatment of social groups within the society. To understand his or her education, we would consider school subjects as representing kinds of knowledge accessible to groups within society on a differential basis. The child's education would be perceived as a reflection of this treatment.

Finally, with the narrative perspective, we understand the child's education in terms of the child's and the teacher's dominant narratives embedded within cultural and historical narratives. The child's education, for instance, is seen in terms of his or her personal narrative and of the meaning this conveys of his or her learning experiences in a particular classroom. The child's education is seen temporally in terms of past, present, and future.

Each of these perspectives adds a kind of understanding of the child's education: an understanding of effective variables, of complex whole, of accomplishment, of generalized school structure and process, of societal forms, and of personal narrative.

It should also be clear that we have, throughout, said nothing of theory. Our perspectives are forms of inquiry that yield forms of knowledge. We have tried to give a sense of these forms. But within each form, different theoretical orientations are possible and, from our point of view, desirable.

SUMMARY

In this chapter we have provided six characteristics of educational research. These six characteristics allow you as a teacher to ask some questions about how research can be used in your curriculum planning.

We then provided an overview of six research perspectives. These research perspectives give you a tool for analyzing and understanding where the research is "coming from." It helps you ask questions about what conception of schooling the researcher holds, what aspects of schooling he or she is examining, and what characteristics his or her research methods have. You then have a basis for understanding what kind of knowledge the researcher is providing.

In the next chapter, Unlocking the Literature, we give you a way to understand what you are reading in the curriculum literature.

RECOMMENDED READINGS

As further reading for this chapter, we suggest you look at one study from each research perspective. Try to see why we feel it fits within the perspective. Then choose an issue of a research journal you sometimes read, such as *Curriculum Inquiry, Teachers College Record, Harvard Educational Review, Educational Leadership,* or *Elementary School Journal,* and see if you can use the research perspectives to classify articles in the issue. Ask yourself what kind of knowledge is produced in the study. Then try to identify what the study has to say about a child's education or about your curriculum planning. When you become familiar with what we have presented in this chapter, you will find that it is a useful tool to use when reading research literature and trying to make sense of it for your own practice. Remember that research asks its questions and you ask yours. They are not necessarily, nor even likely to be, the same questions.

Unlocking the Literature

The field of curriculum is—to put it bluntly—a maze. No two people seem to want the same thing. Although everyone subscribes to a belief in "basic" education, few can agree on what is basic. Pleas and plans are made for grouping; for the priority of language over thought or of thought over language; for goals, objectives, and how to write them; and for defining the roles of teachers, principals, and consultants. Some think policies are too vague and nondirective; others consider them too specific and directive. Some people believe psychology will solve our problems, while others, equally earnest, plead for a return to the academic disciplines. You could, we are sure, continue this litany from your own experience.

Should we throw up our hands in despair? Not at all. What then can we as teachers do? We need first to be clear about the "curriculum maze." The maze is not only the way things are but the way they have to be. Curriculum, including lesson planning, testing, and teaching, is tremendously complex. People naturally express different views—otherwise, new ideas and alternatives would never enter our thinking. Who then sorts it out? In the final analysis, we teachers do. We walk into a class and the clock is running. Even though many other people feel it is their responsibility to get us to do things their way, we are on our own. It is we, not somebody else, who must take action.

But how is one to think curriculum out if it is so complex? One way, we submit, is by the hard yet rewarding work of reading carefully and listening well. One's mind, working with detailed knowledge of a specific situation, can shape what is read and heard into workable directions for curriculum planning. Although we must do the shaping ourselves, we can develop ways of classifying the books, articles, or speeches that we read or hear, and of extracting from them the meaning intended by the author or speaker.

A version of this chapter with the same title appears in *Curriculum Planning for the Classroom* (1980), pp. 35–43.

Try following the set of eight rules or maxims presented in this chapter. You will find that they can unlock the literature like a skeleton key.

RULES FOR UNLOCKING THE LITERATURE

View Articles and Speeches as Prescriptive

Rule 1: *Read and listen to everything as if it were a practical prescription*. Books, articles, and speeches may appear to be purely theoretical, or they may appear to be objective presentations of research findings. Such materials often contain hidden "messages" that are intended to persuade you of the rightness of a particular approach or course of action. Consider Phenix's *Realms of Meaning: A Philosophy of the Curriculum for General Education* (1964). This well-known work is recognized as an important theoretical resource in curriculum studies. Its theoretical, reasoned character is illustrated in the following quotation taken from the book's preface.

> In a somewhat similar vein, the present volume is an attempt to elaborate a philosophical theory of the curriculum for general education based on the idea of logical patterns and disciplined understanding. The central thesis is that knowledge in the disciplines has patterns or structures and that an understanding of these typical forms is essential for the guidance of teaching and learning. This thesis grows out of the concept of human nature as rooted in meaning and of human life as directed towards the fulfillment of meaning. The various patterns of knowledge or varieties of meaning, and the learning of these patterns is the clue to the effective realization of essential humanness through the curriculum of general education. (p. x)

Even though the book has this theoretical quality, it is also clear that Phenix wants to persuade us to think of curriculum in the way he outlines. In the quotation above, for example, this is seen in the part of the passage that reads ". . . an understanding of these typical forms is essential for the guidance of teaching and learning." It turns out that the very first passages in the book have this persuasive, prescriptive character. The first paragraph of the preface reads:

> In the past decade educators and concerned citizens have shown renewed appreciation of the place of the organized disciplines of knowledge in education. To some extent the impetus for this interest has come from the technical and ideological challenges of the cold war. Americans have become aware of the need for the most effective possible educational

system if they are to meet the demands of life in a highly precarious and rapidly changing world, and they see how important knowledge is for meeting these demands. (Phenix, 1964, p. ix)

Thus, while the bulk of this 391-page book has a very definite theoretical and reasoned character, it is set in the context of its imagined practical application. Phenix's justification for writing the book is practical.

Other types of articles may, like cookbooks, provide their readers with explicit directions. Although there is nothing wrong with cookbooks, you should be reluctant to try new recipes without first seeing good reasons for doing so. The directive in the last sentence illustrates the more explicit kind of practical prescription to be found in reading curriculum works.

Determine Theory/Practice Emphasis

Rule 2: *Decide whether the article or speech is theoretical or practical.* If it is a practical article, determine how much theory underlies its prescription. Some articles and speeches are theoretical, some practical, and some a combination (practical-theoretical). Each type requires a different approach. A psychologist, for example, may speak to you about Piagetian child-development theory; but from your perspective, the only reason for paying attention is to see whether Piagetian theory can make any difference to your classroom practice. Only other scholars and researchers need to judge it from the standpoint of its value as theory. Between this kind of "theoretical" article and the strictly practical "cookbook" type is one that prescribes something but also gives reasons for it. This kind, which we term "practical-theoretical," often reads like a theoretical article; but no matter how logical its wording, it is aimed at getting you to do something in a certain way.

Your first step in dealing with written and spoken curriculum material is, then, to peg the author according to whether the work is theoretical, practical-theoretical, or practical. (A useful simplification is to treat theoretical articles the same as practical-theoretical articles.) Since any author will probably include a mixture of reasons and clearly stated prescriptions, the second step is to determine the balance between reasons and prescriptions. Draw a number line and position the author on it (see Figure 9.1).

Phenix's book from which the above quotations are taken would fall far to the left, although even here the practical, prescriptive context outlined in the preface needs to be taken into consideration. This chapter on reading the literature would, on the other hand, fall well over on the practical side, since rules rather than reasons are stressed. The book as a whole is farther to

Figure 9.1: Theory/Practice Number Line

    1   2   3   4   5   6   7   8   9   10
(Theoretical)   (Practical)

the left on the theoretical side, since reasons for basing curriculum on personal experience are given in terms of ideas of curriculum, narrative, and personal practical knowledge.

Classify by Main Topic

Rule 3: *Classify the article or speech according to the main topics in curriculum.* Many writings and speeches that you encounter will be "on the subject of the curriculum." The authors will promote a view of learning, subject matter, teaching method, and so forth. The intention is to prescribe actual school practices that the teacher should adopt. Again, Phenix's book is a good example, since the concern is with the kind and place of organized knowledge in the curriculum. Furthermore, most teaching subject fields such as science, mathematics, English, and social studies have both teacher- and research-oriented grounds. Much curriculum literature is organized this way.

In recent years another kind of article has become popular, as a result of increased emphasis on shared and local ("decentralized") planning of curriculum. It includes writings and speeches "on the making of curriculum." Authors of such writings refer to "curriculum development" and to such matters as curriculum objectives, the curriculum planning committee, the structuring of materials, and curriculum decision making. Hass, Bondi, and Wiles's book, *Curriculum Planning: A New Approach* (1974), and Connelly, Dukacz, and Quinlan's *Curriculum Planning for the Classroom* (1980) are illustrative titles. Generally speaking, these authors seek to prescribe methods you should follow in planning your curriculum.

Closely related but quite different in purpose are articles and speeches "on managing and maintaining the curriculum." These examine the role of superintendents, consultants, coordinators, and principals. They use the word "implementation" frequently and talk about strategies, action research, climate for innovation, teacher conservatism, curriculum resources, and so on.

Fullan's book, *The Meaning of Educational Change* (1982), is a book of this sort, since curriculum implementation is the book's topic. Hundreds of articles of the kind noted here are referenced in the book. Articles "on managing and maintaining the curriculum" may, of course, combine with the topics "on the subject of curriculum" and "on making the curriculum."

Consider, for example, the title of Tamir, Blum, Hofstein, and Sabar's book, *Curriculum Implementation and Its Relationship to Curriculum Development in Science* (1979). All of these topics appear in this title.

From your viewpoint as a teacher, the purpose of these articles may appear to be to persuade you to do as your superiors and others see fit. Most of these articles, however, are not aimed at you as teachers, but rather are prescribing for others in the school system—for example, the school superintendent wishing to develop and implement a new K–6 mathematics program, or a principal interested in strategies for implementing a Ministry or Department of Education Policy guideline.

Finally, there is a class of articles and speeches "on the study of curriculum." These appear in research journals and at academic meetings. Their intention is to prescribe principles, methods, and problems for curriculum researchers. A wonderful recent example is the spirited debate surrounding Heap's article, "Discourse in the Production of Classroom Knowledge: Reading Lessons" (1985). Although you would miss it in the title, this article made the case for a particular form of ethnomethodology in the study of classrooms. Delamont (1986) raised objections in her "Two 'New' Sociologies of Education: A Comment on Heap's 'Discourse in the Production of Classroom Knowledge.'" Heap (1986) responded with an article entitled "Assuming Transmission or Studying Production: A Reply to Delamont," and finally Hammersley (1987) entered the fray with his article, "Heap and Delamont on Transmissionism and British Ethnography of Schooling," to which Heap (1987) replied with his "Sociologies in and of Education: A Reply to Hammersley."

This debate illustrates a point about the topic of articles "on the study of curriculum," and it further illustrates different points of view at an academic level that spans two continents, since Delamont and Hammersley write in Great Britain, and Heap is a Canadian.

The most important of the four topics discussed above is the first one—articles and speeches on "the curriculum." Most articles you encounter will be on this topic. Because of the importance of the topic, two further rules are needed to help you organize your reading and listening.

Identify the Target

Rule 4: *Decide whether the article is about general curriculum concerns or about more specific subject-matter concerns (the "target" of the article)*. Some articles and speeches are clearly general or clearly specific. An article on behavioral objectives, for example, is probably intended to apply to all curriculum areas, whereas an article on the objectives of intermediate-division science is aimed specifically at science teachers. Hunt's (1987) textbook, *Beginning with Ourselves*, illustrates the generalist "target" as is clearly seen in the book's subtitle, *Practice, Theory and Human Affairs*, and in the opening sentence of the book, which reads, "This book describes how practitioners, theorists, and non-professionals can begin with themselves" (p. xi). Hunt's "target" audience is all teachers and others as well. In contrast, the Tamir et al. book above is targeted at people interested in the science curriculum.

Some articles and speeches are not easy to classify, for instance, those on school divisions, such as primary and senior; or on processes, such as reading, or values education. Nevertheless, if you are willing to make rough-and-ready distinctions, you will find it extremely useful to apply rule 4. For instance, it helps you to quickly see which of your colleagues are likely to be interested in a presentation. If an author's target is the content of Grade 13 biology, it is clear which teachers are affected; but if the target is the writing of objective examination questions, and the author uses biology as an example, many teachers of subjects other than biology may be interested. Thus, what looks like a biology article may on closer inspection turn out to be on the writing of examination questions—and may thus be classified as "general curriculum" rather than "specific content."

Identify Point of View

Rule 5: *Determine the perspective (point of view) adopted by the author.* Decide whether the author is writing from the perspective of social science foundation fields, subject-matter disciplines, or personal experience (the "point of view" of the article). Two people writing on exactly the same topic may give very different accounts of it depending on their perspective. Sharp differences are common. It is wise, therefore, to decide the particular perspective used by an author, because this is an important clue to the author's biases and orientations on the topic.

There are, we suppose, as many perspectives as there are people. But many of them are similar and may be treated as one of a kind. Three kinds are suggested here. They are perspectives derived from social science foundation fields, from subject-matter disciplines, and from personal experience.

Those who treat curriculum from the point of view of foundation fields often do so using psychology, philosophy, and sociology, although more peripheral fields such as political science and economics may also be used. Presentations from a foundation-field viewpoint are often written by professors of educational psychology and philosophy of education. Their work frequently displays a touch of zeal; you need to be wary of the persuasive rhetoric. Such articles also tend to stress theory and reasons, and hence may often be classified as practical-theoretical, under rule 2. Hunt's book noted above illustrates a psychology perspective. Hunt, for example, credits the origin of his ideas to the psychologist Kelly when he writes, "My theme, beginning with ourselves, is based on George Kelly's belief that every person is a psychologist" (1987, p. 1). Contrast this psychological perspective with Phenix's philosophical one in his book, *Realms of Meaning*, noted above. His subtitle, *A Philosophy of the Curriculum for General Education*, clearly identifies Phenix's perspective.

Those who treat curriculum from the viewpoint of subject-matter disciplines (such as the arts, science, and mathematics) are often professors in schools and faculties of education. Not surprisingly, such articles are often specific (see rule 4). While focussing on the content of, say, science, they may be writing about science from the perspective (point of view) of the discipline of science itself. A good example is given in Connelly, Dukacz, and Quinlan (1980), Chapter 5, where we read of a group of history professors' criticism of the content of Ontario's intermediate level history curriculum guidelines. The criticism is made from the viewpoint of the discipline of history. The same history guideline could also be criticized from another perspective—for example, from the psychology of learning or even from the experience of the writer.

Less frequently, articles "target" on general curriculum from the "point of view" of the disciplines. Some people may argue, for example, that the entire curriculum should be modified to permit the introduction or expansion of a subject such as Canadian studies. Others insist that the main organizing principle for the curriculum should be the traditional disciplines. Phenix's *Realms of Meaning* is a version of this last possibility in that he provides a discipline-oriented structure for the organization of the curriculum as a whole.

Authors who write or speak about curriculum on the basis of their own experience with it often have about them a ring of everyday practicality. Frequently they are short on theory and reasons, and therefore can be classified as practical (rule 1). Speakers at professional development gatherings, for example, are often asked to describe something successful that they have done. While such speeches may be disparaged as "war stories" or "tricks of the trade," do not be misled: The presentations may prove extremely valuable, particularly if the authors provide enough detail to enable you to match your own circumstances with theirs. We imagine that teachers who take seriously *Teachers as Curriculum Planners* will use their own stories and other reflective experience to argue curriculum matters.

Note that an article or speech may adopt more than one perspective. For example, university curriculum professors who are professors of a content area, such as social studies, may feel that the teaching of their subject matter is best viewed from one or another of the foundation fields.

Thus it is not unusual to find that an article dealing with, say, mathematics content is written from the perspectives of both mathematics and cognitive psychology. The well-known cognitive psychologist David Ausubel, for example, has published several articles on science content based on his psychological theories. In this case only one viewpoint is at work. But professors of science education who are disciples of Ausubel or other teachers of cognitive psychology often mix "good science" with "good psychology" in their arguments about science teaching. To understand their articles fully, you need to be aware of the two points of view.

The same sort of mixing of viewpoints occurs with articles having the "author's experience" perspective. An author may weave personal experiences into an argument written from a foundation or discipline point of view. He or she may argue for the teaching of science from a Piagetian perspective and at the same time draw on his or her own experience with children. In the book you are now reading, for example, personal experience, set in a context of philosophy of knowledge, plays a large role in making the prescriptive, practical argument to the effect that "your personal curriculum is a metaphor for your curriculum and teaching" (Chapter 3).

After all this classifying, what can we now say about an article or speech about curriculum? Well, we might say that a certain article is about the curriculum (rule 3) and is practical-theoretical (rule 2); that is, it gives both prescriptions and reasons. We may also be able to say that the article is on general curriculum (rule 4) and is written from the point of view of both psychology and personal experience (rule 5). (Figure 9.2 provides a sort of map to help you chart your course.) Once an article has been classified, there are a number of other reading and listening steps that will help you "get a handle on" an author. Take an example such as the Phenix book used for illustration above and try to work your way through a complete example. Or, to take an example close at hand, why not try to "map" this book.

Determine Desired Outcome

Rule 6: *Ask yourself, "What does the author want me to do?"* This question follows from rule 1. If we are to approach all curriculum writing as if it were prescriptive, we will be watching out for what the author wants us to do. This is usually easy to determine. Articles or speeches frequently begin with criticism of some practice or view and then proceed to support another. It is quite clear what the author wants the reader to give up and to take on. An author's wording may refer to the "curriculum" or "practices in the field" or "views commonly held." What the author really wants is for you as reader to do something different—or the same, of course, if your

Figure 9.2: Classifying Writers and Speakers on Curriculum*

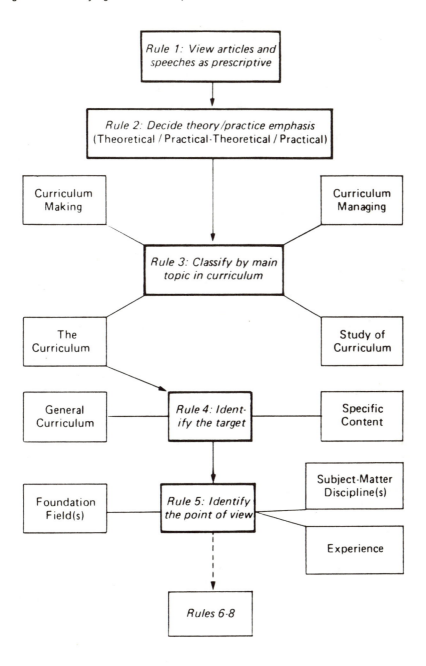

*From Connelly, Dukacz, Quinlan, (1980, p. 43)

practice is in line with the author's ideas. For instance, Phenix wants curriculum to be organized according to the realms of meaning outlined in his book, and Hunt wants practitioners to rely on their own experience.

Rule 6 is easier to apply to writings than to speeches. A reader can skim an article, checking off what the author thinks should be done. Once you have this firmly in mind, it is much easier to follow the arguments used. Indeed, they often make no sense unless you continually remember to ask, "If I were to follow what this author says, what would I be doing?"

Determine Rationale

Rule 7: *Ask yourself, "Why does the author want me to do it?"* This is a fairly simple task with practical articles in which any reasons given are presented in a direct way. The task is more complicated with practical-theoretical articles that emphasize reasons and justifications. But there is a simple tool you can use (see Chapter 7 for details).

Every writer on curriculum, in one way or another, touches on the learner, the subject matter, the milieu of teaching, and the teacher. When you skim an article or take notes on a speech, use the notations "L" for learning, "SM" for subject matter, "M" for milieu, and "T" for teacher to help you see quickly whether an author or speaker is discussing students, teachers, the role of society in learning, and so on. Once you have these pinpointed, you can readily locate the starting point of the argument and see how the author develops it. The starting point (perhaps hidden in the text) might be the view that children (L) are active inquirers. The entire speech or article may follow this up with an account of what the teacher (T) should do to encourage inquiry. Returning once again to Phenix, we note that the second and third sentences of the Preface (quoted above) are clearly identifiable as milieu (M) statements. This gives the "why" of the book. The second paragraph of the Preface gives the "how," that is, the means for accomplishing this purpose. Phenix writes:

> However, there is a far more fundamental justification for basing the curriculum upon the best available results of critical scholarship than the present crisis. This justification is found in the nature of man and of the educative process itself. There are now heartening signs that scholars and educators are drawing together in cooperative effort and in recognition of a common opportunity to make the best that is known as widely and economically available as possible. (1964, p. ix).

This is clearly a subject matter (SM) reason. The entire book that follows is, in effect, a statement of subject matter. A shorthand summary of

Phenix's book, then, might read: "Phenix develops a concept of subject matter (SM) to organize the curriculum for social purposes (M)." Careful and knowledgeable readers of Phenix might well argue with this summary on the grounds that Phenix's key term is "meaning" and that "human beings are essentially creatures who have the power to experience meanings" (p. 5). On these grounds it would be quite fair to argue that Phenix has transformed disciplinary subject matter knowledge into a question of relevant human meanings and that he is, therefore, talking about the learner (L) when he writes about realms of meaning. On this more complex notion, a summary of Phenix's book might read: "Phenix develops an idea of human meaning (L) associated with disciplinary knowledge (SM) in order to organize curriculum for social purposes (M)."

Critique Prescriptions

Rule 8: *Ask yourself, "Do I believe that what the author wants is a good thing? Is it better than what I am doing at present?"* Since an author is prescribing certain things for you, you must decide whether you wish to follow his or her prescriptions. No matter how reasoned and theoretical the article may be, you still must judge whether or not what is proposed is consistent with what you believe to be sound practice. The article may be first-rate as research or theory and still be of no more than passing interest to you. Obviously, of course, you should keep an open mind as you read articles or hear speeches, and be willing to consider alternatives to your own way of thinking and doing.

Rule 8 brings us back to where we began. The literature of curriculum is a complex maze that no one else can sort out for you. The system outlined in this chapter can help you to do the sorting more quickly and efficiently; try it on the next curriculum article you read or speech you hear.

RECOMMENDED READINGS

If you have enjoyed reading this chapter, you will want to read the book on which the chapter is based, *How to Read a Book*, by Mortimer J. Adler and Charles Van Doren.

10

Stakeholders in Curriculum

Newspaper editorials and local television channels often carry stories and comments on what schools and teachers "should" be doing. Frequently they find fault with what we are doing in our classrooms. Our first reaction is often "what right do they have to tell me what to do in my classroom?" But this first emotional response is usually followed by a more thoughtful comment about the concern voiced. For, as educators, we know that many people have a right to make demands on and comments about our schools and what goes on in our classrooms. They have what is called a "stake" in curriculum and we call them "curriculum stakeholders."

By "stakeholder" we mean a person or group of persons with a right to comment on, and have input into, the curriculum program offered in schools. We say they have a claim or a stake in what goes on in our classrooms. Obviously the stakes or claims they have may be very different one from another. Students have one kind of stake in the curriculum, and the Ministry or Department of Education another. Trustees and the business community each have different stakes in what we do in our classrooms, and on it goes. In the next section we examine some of the stakeholders and their stakes in our programs. It is important that we know and understand the various stakeholders and their stakes, for, as we well know, our schools are in dynamic relationship with the society, that is, shaping and being shaped, reflecting the society and responding to it. Our job as teachers is to know who the stakeholders are and what stakes they have in our programs so we can be appropriately responsive.

Given the focus of this book, we must also be aware that, as teachers, our personal narratives are embedded within the historical and cultural narratives of our society. We need to be aware of the various claims made on us by all stakeholders rather than being responsive to only those which are part of our own narrative experience.

WHO ARE THE STAKEHOLDERS?

To gain some sense of the idea of stakeholders let us read the transcript of an elementary school teacher, Marie, as she talks about her classroom planning. The interview was not designed around the idea of stakeholders. It is all the more fascinating, therefore, to see the role various stakeholders play in her thinking. As you read the interview fragments, try to identify the stakeholder whose concern she is addressing. When we come to the end of each fragment, we briefly discuss our own notion of who the stakeholder is and what stake we think that stakeholder has on Marie's curriculum. In a subsequent section we provide ways to help you understand the stakeholders in your curriculum situation.

FRAGMENT #1

This week because I am planning for Grades 2 and 3, what I have done is tentatively skimmed the curriculum guides for all the major subject areas, to see . . . the four to start with. (Just to see what is supposed to be there and what I have to study over the weekend.) On Saturday morning I spent my time reading through the curriculum guides quite closely. So I have done that to see what sort of skill areas they want you to touch on and cover. Then I have quite a few ideas in my head, very major things, like I will use journals. We will use conferencing. First of all I will start with one child sharing a book with a group, the whole group, and then we will break this into smaller groups, so I have these massive ideas in my head. There is nothing on paper yet. . . . First of all, before I set up the curriculum, I need to spend, I think, about a week with those children . . . get to know what they are like. Who are they? What backgrounds do they have? What are their skills? So I need to do miscue analysis in reading to see how well they read. We are going to do a few little diagnostic tests in math to see what sort of skills they've gleaned . . . um, we are also going to do some things that will set up the room. I could do that myself but I think it would be better for the children to take part in it to give it a sense that this is their room and we are all here together.

In this interview fragment, Marie draws our attention to two very important stakeholder groups. We see her noting that the curriculum guides provide boundaries for her curriculum. They can be seen as representing the government's stake in her curriculum. They are, of course, written and developed with professional advice and with political considerations in mind. They are an attempt to balance the claims of various stakeholders. For teachers in their classrooms, what the guides have to say represents an important stake in their curriculum.

But she also points to perhaps the most important stakeholder in curriculum planning, the student. Students are placed in schools for a set number of years, and they expect a number of things from their educational experience that will lead to their cognitive, social, emotional, moral, and physical development. They have a major stake in our curriculum; Marie points to that in her comment about needing to get to know her students. She also knows the importance of helping the children recognize that they have a stake in the curriculum by letting the "children take part in" setting up the room so they know that "we are all here together."

FRAGMENT #2

Jean: What kind of problems do these kids have that you are going to be working with?

Marie: Well, I hear rumors that we're going through a heavy sexual abuse program in the next couple of weeks because I guess there is a fair amount of sexual abuse in the area. The program is being run by the police department.

She refers here to an agency or institution with a stake in what she is doing in her classroom. In this instance it is the police department. Different agencies and institutions at different times and for different reasons have an interest in and a right to influence the classroom curriculum.

FRAGMENT #3

Jean: So there's no expectation made on either math workbooks that they have. . . .

Marie: No, you don't have to. In fact, the principal encouraged me by stressing that "whole language" was what they were going for. So there's, and I don't think that I have, there is no expectation in that area.

Here she draws our attention to the stake that administrators have in her curriculum. While in this fragment she recognizes the stake of an in-school administrator, other school administrators such as superintendents of curriculum also have a stake because of their leadership mandate from the school trustees and, indirectly, to the public.

Marie: There is one area that I am having a lot of problems with and that is having parents in the classroom. Now I certainly understand parental involvement and all of that and I do think the parents have the right occasionally to come in, but I am having doubts about every Monday I have this parent and then Tuesday and then Wednesday and then Friday and then we start the cycle again. I don't know how valuable that is for anyone. . . . So I am having trouble about these parent situations.

Jean: But will you have parents?

Marie: Yes, I will have one or two once in a while, which is okay. I mean I certainly feel that they should be able to come in once a month and see what their child is doing, but as far as getting intimately involved in all the program and all of that, I think we have lost, to me, I think we have lost the objective of the parent involvement. Otherwise, why do we have school at all?

Here she draws our attention to the stake that parents have in our curriculum. Marie recognizes their stake in her classroom. But she also wonders just what the nature of their stake is. Parents depend on schools to provide quality educational experiences for their children; to develop their children socially, emotionally, and morally; to provide physical care and support; and to assist their children toward goals to which they and/or their children aspire.

Yes, I know and I am also signed up for a course with the math consultant on the 4th. . . . She is teaching a math workshop at the resource center. She is doing drills and multiplication and whatnot for grades 2/3 . . . so that would be very specific for me. . . . Math I am worried about because my background in math is not all that great and I am not quite sure how children learn numbers. I have done some reading in it. I read *Children's Minds* by Donaldson.

Here the teacher (Marie) draws our attention to the stake that consultants and school resource people have in our curriculum. They are responsible for providing teachers with information on materials and methods through workshops and professional development days.

So then we have math after recess, because that is what everyone does and I can truly say to everyone, yes, we are hitting the required number of minutes, which is very important. Then I would like to do science in the centers in the afternoon. We would be having science centers about three times a week and have maybe two or three major centers. Now since we don't have any play centers, since I can't have play centers, it is going to be a problem about what sort of centers I will have. I can have puppetry and I can have those two or three science centers and I will have a listening center and . . . painting will be there and clay and those kind of things. They can do their own and then probably two afternoons a week maybe it will be more structured and we will have readers' theater going on and make small groups doing readers' theater. Now social studies somewhere in there, um, probably one, those two afternoons we will do some social studies. I am going to try and integrate as much as possible.

Here Marie makes reference to the amount of time she must spend on each subject matter area. We imagine she is drawing our attention to various stakeholder groups, such as politicians who want to ensure that her curriculum provides students with experience in a broad range of areas that will respond to all societal needs. We might also imagine she is responding to the stake that the community, made up of various occupational groups, has on her classroom curriculum. The demand for academic study rather than "play," as evidenced in her comment "since I can't have play centers," may well be a recognition of the taxpayers as another group of curriculum stakeholders. The taxpayers, who pay for education, want value for expenditures and a voice in curriculum planning.

Um, I am a little worried about venturing into an area that I haven't ever taught before and whether I will be able to hit all those areas I'm supposed to hit. I either say these children are so far behind and what can I possibly do, but then the other point of view is the one that my friend in business is giving me. "Well, why don't you go, do the best you can, and see how far they can come by the end of June." I am also a little worried because I hope that I do really have background. Like I have these ideas. But will I, through my ideas, be able to take it and get the skills, concepts, kinds of things that I would like them to be able to do at the end?

Here Marie draws attention to yet another group of stakeholders, the business community. The business community expects our school graduates to meet the employment needs of their organizations. They expect school graduates to have both the appropriate skills and attitudes to take their place in business. She recognizes that she must acknowledge their stake, in her comment about listening to the "other point of view."

FRAGMENT #8

I have learned that and I am happy to be in a closed classroom because I don't think that I want to take risks anymore with everyone watching. I will do fairly safe lessons that I know that I've done before when people are going to be watching. Although I think when children trust you they will do a lot. They will go with you even in a risky situation. . . . When the trustees came to look at the program that day . . . it was very interesting what the children said at the puppet center; they were making James out of paper bags, they were making the peach and James, and Deirdre (one of the students) said, oh we don't have to make these, Mrs. M said we didn't have to, just if we wanted to do this. And one of the trustees asked "well, why were they doing it?" and Deirdre said because they were reading the story in the morning and they wanted to do a play about it but they don't have to do a play about it. And I was really surprised at how they made it very clear. . . . I am just surprised that they verbalized it so carefully . . . and Deirdre made it quite clear that they didn't have to do this because she was asking them how they chose centers, did they manipulate, essentially were they manipulated into choosing things and. . . .

She draws our attention here to trustees, another group of stakeholders, elected by the community to operate local school systems. They are responsive to, as well as responsible to, the electorate to run an efficient and successful school system. They have a stake in what goes on in the classroom and a responsibility to their electorate to ensure that quality education is going on. In the fragment, we learn that a school visit is one way trustees get to know what goes on and fulfill their mandate.

FRAGMENT #9

All it seems to do to me is reinforce stereotypes so I think there is a lot of other things that we can do in social studies without touching that yet. I don't think they're ready. I mean you have to use some very abstract concepts and I don't think children at 7 or 8 are ready to do that. That's my own view. In fact, I'm really, my first degree was in history and, um, I was amazed when I got to university and I really found out what history was about.

Marie draws our attention here to her sense of the stake the university has to maintain a standard of excellence in all professions, including teaching. It is up to the universities to advance knowledge, conduct research, and provide leadership. She draws our attention here to her sense of that claim.

FRAGMENT #10

What I would like to do in language arts, this is what I was running through my mind just before I got here. I really like doing the news and they truly like it and I truly understand that, talking about themselves and what they have done and it does all those, it covers all those speaking group things that you need.

In this last fragment she draws our attention to her own, the teacher's, claim on the curriculum. Teachers want to provide quality educational experiences for children in their classrooms. This book is basically about the claim that teachers have on the narrative of experience for themselves and for the children in their classrooms.

This illustrative interview does not, of course, cover all stakeholders with claims in all curriculum situations. Marie names many of the stakeholders readily apparent in her classroom planning situation. As we noted above, this was not an interview designed to probe the stakeholders in Marie's classroom situation. The interview was conducted to help Marie reflect on her classroom teaching. It makes use of one of the reflective tools we outlined in Chapter 5. Notice, however, how intuitively Marie recognizes the claims of various curriculum stakeholders. We think teachers recognize spontaneously and intuitively that they work in a prescriptive environment filled with various forces that must be juggled. They recognize various stakeholders and their claims on different aspects of curriculum situations. Think back on the interview fragments and try to see what claims Marie thinks various stakeholders have on her curriculum situations.

Try a similar activity using your own reflective material. As you think about your own curriculum situation and your reflections on it using the tools discussed in Chapters 4 and 5, try to identify stakeholders in your curriculum situation. Go through the data you have now collected about yourself, the interview material, the stories, the journals, and so on, and see if you can identify your own understandings about stakeholders in your situation. As you engage in this activity, you will have new questions to ask about your curriculum situations. Rather than seeing the claims as something to be struggled against, you will be able to identify the various stakeholders and their claims. In the next section we help you work through an analysis of the stakeholders in your curriculum situation.

UNDERSTANDING STAKEHOLDERS
IN YOUR CURRICULUM SITUATION

Your curriculum planning situation can vary from planning your classroom curriculum to program planning with a team of teachers in your school to participating on a local or provincial or state curriculum committee. In the above interview fragments we saw a teacher planning her classroom curriculum situation. Each time you find yourself in a situation where you are working on a curriculum problem, your first step is to understand your curriculum situation.

Ask yourself the following questions. Keep notes on how you respond to each question.

1. What is the purpose of the curriculum situation?
2. If there is a group, what is the makeup of the group? If you are planning with your students, remember to include them as part of your group.
3. Who set up the project?
4. How was the group's membership and purpose established? Even if your curriculum situation is classroom planning, think about the latter two questions. When we think about our classroom planning as a curriculum stakeholder situation (as Marie might do following her interview), we gain new insight into how we understand our classrooms.

Your next task is to understand the stakeholders in your curriculum situation. Your first activity here is to make a list of all of the stakeholders in the particular curriculum situation under consideration. If you are considering your classroom planning, the stakeholders will include the students, parents, and you as teacher. Your list may also include the Ministry or Department of Education (as represented in the curriculum guides), trustees and administrators, and, depending on your situation, any of the other stakeholder groups mentioned above. Think of Marie's list. Be as specific as you can in naming the stakeholders. Is there a particular trustee or administrator that is a stakeholder, for example?

Once you have your list completed, ask yourself the following four questions for each stakeholder. Keep notes on your responses.

1. How accountable am I to this stakeholder?
2. How much will this stakeholder be affected by my decision?
3. How much risk is there in ignoring this stakeholder?
4. How much right has this stakeholder to direct my action?

Once you have worked through the activity, review the list and see which stakeholders have the most significant stakes.

Your next activity is to examine the claims of the four or five major stakeholders in your situation. One approach to doing this is to use an analytic framework based on the curriculum commonplaces (see Chapter 7). Use the four commonplaces of subject matter, learner, teacher, and milieu to probe the claim of each. For example, ask questions such as the following:

1. What does the stakeholder see as the teacher's role?
2. What view of the student does the stakeholder have? What aspect of the learner is stressed by this stakeholder?
3. What characteristics of the subject matter does the stakeholder stress?
4. What does the stakeholder see as the appropriate environment for learning in this situation?
5. What aim for society and/or educated persons does the stakeholder have?

It is important to realize that some stakeholders see their stake as one of managing other stakeholders' claims. The principal, for example, may see his or her job as that of ensuring that curriculum guidelines are implemented. He or she may not see the claim as ensuring a particular view of learner or subject matter but merely as a manager of guideline implementation. In light of this, add one more question to the five above.

6. Is the stakeholder primarily a manager of another stakeholder's claims, and, if so, what is this stakeholder managing?

BANNING BOOKS: AN EXAMPLE

An example of how these questions can be used to understand a stakeholder's claims may be seen by analyzing the following newspaper column. The problem is an old one; "Should certain books be banned from the classroom?" Read the newspaper column and try to identify the various stakeholders and their claims.

Globe & Mail
Saturday, July 26, 1986

SCHOOLYARD PAIN OUTWEIGHS VALUE
OF TEACHING SOME CLASSICS

By Michele Landsberg—New York

In London, England, I've heard, they sometimes read Little Black Sambo aloud in inner-city kindergartens filled with black children. I loved that book as a child; I envied Sambo's radiant clothes, especially his purple shoes with crimson soles and linings; I thought Black Mumbo was a wonderful mama, and when the tigers melted into butter, my joy knew no bounds.

But the book holds no joy for little black kids who are cruelly taunted by white classmates.

The Adventures of Huckleberry Finn is an anti-racist masterpiece whose every word is pure delight to me. But it has proved a torment to West Indian high-schoolers in the Jane-Finch suburbs of Toronto, who only hear, over and over again, "nigger, nigger."

I thought of these school book controversies when the latest one erupted a couple of weeks ago in Waterloo, Ontario, home of one of Canada's largest school boards. A parents' group pressed the board to stop teaching Shakespeare's Merchant of Venice in Grades 7, 8, and 9.

People tend to jump into fixed positions in these disputes, and the media have their own biases. As usual, the trustees were portrayed as grovelling political cowards, the parents as overemotional and unenlightened, and the great work of literature as a battered and bleeding victim.

"Another school book ban!" complained radio and press people.

But there is no ban.

The trustees have asked the Ministry of Education for proper guidelines on how to teach the play . . . thus leaving everyone unsatisfied. The protesting parents had not asked for a ban, and they had not asked for guidelines either. They argued, with what seems like plausible evidence, that teaching this controversial play in Grades 7, 8, and 9 was counterproductive. Jewish students, a tiny minority in the area, were being called "Shylock" and "dirty Jew" by other students after the play was taught. Some Jewish students even had coins thrown at them by sneering classmates.

I don't have to guess how those kids feel. I know. I remember how I yearned to belong in Grade 9 (I bought the saddle shoes and the ribbons in school colors to pin to my shoulder), and how cold a spotlight fell when the teacher turned her mild and kindly face to me, the only Jew in Grade 9, and said: "Stand up, Michele, and explain to the class about Jews . . . about usury . . . about the pound of flesh. . . ."

Had the play been taught in Grade 11 or 12—which is, by the way, just what the Waterloo parents are requesting—I would have been more worldly (and so would my classmates) and better able to bring some historical perspective to bear (and so would they).

The trustees in Waterloo have reacted with what we have come to recognize as predictable doltishness. One, a bold innovator, said, "It's been taught for decades and there's no reason to change." Another said, "The parents are over-reacting." This is a familiar Canadian theorem: "I am sensitive, you are over-reacting, she is hysterical." The board voted to have the Ontario Human Rights Commission rule on whether the play is anti-Semitic, a move of such staggering irrelevance that it leaves me breathless.

What matters is not whether the play is anti-Semitic, which is quite likely indeterminable, but that students are a captive audience. There must be sound educational reasons—and none have been convincingly argued—for the choice of materials.

"They have to learn about racism," said a Waterloo education official. Another irrelevance. If the authorities are burning to teach about racism, let them teach history courses on slavery, on the Holocaust and on what Canadians did to fellow Canadians of Japanese extraction (during World War II). The Merchant of Venice is a very bad vehicle for teaching about racism to confused youngsters, because it seems to give the imprimatur of the great playwright (and of the school) to the most virulent of stereotypes, as columnist Gunther Plaut pointed out in this newspaper last week.

"Huckleberry Finn is a masterpiece," argued a chorus of self-righteous voices during the similar furor in Toronto's Jane-Finch immigrant suburb a year or two ago. Of course it is. So what? There are a thousand other masterpieces; why do schools have to pick one that will humiliate, wound and alienate their youngest and most vulnerable students?

Schools have a fine line to walk between responsiveness to students and parents, and their duty to intellectual freedom. It seems to me that when they move a highly controversial work to a higher grade, that's a responsible educational decision. Such choices are made constantly: at most, five of Shakespeare's plays are taught throughout high school.

Romeo and Juliet, for example, is not widely taught in Grade 9 though I would have thought it highly relevant to the seething concerns of 14-year-olds. Does anyone protest that it is "banned"?

Nor is there a real parallel to the frequent flare-ups when fundamentalist groups seek to banish Margaret Laurence's works from high school curricula. There, indeed, is a censorship issue: such pressure groups (often they are not parents of students at the school in question) try to proscribe the entire work of one of our stellar Canadian authors. No such repressive impulse is behind any of these current ethnic imbroglios.

Schools are not libraries, where citizens freely come and go and read (or do not read) what they please. Our concern should focus on those who have neither voice nor vote nor any choice in the matter: the students who must sit there and hear themselves demeaned, and who have to brave the schoolyard afterward, while the teachers adjourn to their lounge.

In the column we learn that parents in a school jurisdiction want a particular play, *The Merchant of Venice,* taken out of the Grades 7, 8, and 9 course of study and taught instead in Grade 11 or 12. They have made their request because of the younger students' reaction to the play and with particular concern for the Jewish student minority.

The trustees, on the other hand, see the curriculum situation as one in which teachers need only proper instructional guidelines and the board needs knowledge of whether the play is anti-Semitic. We assume that if they found the latter to be true, they would ban the study of the play.

The students, as represented by the columnist's memory of her own school experience, are seen to be at that age lacking in "worldliness" and "historical perspective" to understand the play. They are a captive audience for whatever is taught.

What is evident in the debate as represented in the column is that the trustees and parents have a strong stake in the curriculum situation. Let us try to analyze the curriculum situation using two of the six questions provided above. You may want to finish the analysis of this situation on your own. Our analysis will give you a feel for what we mean.

For example, what does the stakeholder see as the teacher's work or role in this situation? The trustees see that teachers need appropriate instructional guidelines with which to teach. Given those, they can teach any literature (subject matter) to students. The parents see that teachers must judge the appropriateness of particular literature (subject matter) by understanding its impact or influence on their students.

Further, what view of the student does the stakeholder have? The trustees see students as able to understand literature (if properly presented) regardless of their age, developmental level, or experiential background. The parents see students as needing a certain degree of worldliness and perspective in order to understand some literature.

If you are interested, go on with the analysis. Our analysis merely provides a start. We encourage you to complete such an analysis for your own curriculum situation. When you have done so, you can gain a sense of a "match" or "mismatch" among the stakes held by the various key stake-holders. You then have enough information to discuss with colleagues and others what to do about a mismatch.

As another step in analyzing your curriculum situation, you may wish to list your own responses to each of the six questions. What are your views as a stakeholder in the situation? In that way you can compare your own views with the views of the other stakeholders (the principal, the guidelines, the parents, and so on) in your situation.

WHAT NEXT?

At this point you are on your own. You have a great deal of informa-tion about your curriculum situation and are now ready to make planning decisions based upon it. If you are making plans for your classroom, you are now ready to consider how to proceed on your own and in consultation with colleagues. If you are on a curriculum committee, your committee now has some shared ground from which to deliberate on the necessary next steps of planning. You now know who wants what and how much attention each stakeholder must be given in your planning situation.

RECOMMENDED READINGS

There are no books that deal specifically with the topic of this chapter. But there are works that stress the "politics" of curriculum planning. Two interesting books in this respect are Lawton's *The Politics of the School Curriculum* and Becher and Maclure's *The Politics of Curriculum Change*.

11

Curriculum Materials

Curriculum materials are central to the learning process. Ordinarily we tend to think of textbooks when we think of materials, but we might just as well think of films, papers, workbooks, newspapers, laboratory equipment, lakes, ponds, and street corners. Chapter 1 set out a curriculum idea that made "things," called "curriculum materials" in this chapter, integral to the curriculum process. After all, people do not experience in a vacuum. Think of an art object. It is an idea worked out in a material medium of paint, glass, and so forth. Think of a building, an idea made real through concrete, glass, and steel. Think of the curriculum, of experience and thinking. We readily see that experience takes place through processes of interaction with things, things we call "curriculum materials." For a person, growth into the future through experience in the curriculum is, therefore, a process of interacting with curriculum materials.

That is the general idea, given the concept of curriculum in this book. But it is an idea that at first may seem humdrum if we think of materials only in terms of textbooks. An inexperienced teacher may see little other than security in materials. They are a comforting source of activity, teaching, and assignments. An experienced teacher might have a sense of resignation about the faith that curriculum reformers seem to have in curriculum materials changing education.

Curriculum materials will make everything better! Or so school reformers seem to think. Reformers, at least those with money, inevitably turn to "curriculum development" and "curriculum implementation" when they sense that something is awry with the schools. The 1960s and early 1970s were the years in which the greatest effort in North America, and abroad, was made to reform education through curriculum materials. It was a time of the "alphabet soup" courses in the United States— BSCS Biology, PSCS Physics, CHEMstudy Chemistry, AAAS Science, and DISTAR reading. The list goes on. These were curriculum materials produced by national organizations with millions of dollars of funding. The results were less than spectacular, particularly from the point of view of the developers and implementors of these programs. Why should that be so? After all, a great deal of money was put into the production of the materials. Top people from the academic disciplines, from education, and from support disciplines such as psychology and philosophy participated in the process. And a great deal of money was spent on implementation. The answer, as far as we are concerned, is a curricular one. The experience of teachers and students in their curriculum situations was overlooked and often dismissed.

As teachers we need to understand how curriculum developers and implementors have thought of classrooms, because those ideas are still in existence. When national organizations, local boards, or even consortiums of teachers gather together to reform the schools, they often do so in ways that relive the development and implementation years of the 1950s to 1970s. You will be better prepared to cope with curriculum developers and curriculum implementors if you have a grasp of their ideas of curriculum and the classroom. In this chapter we describe an array of possibilities, all of which revolve around varying degrees of acknowledgment of the curriculum as an interactive experience of teachers, students, and materials set within the biographic context and the intentional futures of those situations.

TEACHER-PROOF MATERIAL

As we write this book in the 1980s, we look back with a sense of disbelief at the "teacher-proof" literature. The idea was quite simple, as seen in Figure 11.1. After it was decided what needed "fixing" in the schools, materials were developed as the treatment. Teachers were seen as modifying screens of the purposes built into the materials. Various strategies were undertaken to minimize teacher influence; hence the name, teacher-proof materials. These notions were found in programmed learning textbooks, some versions of computer-assisted instruction, and highly prescriptive textbooks detailing what the teacher should say and do at particular times and giving answers to questions teachers might pose to students. A particularly vivid example of the latter were the teachers' manuals that accompanied publishing houses' basal reading series.

Remnants of the teacher-proofing idea are still found in government policy documents, perhaps more frequently in centralized countries than in more decentralized countries such as Canada and the United States. Still, in these latter countries, provincial and state governments and large school boards often act as the "country" and produce detailed curriculum guidelines. Teacher-proofing remnants are also found everywhere in professional development and teacher workshop activities. Too often these activities are not curricular and educational in the sense described in this book but are,

Figure 11.1: The Idea of Teacher-Proof Materials

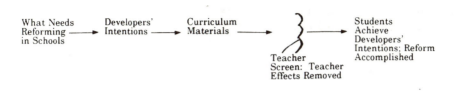

instead, efforts to get teachers to teach specific things in specific ways. Recognizing the virtual impossibility of preparing curricular materials on which teachers could not imprint their personal stamp, the workshopping/professional development idea is often used as a teacher-proofing backup. The idea of spending time and money on the training of teachers is often not so far removed from the idea of ignoring them altogether in the production of teacher-proof curriculum materials. If workshops train teachers to teach in certain ways, how is this any different, in principle, from bypassing teachers altogether in teacher proofing of curriculum materials? There are, of course, many excellent professional development and teacher workshops. We want teachers to be able to judge for themselves whether the professional development activities in which they engage are educational or whether they are designed as an alternative to teacher proofing. It is your professional development. You must judge.

SELECTING, ORGANIZING, AND ADAPTING CURRICULUM MATERIALS

The title of this section names the heart of the idea of curriculum that most of us are taught. Because there are a wealth of curriculum materials available, and because most of us are not required by government and/or board of education policy to use specific materials, the problem often becomes one of selecting, organizing, and adapting materials for our own use.

Figure 11.2 summarizes Ralph Tyler's classic statement (1950) on this general idea. Understanding this idea will pay curriculum dividends. It has a utilitarian side to it, and you may find it useful in certain circumstances. Just as important, however, is that you think through some of the limitations of the idea. Let us explore it further.

Figure 11.2: Tyler's Classic Formulation Summarized

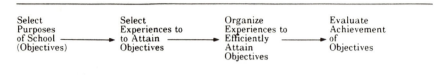

Selecting Objectives

As with teacher proofing, this is a "logical" notion and has a comforting ring to it given the everyday complexities of the curriculum. Choose your objectives, select and organize your classroom activities, conduct them, and evaluate using specified objectives. Straightforward and to the point. Notice also that it is a one-way street from idea to classroom, similar to the teacher-proof idea. The interactive sense of the concept of curriculum advanced in Chapter 1 is missing.

Still, there is much good common sense in the Tyler idea, and some aspects of it are consistent with the idea of curriculum in this book. An objective is something that is intentional. It points to the future, and being self-conscious about our future is, after all, one of the purposes of a narrative understanding of curriculum. Tyler suggests a specific methodology for obtaining objectives. There is to be an assessment of learner and societal needs and characteristics, and a study of the nature of subject matter. These are to be filtered through what is known psychologically and philosophically about people and society. From this, choices are made that yield objectives.

The method is fine as far as it goes. But how far does it go? Notice that this is an "objective" process of obtaining objectives. After reading this book, especially Chapters 1, 3, and 6, it is clear that what is missing is the situational and the personal. It is a "rational," "objective" process, and it is probably for this reason that curriculum development committees are so fond of it. After all, someone developing curriculum for another person cannot deal with personal knowledge or with the details of particular situations, even if he or she wants to. So the process must necessarily be depersonalized. For these people, Tyler's idea probably makes a great deal of sense except, perhaps, for one other thing. Tyler goes on to say that the *way* to state an objective is to write it as a statement that contains both content and behavior. That is, the author of an objective must say what a student is able to do with a certain content. A unit, or an entire course, may therefore be set up in a two-dimensional grid, listing all of the content areas on the y-axis and all of the behavioral objectives on the x-axis. Every cell thereby formed becomes an objective. Indeed, an entire course boils down to this two-dimensional grid.

Suppose the topic is Mendelian genetics in secondary school. The statement of objectives might read: "The student is able to calculate F1 genotypic ratios given the genotypes of the parents." Or, for the same content but a different point on the y-axis, one might write: "The student is able to write an essay on the genetic consequences of in-breeding." This way of setting up a unit or a course can be a handy "objective" reminder. But notice it is "objective"; it speaks of students in behavioral terms (something altogether different from "personal practical knowledge" as described in this book); and there are no rules for deciding just how finely the x-axis and the y-axis may be divided. You might do an interesting exercise by yourself. Take a topic of interest to you, let us say, mathematics at the elementary school level. Then think of every possible breakdown of that topic for elementary school. Now, for the y-axis, think of every possible behavioral objective that might be stated. How many cells did you obtain? 4, 4^2, 4^3, 4^{10}? Some curriculum committees that have taken this exercise seriously end up becoming lost in a sea of objectives. There are some humorous examples on library shelves. You might find it interesting to try to read one or two to see just how far this idea can go.

Selecting Experiences

A key term for Tyler is "experience." This perhaps is not so surprising, since John Dewey taught for a number of years at the University of Chicago where Ralph Tyler worked and wrote his famous book. When Tyler turned to the topic of selecting learning experiences, he began with a preamble that could serve for this book. He says, for example, "It is possible for two students to be in the same class and for them to be having two different experiences" (p. 64). He then shows how this is true. His definition of experience involves "the interaction of the student and his environment" (p. 63), and this "implies that the student is an active participant" (p. 64).

The difficulty with Tyler's idea is that as soon as he says these things, he gives up hope of doing anything about it. Instead he turns to "general principles in selecting learning experiences." These are principles, he says, that apply to all learning experiences whatever the objectives may be and to all students no matter who they may be. Here are the five principles he names:

1. The learning experiences must give the student opportunity to deal with the kind of content implied by the objective. If the objective is to learn to read then the student must be given exercises in reading, not just be told about reading.
2. Learning experiences must be such that the student obtains satisfaction from carrying on the kind of behavior implied by the objectives.
3. The student reactions desired in the experience are within the range of possibility for the students involved.
4. There are many particular experiences that can be used to obtain the same objectives.
5. The same learning experiences will usually bring about several objectives. (Tyler, 1950, pp. 65–68)

(This last statement is significant beyond its appearance and is at the basis of what we later call the "hidden" and "null" curriculum.)

It is worthwhile in your curriculum work to pay attention to these principles. The first three basically say, and remind us as teachers, that students should practice what they are taught, that they should enjoy doing it, and that the activity should not be too difficult. If you think hard about this, it may be a surprise to discover how much of the curriculum fails to meet the principles. The fourth and fifth principles are versions of the old maxim that there is more than one way to skin a cat. These are worthwhile lessons since too often, particularly in teacher inspection and evaluation work, it is thought that there is only one way to do something. If a teacher is teaching in a way that an inspector, superintendent, or evaluator disapproves of, the teacher is likely to be negatively evaluated. We are also reminded here of the hidden curriculum—the idea that we teach a great many things we do not realize we are teaching. Some of those "metalessons" may be added bonuses; other may not.

Organizing Experiences to Attain Objectives

The problem of organizing experiences and/or curriculum materials may be thought about in two different ways: the organization of the conceptual content, *and* its vertical and horizontal distribution across the curriculum.

Conceptual organization. Tyler's breakdown is a traditional one and will profit any teacher thinking about the conceptual organization of material. His three organizing categories are "concepts," "values," and "skills, abilities and habits." Thus, for any subject field to be taught, for example, mathematics in the elementary school or social studies in the secondary school, the teacher planning a curriculum asks:

What are the major concepts in this field?

What are the major values in this field, or to which this field might apply?

What skills, abilities, and habits are basic to this field?

The significance of asking these questions is easily seen when one reads the table of contents of most curriculum materials and sees only a listing of concept categories.

You will undoubtedly wish to extend this breakdown of the conceptual content, particularly if you are a secondary school teacher. There it becomes particularly important to distinguish among theories, hypotheses, concepts, principles, facts, and history of inquiry.

Again, you will wish to ask yourself the same question of each subject field, for example, "What are the major theories in this field?" But you need to do more than this. You need to understand the differences among these conceptual categories. We think you will be genuinely surprised, if you have not thought about this before, to learn how difficult it is to keep even such apparently distinct matters as fact and theory separate. Many working scientists, for example, will say that once a theory has been proven it becomes a fact. For them, the idea of fact is something that is true rather than something on which a theory is based. Most philosophers who write on the nature of knowledge would, of course, disagree with these scientists, holding instead that facts and theories are two different things. You need to sort out in your mind exactly what you think these terms mean and then be able to apply them consistently. This problem is made even more difficult by the addition of the concept of "history of inquiry," because you will frequently see that what you thought was factual in and of itself is actually something defined as factual by virtue of its role as such within a theory. We saw excellent examples of this in the educational literature described in Chapter 8. There, you will recall, what passed as a fact was defined by the perspective at work. A different perspective yielded different facts. But this is just as true in the sciences. Indeed, something that amounts to a discovery for one researcher may not even be recognized by another researcher. The failure of certain molds to grow on agar plates as the triggering fact in the development of penicillin is an example. Many people had made this observation. But it did not register as a "fact" until it was connected to penicillin by-products in mold growth.

Give this problem hard thought. Facts turn out to be quite ephemeral and difficult to define. Likewise, theories are often defined in terms of the facts that particular patterns and histories of inquiry choose to recognize as facts. Many of the "alphabet soup" science and social science courses, noted above, illustrate this interdependence of fact and theory. You need to sort it out in your mind and for your own curriculum, and you need to be able to assess curriculum materials to discover the implied views of fact and theory contained therein.

Vertical organization.   The sequencing of content throughout the curriculum is called vertical organization. In the most general sense, this refers to sequence across grades. In its more detailed sense, vertical organization refers to the development of ideas within a particular lesson.

This idea has been in great favor with those favoring logical development of the curriculum. Gagne (1964), for instance, taught curriculum developers to ask what the prerequisite behavior for any behavior was. For example, if the "terminal" objective was throwing a ball, then the prerequisite behavior was orienting the arm and body in a certain way. One kept asking these questions, thereby building up sequences of behaviors tied to content. The most notable example of this mode of curriculum planning was, perhaps, the American Association for the Advancement of Science's elementary school materials. At one point their entire curriculum was laid out on a huge chart containing long sequences of prerequisite behaviors. Notice that in this plan the curriculum developer specifies a final or terminal objective and then keeps asking questions that lead up to the entry behaviors. Students, of course, following along with this idea, proceed the other way around in their learning. The idea is that they begin with the prerequisite entry behavior and work toward the final or terminal behavior.

When this vertical sequence of prerequisite content and behaviors is turned into a vertical sequence throughout the curriculum, we see that it lends itself most effectively to centralized educational systems. In such systems it is possible to say that students will be at a certain point at the end of each year, and so on down the line as the years are broken into major blocks of time such as semesters, and these into months, and months into weeks, and so forth.

Again, this vertical sequencing has the appeal of objective logic. An interesting exercise would be for a group of two or three teachers to pick a topic and specify and agree on a terminal behavior, and then for each teacher independently to write his or her own vertical organization. What do you think the comparative results would be when the two or three teachers came together? What would happen when these three teachers told stories about the vertical organization of subject matters? They would not have only *one* logical organization in which one part necessarily presupposed another part. Our point here is that any vertical organization is based on an organizing assumption and there are more than one for any field.

If one person makes an assumption, then one kind of vertical organization occurs; if another person makes a different assumption, another kind of vertical organization occurs. As always, when "objective" logic is the basis for curriculum planning, difficulties emerge because of competing logics and because the curriculum logics and what some have called "psychologics" are not taken into account. You may be sure that when one vertical organization predominates in your school, board, state, or province, it is held together, for the most part, by political considerations of one sort or another. Chapter 10 on stakeholders helps to explain this phenomenon. In the end, what appears to be a logical organization of subject matter in curriculum materials is really a political organization.

The two main educational reasons behind the political choice of one or another logical vertical organization are that students need both to build a reasonable, coherent learning structure and to be able to transfer from school to school or community to community with minimal interruption in their learning. These are not easily overlooked considerations and haunt teachers who think beyond particular courses and grades they may teach.

Horizontal organization.   The integration and balance of one part of the curriculum's content with another is known as horizontal organization. The introduction of new curriculum content such as "values education" in the elementary school, environmental studies in the secondary school, or computer literacy at all levels highlights the horizontal organization problem. Questions having to do with age-grade level, instructional time, and effects on other subjects come to the fore. In addition, matters such as the possibility of overlap, redundancy, and support for the new content in other parts of the curriculum are at issue.

The two main ideas that need to be considered in planning the horizontal organization of curriculum are balance and integration. *Balance* refers to the relative emphasis given to each subject in the curriculum. Balance is almost always treated as a temporal matter. In the secondary school, for instance, a standardized unit such as a credit or a course may be defined. The standardized unit will then be defined in terms of the number of instructional hours to be given to it. In Ontario, for example, a credit system is used in which a credit is defined as 120 instructional hours. Since it is known how many instructional hours there are in a year, balance is defined in terms of the number of credits to be given to each subject.

Vertical and horizontal organization come into play because often the deciding factor in any one year is a combination of both. For instance, it may be decided that high school students (Grades 10–12) ought to receive four credits in English, three credits in mathematics, four in the sciences, two in language, and so forth, over the three years of high school. If a subject is rigorously defined in terms of vertical integration, such as mathematics might be, then one credit will be given to mathematics each year.

Students might be given the option of when to take their English credits, perhaps even grouping them in two years if no necessary vertical integration of them has been defined. In any one year, then, the curriculum experienced by a student is a mix of these vertical and horizontal considerations.

As described above, balance considerations are often in the hands of curriculum committees rather than individual teachers. In fact, once a secondary school has settled its vertical and horizontal specification of the curriculum, teachers are hired to fill the ensuing blocks of time. But at the elementary school level the problem becomes more crucial to individual teachers. The curriculum is rarely specialized, and a single teacher is often responsible for most of the class's content. Sometimes, government, board, or school policy may define the number of hours to be given to science, language arts, and so forth, in somewhat the same way that the credit and/ or course system described above works at the secondary school level. But frequently this specification is missing. Even when it is present, elementary school teachers frequently have much more leeway than do secondary teachers in adjusting the balance depending on their own teaching interests and expertise and the needs and interests of their students.

Integration refers to the possibility that the curriculum is defined more in terms of student needs and/or possibly content processes so that different teachers in different subject areas may be said to be teaching the same thing. In the secondary school it is common, for example, to have social studies courses. These are often based on the idea that there are certain social concerns that form the curriculum and that the traditional subjects of geography and history contribute equally to those topics of concern.

At the elementary school, integration is more often a living everyday concern as teachers tend to focus on social skills, language development, attitudes, and so on. An excellent example of integration at the junior high level was seen in Kroma's letter to Bruce, described in Chapter 6.

Various ways of organizing curriculum, as well as print materials, have been designed to cope with questions of balance and integration. The notion of team teaching is one such plan. Open concept schools are another. You will undoubtedly confront the problem of horizontal integration on a day-to-day basis if you are an elementary school teacher. It is a problem also frequently faced by planning and curriculum committees. Many of the battles over what ought to be in the curriculum may be understood in terms of competing stakeholder claims (see Chapter 10).

Evaluating Curriculum Experiences and Materials

Tyler's idea of evaluation, somewhat like Dewey's notion of curriculum, has mostly been misunderstood. Basically, people have set up a simple equation between objectives and testing, and this has *seemed* to fit the Tyler model. To an extent it does. Tyler argues that the purpose of objectives is to specify changes in behavior and, therefore, evaluation is the process of determining whether or not behavioral change has occurred. The degree of change may be used to pass or fail students, *or* to evaluate the success of the teacher or even of the curriculum. But Tyler writes about evaluation in a more developmental way than this simple logic suggests. He asks that assessment come not only at the end of teaching but during the process. Indeed he asks that assessment occur at the beginning so that one knows where one is starting with each child. Furthermore, while most testing is restricted to content and some to skills, Tyler asks that people undertake observations of students to understand their habits, and interviews to understand their attitudes, interests, and appreciations. He asks people to consider a wide array of evaluation devices, for instance, objects made in a shop, books withdrawn from a library, cafeteria food selection, health records, and so forth.

Finally, while evaluation according to the objectives model is usually aimed at student promotion, Tyler describes the possibility of using evaluation to diagnose students' learning needs. Thus, Tyler had more educational uses in mind for evaluation than the achievement testing movement would suggest.

While Tyler did not go as far as we would like, he did come part of the way. What is next? Given the idea of the curriculum in this book, the ideas of objectives and of evaluation are concrete curricular ways of moving into the future and of reflecting on the past. Objectives have an intentional, directional future orientation, and evaluation is a way of continually moving back and forth from the future to the present in a kind of never-ending cycle to adjust and fine-tune curriculum situations along their temporal dimension.

The difficulty with the Tylerian model, then, is partly in its conception and partly in its use. It is conceived as something logical, linear, and objective. And it has been used in such a way that one's mind, one's personal practical knowledge, has been reduced to mere behavior. Furthermore, the future has become overly fragmented in endless statements of objectives. Evaluation has been seen less as feedback and diagnosis and more as a matter of achievement and promotion. So you must read Tyler carefully. Do not take for granted someone else's Tylerian idea of what it means to write objectives, select and organize materials, and evaluate outcomes.

TEACHER AS CURRICULUM DEVELOPER

We are interested in shifting the curricular emphasis from the prescriptions of outside developers, policy makers, academics, and others to the decisions of teachers. We can, of course, imagine an active teacher role following Tyler's idea. But in practice this idea has become strongly equated with the idea that the teacher is someone else's servant.

The choice that school administrators face with new curriculum materials is essentially one of how to treat teachers. Are they to be seen as screens whose effect is to be minimized, as in teacher proofing and most notions of the Tyler idea? Or are they to be seen as integral parts of the curriculum situation and therefore encouraged to explore and realize the curriculum potential of curriculum materials? If the first answer is given, then a great deal of "explaining" to teachers will occur. They will even be encouraged, perhaps, to try out the materials in field tests similar to those in secondary school science laboratories where students do an "experiment" to "demonstrate" an idea in the book. Of course, most of us have been in implementation situations that were not as extreme as that. But we think that if you probe beneath the surface, this is what you will often find is going on. Remember, program implementation may be done in heavy-handed ways or in very subtle ways. The trick for an intelligent teacher-participant is to find out exactly what is happening. Do the people running the program want teachers to put their own stamp on the program? Or do they simply want teachers to bring their personal traits to bear on doing something that the implementors have defined?

In the following sections we describe three ideas that shift the curricular emphasis to the teacher (see Figure 11.3). We contrast these ideas with the idea of implementation, a process that is a version of the teacher proofing of materials.

Curriculum Potential

Using the temporal idea of curriculum described in Chapter 1, we showed in Chapter 3 how it is possible to say that any one individual is a different person in different curricular circumstances. The situation "pulls" different things out of each of us. This same idea applies to curriculum materials. Accordingly, it may be said that different curriculum situations "pull" different things out of a given set of curriculum materials. It is this characteristic that so upsets curriculum implementors who wish their materials to serve specified objectives and to be used in only certain ways. But while this is a tragedy for those who think teachers and curriculum should be controlled externally, it is consistent with the narrative notion of curriculum. It is something to be celebrated.

Ben-Peretz (1975) developed the notion of "curriculum potential" to name this characteristic of curriculum materials. She points out that curriculum materials are more than the embodiment of their developer's intentions, as the notion of teacher-proof curricula and most uses of the Tyler idea would have it. It is not only what may be "read out of" curriculum

Figure 11.3: Choice on What to Do With a New Program

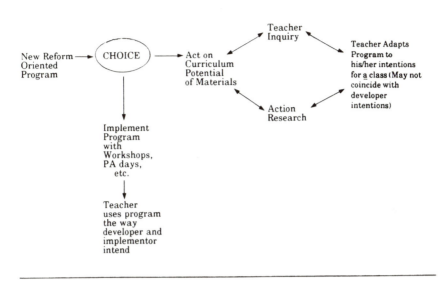

materials, as implementors would insist, but also what may be "read into" them. Everyone who has read a favorite book several times at different stages in life realizes that the same book is many different things, even to one person. What must it be for others? A book is not one thing to be read in exactly the same way by everyone. Books are that, to be sure, but they are much more. We all read a book according to our own personal practical knowledge. Accordingly, different people read the same book differently. And because our narratives evolve and grow through life, we read the book differently at different times in life. Curriculum materials are no different in this respect, and, while they may be an expression of the developer's and implementor's intentions, we teachers also make of them different things depending on our purposes (see Chapter 7).

Ben-Peretz gives a concrete example from the so-called "new mathematics":

> The intention of the developers is to teach "invariants of reflections" as an intuitive preparation for the learning of geometry and functions. The teaching strategy chosen by the developer is individual student work, each child learning and testing his progress independently with little teacher intervention.

The curriculum material is nonverbal and the figures chosen are abstract so as not to distract learners from their tasks. The target population is children at the age of eight with no prior knowledge or experience in this field. Trial implementation of the material has revealed possible uses and learning outcomes not intended by developers. Experience with these reflection cards has shown that, while intended for development of mathematical concepts in an intuitive setting, they can also be used in different subject-matter areas such as language and art.

Although the developers had not intended that teachers intervene in the learning process, some teachers did so. Some told stories to promote understanding; others encouraged children to name the figures they produced with the reflection cards, and to express their reactions in writing or painting. The cards thus became stimuli for creativity.

The target population was children at the third-grade level of primary school. The curriculum potential revealed during implementation trials points to the possible use of the material with younger age levels or with handicapped children. (1975, pp. 155–56)

Ben-Peretz (1975) gives another example using the secondary school biology curriculum. You may wish to read this second example because it illustrates a notion closely aligned to the ideas of this book. She describes material aimed at a "narrative of inquiry" in biology.

How far can one go with the idea of curriculum potential? No doubt, the higher the quality of curriculum materials, the easier it is to create productive curriculum experiences. But it is possible to use poor, standard materials and to create vivid curriculum experiences. Almost all of us know of teachers who work in remote areas, inner-city environments, or private school settings where the quality of available materials is not high, and yet these people create vivid and compelling curricula. Gino, an experienced teacher in one of our graduate courses, told a story (Chapter 5) of his first year of teaching. He remembers it as an especially vivid story. The story is as follows. He was in his first year of teaching and was assigned a class of approximately 50 students in a temporary school building designed for 30. A new school with larger rooms was being built, but it was two months before it could be occupied. Furthermore, books and other resources were not available until the move. He was compelled to teach his classes using resources outside the school. He took the students into the community and his materials became the community resources. He claims that he was left entirely on his own for those first two months of his teaching career. The upshot was, he says, his "first, and likely best, integrated (Grades 7–8) unit of my teaching career, incorporating activities in language arts, science, and geography." When the class moved in to the new school, he says that "this is where the irony comes in. For a variety of reasons we reverted to a more traditional method of instruction, but we now had all the space and supplies we wanted." In this process, Gino learned a great deal about his own strength and about the potential of curriculum materials. Gino is not likely a teacher who has felt constrained by curriculum materials throughout his career. He is aware of their potential and is also aware that he can radically alter the way in which they may be used.

It might be interesting to try a "thought exercise" on some particularly mundane set of curriculum materials. Imagine all the things you might do with them. You will, we think, gather some feel for the idea of the curriculum potential of instructional materials.

Curriculum Inquiry

Curriculum inquiry is a process in which teachers read and study curriculum materials in the same way that they would read and study potentially interesting texts. Part of the purpose, therefore, is to "recover meaning," as described in Chapter 7. This much of the task is not inconsistent with the implementor's purpose, because understanding at the level of the text is partly an effort of finding out what intentions are built into the material.

But even here, notice a fundamental point of difference between implementation as it is usually treated and curriculum inquiry. In implementation, teachers are told, perhaps even exhorted, to learn and act on what is intended, whereas in inquiry teachers work out for themselves, under guidance, the meaning of the text.

Furthermore, recovery of meaning, as noted in Chapter 7, is only half the story in curriculum inquiry. The other half is reading those materials from a personal point of view. The questions one continually asks are "what do these materials mean for my curriculum situation?" and "what can I do with this material?" Again, as Chapter 7 made clear, the inevitable tension that comes from reading a text in its own terms and reading it in our terms creates a kind of third possibility, one that is neither the text as intended by the developer and the implementor nor one that is merely a reflection of our own prejudices. It is, rather, something new resulting from the interaction of reader and curriculum materials as text. And just as any text may be read in different ways by the same person, it is possible that any one teacher will discover and create a variety of potentials in the text depending on his or her particular curriculum situation, the students, the community, and so forth. This matter of different readings is multiplied when we think of the consequences of this notion for different teachers reading the same text, each of whom may have multiple readings of the materials.

Would this process result in chaos? We think not. We think, in fact, this is what happens in practice. It explains why so many curriculum implementations are thought to be failures. They are thought to be failures because the intentions of developers and implementors do not show up unambiguously in classrooms. Given the concept of curriculum in this book, it is clear that these various differences are expected. Furthermore, we want them to occur. As teachers we must trust our own personal practical knowledge, understand our narratives, and decide what is needed in the particular mix of our classrooms. We do not want these matters decided by others. Good curriculum materials have many different potentials for different people in different circumstances. As teachers, we must realize this potential.

Action Research

Action research refers to teachers studying and trying something out "on the fly" in the classroom. Hopkins (1985) defines it as "an act undertaken by teachers either to improve their own or a colleague's teaching or to test the assumptions of educational theory in practice." From the point of view of this book, action research is simply an extension of the notion of curriculum inquiry and is built on the idea of potential in curriculum materials. It names the process that innovative teachers do as a matter of course. They try out new materials to see how the materials work for them in their classrooms.

Some, however, see action research as another way of implementing new curriculum materials. When this idea governs the process, the teacher's innovativeness is minimized. Developers and implementors control the research process and obtain feedback from the classroom. This feedback is obtained either to further modify the materials to ensure minimal influence by the teachers and/or to give corrective advice to teachers on how to use the materials. Be on the alert for this misuse of the idea of action research! It is easy to be trapped by this misuse because it is rewarding to have extra attention paid to your classroom as the developer and implementor provide feedback during the tryout of new materials. And it is easy to be blinded by the praise that developers and implementors will give as you narrow in on the intentions they have in mind. These situations may be pleasant for a teacher. But are they educational? Are they experiences that expand your capabilities and, through the educational growth involved, increase your ability to create rich learning experiences for your students? You must be prepared to dig beneath the surface of attention and praise that may be part of the implementation setting and ask: "Is this activity built on the idea that these materials have multiple potential? Is this activity based on the idea that my personal practical knowledge is to be trusted? Is this activity based on the idea that the test of action research is how imaginatively materials are used for particular situations, rather than how well the intentions of the developers are fulfilled?"

If the situation is genuinely an action research situation, that is, where you as the teacher are the inquirer and not merely the research assistant for the developer and implementor, then the course of the inquiry is in your hands. And because it is in your hands, you, and therefore your students, will be the beneficiaries. You will be educated in the process, not merely trained, as you would be in an implementation setting.

How do we understand this notion in terms of the idea of curriculum and of narrative advanced in this book? As Clandinin wrote, "the narratives of all of us are complex and contain various threads that knit a kind of continuity and unity in our personal professional lives . . . they are particular orderings of prior experience, brought to bear on new situations. As such these orderings yield new ways of telling a story of who we are and how it is that we are doing what we were doing" (1986, p. 11). Action research is, therefore, a deliberate way of creating new situations and of telling the story of who we are. Action research consists of deliberate experimental moves into the future, which change us because of what we learn in the process. This is not so surprising to anyone who has studied the literature of curriculum development and innovation. It is always the developers and innovators who benefit most. They are the ones who say, "The development process was marvellous. I learned so much from being on that committee." You will find the same thing as you bring this process to bear in your own classroom. You will learn "so much." But you will learn only if it is a genuine inquiry. If you are controlled by developers and implementors, you may be trained rather than educated.

THE HIDDEN AND THE NULL CURRICULUM

Elliot Eisner (1979) makes the point that all schools teach three curricula: the explicit, the implicit (i.e., the "hidden"), and the null. The explicit curriculum is the curriculum as stated, including the intentions of developers, policy makers, and others. It also includes lists of content and so forth. The implicit, hidden curriculum names all those things that are taught even though we do not set out to do so. The null curriculum refers to those things deliberately excluded. Whenever something is taught, something else is deliberately not taught. These ideas are connected to the notion of curriculum potential.

Let us take the *null curriculum* first. People who argue strongly that specific things should be taught and that specific intentions should be met are, although not saying so deliberately, specifically excluding other things. Anyone who has participated in a curriculum committee has a good sense of this from seeing members battle over what should and should not be included in the curriculum (see Chapter 10). No curriculum can contain everything. Every intended curriculum leaves out more than it contains.

Leaving things out of the curriculum is not only a matter of excluding certain lists of content. It is also a matter of excluding certain ways of thinking about things. Suppose, for example, a curriculum is explicitly built on the idea of behavior as seen in Tyler's plan. We teach people that what matters is whether something can be seen to be done. Terms such as "understanding," "truth," and so forth, are not part of the curriculum. Rather, we look for evidence of performance. Such a curriculum excludes a view of knowledge and knowing based on the mind. Another curriculum at another school with the same age-grade students might have a curriculum built on discussion, reading, and memorization of concepts and ideas. These students, while being taught the same content as the first, are learning something entirely different. What is excluded for one is included for the other.

There are almost endless possibilities as one thinks about the null curriculum. Try thinking about your own teaching. Make a list of things not taught but that could be. Make sure your list includes ways of thinking as well as what is taught. You will find the exercise illuminating. The exercise will also suggest an important question for you when you are asked to use a set of new curriculum materials. In addition to asking the various inquiry questions noted above, you also want to ask, "What does this set of materials not do? What is excluded?" These questions are especially important given the notion of curriculum potential. Once you discover the "null" side to curriculum materials and decide you wish to make some parts of the null curriculum explicit, then the potential inherent in the interaction between you and the materials will make it possible to use the materials to teach things deliberately excluded by developers and implementors. Of course, those who have a real urge to control teachers in their classrooms know that good teachers do this all the time. It is troublesome to them. But remember, it is your classroom. It is you who must decide what should be included in the curriculum.

The *hidden curriculum* is a closely connected idea. Mostly, this term applies to you as the teacher rather than to the developer, as was the case with the null curriculum. Generally speaking, people think of the hidden curriculum as falling in the area of attitudes and values. Think of this obvious example. We say a teacher who has a love of the subject brings life to the classroom. The hidden message is that studying the subject is fun, enjoyable, rewarding, and worthwhile. Often when we look back on good educational experiences in our own lives, we find ourselves talking about hidden things in those experiences. Teachers who cared, although caring was not an intention; love for the subject, although knowledge may have been the goal, and so forth.

But the hidden curriculum may as easily be negative as positive. Think of the two or three children in a class at whose difficulties in learning a teacher may continually show exasperation. And think of this repeated by other teachers and throughout the grades. The hidden message is that these children are not as worthwhile as others, and they learn to value themselves less, to have a lower self-image, to defer to others.

The only way to be sensitive to the hidden curriculum in our own teaching is to be reflective and to use the tools of Chapters 5 and 6. We need to ask, "What are the meta-messages in my teaching?"

Radical educators in recent years have approached this problem as a social rather than a personal matter. They say various forms of streaming that go on in schools are "hidden" ways that ruling social classes use to educate their young, thereby keeping them in control of society. They argue this on the grounds that students streamed into nonacademic curriculum routes are trained in the ways of following and serving, while those in the advanced academic routes are trained in the ways of dominance and leadership. The same curriculum materials may be found in two separate classrooms. But, because of streaming and, therefore, the "hidden" messages given to the students in different classes, the potential is realized in radically different ways.

The idea of the "hidden" curriculum for radical educators is that society "reproduces" a hierarchical social structure that benefits some at the expense of others. This, of course, is not an intention nor is it something that is left out in the "null" curriculum. It is a hidden lesson not only in individual classrooms but throughout society. Similar observations are made, for example, about the teaching of science and mathematics to boys and girls. Many believe these subjects are made "masculine" in subtle, hidden ways in instruction. We expect boys to do well in science and girls to do poorly. No one would state this as an explicit learning goal, but many argue that it is the hidden message that comes across in science and mathematics curricula. Again, one can only be aware of these hidden cultural messages by reflecting in detail and in depth on their own classes. Ask yourself, "Do I treat children of different cultural backgrounds and of different sexes the same way?" Because the message is hidden, you will need to look closely at your language, your bodily behavior, your instructional practices, and so forth.

We see, therefore, that curriculum materials that may be entirely neutral with respect to these "hidden" messages may, because of their potential, be taught in such a way as to differentiate between cultural classes and between sexes. Curriculum potential, then, is a mixed blessing that creates power for educational growth but, as seen in the negative instances of the hidden curriculum above, also creates potential for miseducation. The uses of the notion of potential for curriculum materials are in the hands of teachers.

RECOMMENDED READINGS

Every teacher should have Tyler's classic book, *Basic Principles of Curriculum Instruction*, on his or her shelf. Another excellent little book that details various ways of analyzing curriculum materials is Eraut, Goad, and Smith's *The Analysis of Curriculum Materials*. Elliot Eisner's book, *The Educational Imagination: On the Design and Evaluation of School Programs*, is well worth reading on the ideas of the null and hidden curriculum. An edited book that contains several chapters on the uses of curriculum materials is Ken Leithwood's *Studies in Curriculum Decision Making*. Those particularly interested in the hidden curriculum arguments of the radical educators will find Apple's *Ideology and Curriculum* a useful place to start. You will, of course, want to read Ben-Peretz's article, "The Concept of Curriculum Potential," and Clandinin's article, "Classroom Research: Teaching and Change," which sees action research in narrative, curricular terms. Goldstein's *Changing the American Schoolbook* is useful for those interested in textbooks. Several articles of interest are Flinders, Noddings, and Thornton's "The Null Curriculum: Its Theoretical Basis and Practical Implications," Connelly and Elbaz's "Conceptual Bases for Curriculum Thought: A Teacher's Perspective," and Connelly's "The Functions of Curriculum Development" and "Curriculum Implementation and Teacher Re-education."

Part IV

UNDERSTANDING YOUR NARRATIVE: CURRICULUM PLANNING IN THE SCHOOL

One of the great learning devices is the exemplar. Good writers illustrate sentences, paragraphs, chapters, ideas, and books. In educational studies there are no better exemplars than the case reports of the education of individual persons. For teachers and curriculum, this means case reports of specific teachers doing specific curricular things. This part, even more than the rest of the book, is filled with exemplars of teachers' planning, administering, and working with students.

12

Planning Lessons: Cycles and Rhythms in Stephanie's Classroom

In this part of the book, we begin a series of case studies, stories about teachers working in curricular situations. Chapters 12 and 15 present stories about teachers engaged with their colleagues in working through curricular problems or, as it is more traditionally called, working on curricular reform in their schools and classrooms.

In Chapters 12 and 13 we look within Stephanie's classroom to tell stories of her planning. You have met Stephanie, a primary teacher, in earlier chapters. In Chapter 12 we look at Stephanie planning her lessons in the day-to-day planning of teaching, the planning done "on the fly" so to speak. In Chapter 13 we examine interlocking or embedded narratives as we look at Stephanie planning with her students in her classroom. These chapters illustrate some of our ideas of curriculum developed through our work with teachers.

But let us begin with the story of Stephanie planning in her classroom. We told part of this story in Chapter 6 when we wrote about rhythms in our practical language of schooling. Our story begins with a classroom celebration to mark Hallowe'en. We tell the story through excerpts from a narrative account, a letter written to Stephanie.

My next day in your room, Friday, October 30th, 1981, was the culmination of the week of Hallowe'en activities. Your enthusiasm for taking part in the festivities and the extent to which you go to make the celebration memorable were remarkable to me. The children brought in food; you had me cook the pumpkin seeds and later I took over the class while you left to gather more party supplies. In checking my notes I find that I wrote: "When I arrived back in the classroom, several children were hanging balloons, Wallace's table was being covered with a black tablecloth made of crepe paper, Gail and another student

159

were sorting apples for bobbing and there was much party activity going on. (Field notes, October 30th, 1981)" (Narrative account, January 1982).

This is a partial record of a lesson in Stephanie's room. It is not a lesson we saw everyday, but, as we worked with Stephanie, we understood that as each holiday on the school calendar was celebrated, we would see something similar. We knew we would see similar elaborate preparations: the classroom being taken over by activities that have traditionally marked the holiday, and all classroom activity directed toward the holiday celebration.

To understand Stephanie's classroom planning, both for daily lessons and for the year, we need to explain what we see as the cyclic temporal order of schooling. It is within school cycles of the year, week, day, lesson, and so on, that we see teachers' rhythms of teaching develop. We wrote about rhythms briefly in Chapter 6 as part of our developing language of practice. Here we see how these rhythms give us insight into Stephanie's and other teachers' planning.

THE CYCLIC TEMPORAL ORDER OF SCHOOLING

Schooling exhibits a periodic cyclic temporal order. Schools are ruled by the clock on a daily basis and by promotion on an annual basis. Annual and daily cycles reflect more general social cycles, some of which are natural, such as the seasons, and some of which are conventional, such as the yearly calendar. Looking inward at the workings of schools reveals grand epicycles such as primary, junior, intermediate, and senior divisions within a twelve-year cycle of schooling and miniature cycles such as the six-day cycle and the duty cycles of teachers. Altogether, we identified ten school cycles according to their temporal duration: annual, holiday, monthly, weekly, six-day, duty, day, teacher, report, and within-class cycles. These cycles vary not only in duration but also according to sequence, temporal location, and rate of occurrence. Cycles of a certain duration, therefore, determine a characteristic sequence of events, at a certain point in time and at a certain rate of occurrence. For instance, the school's six-day cycle orders the socio-temporal reality of different groups of participants—the students, teachers, administrators, and support staff—in school over a succession of six-day periods. Thus, what may appear on a curriculum planner's desk as a linear temporal structure of schooling is experienced by teachers and others as a cyclic temporal order.

Time, and therefore the idea of rhythm in the narrative of teaching, is based on a complex of interacting cycles. For this reason, the terms "cycle" and "rhythm" are often used almost interchangeably. But they are not the same thing. The experience of cycles with their endless repetition of events would lead ultimately to a dulling of experience, just as the ticktock of a clock or the dripping of a faucet eventually becomes maddening or numbing in and of itself. What saves the experience of school cycles from these unhappy ends are the participants' rhythms, which penetrate cyclic repetition and create a sense of narrative purpose. Let us look at how these ideas unfold in Stephanie's classroom planning.

Stephanie's Rhythmic Experience of the Cycle of Holiday Celebrations

Stephanie, of course, participates in and experiences the full range of school cycles. But it is the cycle of school celebrations that dramatically serves to account for her structuring of curricular time. To understand Stephanie's classroom it is necessary to understand how the sequence of school holidays—Thanksgiving, Hallowe'en*, Christmas, Easter, and summer—defines reference points by which the curriculum is organized and to which curriculum and instructional energies are devoted. The idea of Thanksgiving is introduced early in September, and students plan for the Thanksgiving celebration; Hallowe'en follows Thanksgiving; the idea of Christmas is introduced immediately following Hallowe'en, and the class is reoriented in its thinking to the Christmas celebration.

Frank Kermode (1967) describes the endless cycle of life and fiction as being structured by beginnings, intervals, and endings. He adopts a ticktock metaphor and refers to "tick" as "a humble genesis" and to "tock" as "a feeble apocalypse," the two constituting the basic structure of a narrative plot. In Stephanie's classroom, the humble genesis occurs immediately following a major celebration such as the Hallowe'en celebration described above. Our field notes of November 2, 1981 are telling.

When we were chatting Stephanie told me that Connie, the other Grade 1 teacher, was coming in that morning to observe. Stephanie said that she did not know why she was coming. Stephanie said that she did not have anything special ready and she tried to tell Connie that she was all Hallowe'ened out . . . . Later that morning, Stephanie asked the students to tell what they were dressed up like for Hallowe'en. After a few minutes of this, she asked them what else had hap-

---

*According to the Canadian calendar, Hallowe'en follows Thanksgiving, unlike in the United States.

pened on the weekend. She wanted them, of course, to say that it had been the Santa Claus parade. Stephanie had told me earlier that she had gone, by herself, to watch the Santa Claus parade. (*Notes to file, November 2, 1981*)

This is the downtime in Stephanie's cycle of curriculum planning. Hallowe'en had just been celebrated and she was not anxious to have Connie visit her class since this was not a time of excitement and activity. Instead, it was a time of "humble genesis" when the cycle begins again and Stephanie begins to rekindle the students' enthusiasm for the next celebration, Christmas.

The party, described above, had been on Friday, just the weekend before. Then the classroom had been an entirely different place and Connie would have been welcome to visit it. In the account of the party, we have the sense of an ending, a climax, Kermode's "feeble apocalypse." Events have come to a close and the Hallowe'en celebration marks the ending of the cycle.

This cyclic "ticktock" of beginnings and endings fairly represents Stephanie's temporal and curricular experience of the year. She knows the year as a cycle of school holidays punctuated by downtimes, with an accompanying sense of expectation, and uptimes, with an accompanying sense of ending.

Teachers' Rhythmic Knowing of the School Year

But, as we noted earlier, there is more to the story of the year than the repetition of the cycle of holidays. There is a rhythm (see Chapter 6) found, created, and felt by participants in the interval between "tick" and "tock," in the time referred to by Kermode as "significant duration." As he puts it, one has "to defeat the tendency of the interval between tick and tock to empty itself; to maintain within that interval following tick a lively expectation of tock, and that however remote tock may be, all that happens, happens as if tock were certainly following" (1967, p. 46). In Stephanie's classroom a structured sequence of events prevents the interval from "emptying." Typically, as seen in the November 2 note, she begins to draw out a sense of expectation by gently turning the children's thoughts from the excitement of Hallowe'en to the happenings of Christmas. Three events are particularly important in this respect. We noted them briefly in Chapter 6. Consider the following notes, which refer to the interval leading up to Hallowe'en.

The transformation of the classroom. On the morning of Monday, October 26, 1981, the room had been transformed for Hallowe'en.

I was immediately struck by how much had happened in the room over the weekend. The farm display at the back was set up; the pictures were off the back wall; there were criss-crossed clothes lines hanging from the ceiling with Hallowe'en displays; the Hallowe'en words were up for display; the front board displays were all arranged; and the math center was cleaned up. (*Notes to file, October 26, 1981*)

In these notes we capture Stephanie's remaking of the classroom for each celebration. For the transformation of the classroom, she comes in on the weekend and does much of the work herself. Students, of course, add their own work to it as the cycle of events proceeds. A number of discrete activities compose the events. The weekend redecoration, taking things off the walls, and subsequently adding student work to the walls and windows are part of it. For Stephanie, special attention is given to the door. Her room is at the end of a long hall, and is entered through a door in the side wall. The door, elaborately decorated for the celebration, is left open so that it may be seen by anyone coming down the hall.

Counting the days to the next holiday.   In Stephanie's classroom, each school day begins with a class discussion of the day of the week, the month, the date, and the weather. This "date and weather" discussion focusses on Hallowe'en in the following note:

Stephanie's discussion with the students around the number of days left until Hallowe'en took up until recess time. She was just showing them their number books and showing them how to go about making the pumpkins when the recess bell rang. They changed quickly and went out for recess. (*Notes to file, October 26, 1981*)

This event contributes to the sense of building up to the celebration as each day's countdown is marked.

Organizing the curriculum around a celebration.   The following field note captures an event occurring later the same day. The mathematics curriculum is at issue. We note:

She was working on the concept of "more than" and "less than." They were working on this activity using pumpkins. She was going to have them do a cut and paste exercise with the pumpkins. (*Notes to file, October 26, 1981*)

The organization of the math curriculum around Hallowe'en is similar to most of her curriculum planning activities. For example, the "Boo" books that became the basis for the language arts program that week were started. Other similar events occur in any number of activities in the interval leading up to the celebration.

More generally, the overall curriculum is planned and takes shape within the context of the cycle of school holidays. For instance, early in October of the year in question, Stephanie planned her fall term curriculum. The following note is illustrative:

> At one point in the morning, Stephanie sketched out a rough plan of the next few months. She said that after Thanksgiving came Hallowe'en. It would not be until November that they came back to leaves. She wanted to make sure that there would still be some leaves around when it came time to do them. She mentioned doing the wax paper as well as shading the leaves. Somewhere in there she also wanted to do the apples. (*Notes to file, October 5, 1981*)

This note fairly represents Stephanie's frame of reference for curriculum planning. When she imagines a program of studies, she first imagines the upcoming holidays and considers the sorts of activities appropriate to them.

RHYTHMS IN TEACHING

A narrative understanding of Stephanie's classroom rhythms leads to an understanding of her teaching rhythms in terms of her life more generally. This understanding imbues the narrative with deeper meaning than may be achieved by a mere study of teaching itself. Earlier, in Chapter 6, we explained our understanding of teaching rhythms as an expression of some part of the narrative unity arising out of the person's past and embedded in cultural and historical narratives. The picture that emerges is one of the social and personal intimately connected in the narrative.

The cultural origin of Stephanie's classroom planning rhythm was captured by a colleague some 2000 miles distant from the classroom, reacting to a set of narrative notes on Stephanie's school year as a cycle. He wrote:

> . . . the school year being a cycle of big events, Fall, Thanksgiving, Hallowe'en, Christmas, snow and so on. I would like to ask whether the author might see Stephanie and ask her whether this isn't a reflection of the way in which the Jewish religion tends to make Jews think of the

year as divided by holidays. Incidently, there are many such and several of the ones the author mentions like Thanksgiving, Christmas and so on have their Jewish correlates. So, the family Judaism that she represents may have been another factor in contributing to the images which control her judgments. (Schwab, personal communication, 1983)

Stephanie is Jewish. She lives out her Jewish cultural narrative by celebrating her own holidays. In fact, the celebration of these holidays takes precedence over the school cycles. For instance, she takes a two-day leave for the celebration of Rosh Hashanah. Our notes in September 1980 show that

She feels quite badly about leaving the class while they are being reorganized but she refuses to give up her holidays. She made some comment about not giving up her religion for this. (*Notes to file, September 28, 1980*)

This note demonstrates the significance of cultural events in Stephanie's rhythm of living. In this particular case, when Bay Street's classes are undergoing their annual reorganization in September, the cultural rhythm conflicts with the school cycle. But, for Stephanie, this is unusual. Instead, she is, for the most part, able to accommodate her school planning to her sense of rhythm established around the school cycles. Furthermore, it is not only the main cultural holidays and her own Jewish celebrations that are brought into rhythmic play, but also those of individual children of other cultures in the classroom. The result is a more complex class rhythm in which significant cultural events for students take their place in the curriculum planning process. We will have much more to say about this in Chapter 15.

RHYTHMS AND CLASSROOM PLANNING

We find that this understanding of teachers' rhythmic knowing of their classrooms changes the way in which we think about classroom planning. Curriculum scholars and supervisors have often thought of classroom planning (described in Chapter 11) as a process in which one chooses objectives, selects and organizes classroom activities, and then determines an objectives-based evaluation process. Teaching follows the process laid out in the plan. As noted in Chapter 11, in this planning process there is a sense of past (with assessment of where the learner is prior to the instruction) and of present and future (as noted by the intention and direction in the objective). Understanding teachers' rhythmic knowing of their classrooms is consistent with this, but it is much more. We can see within the teacher's rhythm the ways in which her narrative directs present and future action and the ways in which the classroom rhythm becomes a more complex rhythm of students' and teacher's rhythms.

What we learn from this analysis of Stephanie's classroom is instructive. From an analysis of her overall curriculum planning, we see how Stephanie's rhythm helps us understand the way she plans lessons within the holiday cycle. But the understanding of Stephanie's rhythmic knowledge of teaching also gives new insight into how we might understand weekly and daily planning. Each day for a teacher has a rhythm. In the ending of each day we have the "humble genesis" as the teacher reminds the children of what they have done that day and turns their attention to what they will do the next day. With the beginning of the next day the teacher again turns their attention to the day with a gentle reminder of what will be done that day as they work toward the "feeble apocalypse." In the following description of events taken from our field notes of Stephanie's classroom, we see an example of Stephanie's rhythm of daily classroom planning:

> On Tuesday Stephanie had dismissed the students by telling them that now that they had counted the apples, they were going to make applesauce with Miss Jean the next morning. They had picked 57 apples on their trip to the apple farm on Friday. She told me as I walked into the classroom this morning that "you're going to make applesauce this morning" . . . . We talked then about making the applesauce. Stephanie had already taken a bin of apples up to the special education classroom where I was going to make the applesauce with the children . . . . When I returned to the room, Stephanie was discussing the morning activities which included the applesauce making with the children. (*Notes to file, October 14, 1981*)

In this field note segment we get an account of the "humble genesis" in Stephanie's rhythm, when at the Tuesday afternoon dismissal, Stephanie reminds the children of their work in counting the apples that day. She then turns their attention to the next day's activity, which will be using the apples to make applesauce. With the beginning of the next day, she draws their attention to the day's plan to make the applesauce, as they work toward the eating and sharing of the applesauce, the "feeble apocalypse." And even as that "feeble apocalypse" occurs, the "humble genesis" is closely tied to it in Stephanie's rhythm. In Stephanie's classroom, even as the children ate their applesauce that Wednesday afternoon, they knew that Thursday morning they would write about it in their journals.

In our account of planning, the objectives of each new day do not begin afresh, for they are begun with the "humble genesis" of the previous day. We often see a rhythm within the rhythm in elementary school classrooms, when children leave the class at noon and return after lunch. There is often a similar rhythm with its "humble genesis" and "feeble apocalypse." Thus, in Stephanie's classroom, as she winds down the excitement of the center activities of the morning with the reading of a story, what we might call a "feeble apocalypse," there is also the "humble genesis" as she talks about the afternoon activities and the planned visit to the library. We see this in the following field note segment:

> The clean-up went very smoothly. The students had the centers cleaned up and put away in about five minutes. The task was accomplished quite quietly and efficiently. Stephanie gathered the students on the carpet in front of her for a story . . . she read a story that she said seemed to suit her that morning. It was titled TOO MUCH NOISE . . . . At the end of the story about 11:52 or so, she told them they got their very first visit to the library . . . . After that, she told them to line up and get ready to go to lunch. (*Notes to file, September 14, 1981*)

We see the "feeble apocalypse" in the clean-up and the story, particularly appropriate after a noisy center time early in September and prior to the first visit to the library, and then the "humble genesis" as Stephanie draws their attention to their experience with other books and stories and the planned afternoon visit to the library.

Experienced teachers have a sense of how to begin so that the momentum is there until the day's end. Many teachers have "rules" (Chapter 6) that come into play here and serve as ways in which they can talk about their rhythms to others. For example, a kindergarten teacher has said she has a rule to always bring the students together for a whole class sharing time at the end of the day. She does individual and small group tasks earlier in the day. We imagine that, for this teacher, the large group sharing time provides the ending for each day. The individual and small group work is reported on and shared in that final activity. This teacher's rule gives her a way of talking about her daily teaching rhythms to others.

DEVELOPING RHYTHM:
STUDENT AND NOVICE TEACHERS
LEARN TO PLAN

It is interesting to reflect on the experience of student teachers and novice teachers and their way of knowing the classroom. Initially they see their main task as one of the application of some theory or other. It is either a theory such as Tyler's theory of planning noted above or a series of rules adopted from a cooperating teacher or methods course instructor. The teacher's task, for the student or novice, is seen as one of applying the appropriate theory of lesson planning. We wrote about the theory/practice relationship in Chapter 7. Student and novice teachers see the task as organizing some content into a particular form they have adopted. Some, of course, know the form and content better than others, but they know it in the sense that we can test their recall of it. They can recall the information and apply it to a particular concept they want to teach. They have their plan, so to speak.

Competent student and novice teachers see the lesson as having certain component parts: the objectives, the concept to be taught, the introduction (called variously the motivation or the advance organizer, depending on the theory being used), the development of the lesson (the activities), and the closure to the lesson, with the attendant way they will evaluate whether or not they have achieved their objectives. Most students and novices are able to write these plans, some more competently than others. It is in the teaching that they often experience difficulty; usually the most difficult part for them is what teacher educators call "closure" and what we call the "ending." Cooperating teachers with whom we have worked closely often note that students, even the most competent ones, frequently have trouble with pulling the threads of a lesson together so it builds to what we see as the "feeble apocalypse." They cannot, without that sense of apocalypse, have the sense of "humble genesis" where in the ending the beginning is found.

Two points are related to this. One is that student and novice teachers have not developed a rhythm of teaching because they have not lived through this before. As practiced teachers, we experience the school cycles rhythmically. The cycles have meaning in the ways that we know our teaching situations. To a beginning teacher they appear meaningless. They are blocks of time to be filled with lessons of certain instructional content. The transformation of teachers' understanding of cycles from meaningless, fragmented, and objective impositions to events having personal meaning in the ways they "know" teaching occurs through the teacher's narrative of his or her lived experience of teaching. In the narrative of experienced teachers, there is an annual reconstruction of experience, and it is through this cyclic repetition of school life that teachers come to "know" their classrooms rhythmically. This knowledge recollected as they teach allows them to cope with variations as they reconstruct a story already lived out. This living out of the narrative is modulated rhythmically. They know the downtimes will be followed by uptimes; they know that cyclic disruptions are temporary; they know that the end of a cycle, whether it is day's end, week's end, or year's end, is characterized by special features and that activities will be experienced differently at these times.

Student and novice teachers are living with the experience of teaching in schools with the cyclic nature for the first time. For them the school cycles do not yet have meaning in the way that they "know" their classrooms. Their narratives as teachers have not yet been experienced cyclically. It is in living out their narratives in school life that they develop a sense of the school cycles and a rhythmic knowledge of teaching.

The second point is that student and novice teachers do not yet know teaching in the way that we talked about it in Chapter 7 and have illustrated it in our account of Stephanie and her planning in this chapter. It is, for them, still recalled theory and not embodied knowledge worked out in practice. The first years of teaching are crucial to becoming a teacher for it is in those first years that a teacher develops his or her rhythmic sense of knowing the classroom and of knowing how to teach. For those of us with more experience, seen in our account of Stephanie's narrative, it is important that we come to understand the power of our own rhythmic knowledge of teaching and the ways that it is played out in our teaching practices.

SUMMARY

In this chapter we explored Stephanie's planning in order to illustrate the ways in which we have come to see planning from a narrative perspective. We understand from our work with Stephanie and other teachers that planning and teaching are expressions of each teacher's rhythmic knowledge of teaching. We began this chapter with an account of Stephanie's rhythmic knowledge of teaching around the holiday cycle of schooling. We explored here Stephanie's rhythm as expressed in her planning practices. We then gave an account of the way in which Stephanie's rhythm is grounded in her past and is embedded within cultural and historical narratives. Finally, we explored rhythm as a way of understanding classroom planning and examined the ways student and novice teachers learn to plan.

RECOMMENDED READINGS

We are just beginning to explore the notion of teachers' planning as it connects with the cyclical nature of time in schools. For further work on these ideas, see Clandinin and Connelly (1986), where we lay out in more detail the notion of rhythm. Clandinin (1987) offers a case study account of a beginning teacher's developing rhythmic knowledge of teaching.

13

Curriculum Planning as Curriculum Inquiry: Bay Street School and Its Curriculum Center

In Chapter 12, we gave an account of one teacher's, Stephanie's, rhythmic knowledge of teaching and the ways in which that knowledge was expressed in her planning. In this chapter, we offer another account of Stephanie's work in curriculum planning. Our focus here is on curriculum planning as curriculum inquiry, that is, on understanding Stephanie's planning as a form of inquiry into curriculum practices. The context for the aspects of Stephanie's work described in this chapter is Bay Street School's Curriculum Center. We explore Stephanie's inquiry into her teaching and, as a result of that inquiry, curriculum reform in her classroom.

The view of curriculum planning in this chapter is different from the kind of planning curriculum developers had in mind when they developed teacher-proof materials (see Figure 11.1). Those developers wanted to leave little place for teachers to adapt or change what they saw as well-developed materials that taught specific things in specific ways. Curriculum planning as curriculum inquiry also differs from most people's idea of Tyler's formulation of curriculum planning (see Figure 11.2). In Chapter 11, we wrote about his planning model as logical, linear, and objective. Planning, using an application of Tyler's model, was a process of writing objectives, selecting and organizing materials, and evaluating outcomes. In such a process there is little room for a teacher's personal practical knowledge and a narrative understanding of curriculum.

In this chapter, we use our work with Stephanie to illustrate what we mean when we talk about curriculum planning as curriculum inquiry. In Chapter 11, we said that curriculum inquiry is a process in which teachers read and study curriculum materials in the same way they would read and study potentially interesting texts and a process in which they read curriculum materials from a personal point of view. Figure 11.3 illustrates the possibilities for thinking about teachers engaging in curriculum inquiry. This bringing together of the two readings of curriculum materials creates, we said in Chapter 11, something new resulting from the interaction of reader and curriculum materials as text. For us, a curriculum text may be our experience in the past, present, and future as it unfolds, or it may be what it usually means, printed pages. See again Chapter 7. It is this sense of curriculum inquiry that lies behind our understanding of curriculum planning as curriculum inquiry. From this perspective, curriculum planning is a kind of action research, as described in Chapter 11.

This chapter has four main parts. We give a brief description of the Curriculum Center at Bay Street School, the Center that provides the broader school context in which Stephanie works. We introduce you to Stephanie first in a grade meeting sponsored by the Curriculum Resource Teachers in the Curriculum Center and follow her as she begins to inquire into her curriculum practices. We then focus on one month of Stephanie's planning for language arts and the ways in which her planning is a kind of inquiry that leads to curriculum reform. Finally we briefly explore the ways in which the Curriculum Resource Teachers in their work with Stephanie have an understanding of work with teachers that allows for this planning process.

We turn first to a brief description of the Curriculum Center and of the various activities supported within, and by, the Center and briefly introduce the two Curriculum Resource Teachers who work in the Center.

THE CURRICULUM CENTER

The Curriculum Center at Bay Street School was set up under the auspices of the Inner City Language Project, which was established to provide special resources for inner-city children. Bay Street School met the established board criteria for language project schools and became a project school in September 1981. As part of the special funding provided under the project, two teachers were hired as Curriculum Resource Teachers and other teachers were designated as classroom release teachers. The Curriculum Resource Teachers were charged with "implementing" the project. The release teachers were available to release classroom teachers from some regular classroom teaching duties to enable them to engage in various activities.

Two large classrooms were designated as project space at Bay Street School. In addition there was project funding for extra books and for some outside "expert" assistance for professional development days. The project was intended to have far-reaching implications for Bay Street School reform. The direction of the reform was geared toward language and literacy development, with the general focus set by the direction established in a board pilot school.

Stephanie, then, was working in a highly reform-oriented school context. Change was in the air. People, particularly the Curriculum Resource Team, were hired to "make change happen." The school board had determined some sense of what changes were necessary through the results of the pilot school work they had completed and through the "expert" advice they had obtained.

In addition to working with the Curriculum Resource Team, Stephanie was involved in a research project with Clandinin. Clandinin worked in. Stephanie's classroom as a participant observer for three half-days each week. This intensive involvement with Clandinin, begun before the inner-city language project began, had already led Stephanie to question her practices. In this chapter we focus on Stephanie's work with the Curriculum Resource Team in November, although we recognize that many classroom practices had been under inquiry in Stephanie's planning since the beginning of the school year.

The Resource Team

The "implementors," Grace and Judy, the Curriculum Resource Teachers, could have worked with the Bay Street School teachers in different ways. We might imagine them viewing the teachers as screens to successful curriculum reform or, alternatively, as integral parts of the curriculum situation. We wrote about these alternative ways of viewing teachers in Chapter 11. The Curriculum Resource Teachers adopted a view similar to the latter and, in doing so, created a situation in which Stephanie (and other teachers on staff) could engage in "curriculum planning as curriculum inquiry."

To give a sense of the ways in which the Curriculum Resource Teachers saw their work with teachers, we have included some field notes made at one of their September meetings. They wanted to introduce some of the ideas from the report of the board's pilot school and also to find out how Bay Street teachers were understanding their own teaching. The two kinds of meetings, grade and division meetings, provided forums for dialogue between the Curriculum Resource Teachers and the teachers.

There was, apparently, a discussion with the Assistant Principal and it was decided to hold lunch hour grade meetings between 12:10 and 12:50. At first, I understood these meetings to be for individual grades but the first meetings are to be division meetings, that is, for the primary, junior, intermediate divisions. On Monday the primary and the kindergarten have their meeting, on Tuesday, the junior division, and on Wednesday, the intermediate division. The agenda will be the same or similar for all meetings. At all three meetings the relationship between the language arts workshop and the pilot school report will be discussed; program needs will be discussed and the Canada Festival, an upcoming board celebration, will be discussed. At the junior and intermediate meetings, initial assessment will be discussed . . . . There was then a discussion about the kindergarten–primary division meeting on Monday at lunchtime. Grace said that one of the things that the pilot school report recommended was keeping a file of the children's work. This was a better way of doing evaluation than doing standardized testing. She said that to give the standardized tests was not good after the children had had two months of holiday. She then commented on the stressfulness of a testing situation . . . . They want to discuss this at their division meetings as well as to look at teachers' needs. They commented that they had to start from where the teachers are at. (*Notes to file, September 18, 1981*)

The Curriculum Resource Team's approach was one in which teachers were not to be told what to implement, but one in which the team would work with teachers in their own curriculum situations. Teachers were to bring their own knowledge of their classrooms up for discussion as well as to hear about new ideas. The Curriculum Resource Teachers saw themselves working with the teachers in a number of ways. They structured a series of meetings at both the grade and division levels; they released teachers to come to the meetings and to visit other schools and classrooms; they had funding for buying books and classroom supplies; and they provided consultation for teachers who wanted help with certain aspects of their programs. With this brief introduction to the ways in which the Curriculum Center planned to work with teachers, we turn to Stephanie at an early November Center meeting.

Stephanie at a Grade Meeting

Stephanie, in her work at the grade meeting, allows us a glimpse into how she was planning for language arts. The Curriculum Resource Teachers arranged the meeting to address the Grade 1 language arts program. Various language arts practices came up for discussion. Some practices were brought up for discussion by the teachers, while others were raised by the Curriculum Resource Teachers. Stephanie was particularly interested in questioning the use of Big Books, new material unfamiliar to her, which the

Curriculum Resource Teachers were introducing. We might imagine that some developers and implementors of Big Books would see the use of the materials as a matter of adding a 10- or 15-minute session of Big Book activities to each day's program. As we shall see, Stephanie's curriculum planning as curriculum inquiry did not follow such a logical, linear sequence.

> The discussion at that point was on Big Books. The Curriculum Resource Teachers were just saying that they had gone with the Assistant Principal to Scholastic Books and had ordered a great amount of material. One of the things they had ordered had been Big Books for each grade . . . . They made reference to the John Ross Robertson teacher who made her own Big Books. She is apparently a speaker at the Canadian Association of Young Children [CAYC] conference. Stephanie indicated to me that she was going to hear her when Stephanie was freed from classroom teaching to attend the conference. The group discussed the possibility of making their own Big Books as well as the possibility of making a library of story tape recordings. (*Notes to file, November 4, 1981*)

The idea of using Big Books in her classroom obviously interested Stephanie as she made plans to learn more about the possible ways to use them. She had other questions as the meeting progressed. She asked about how she could plan using the new practices instead of familiar ones. Remember that Stephanie had been working with Clandinin for several months and during that time she had made curriculum changes such as using more activity centers. With this change to using activity centers, Stephanie found it difficult to plan her language arts program as she had previously planned it.

> Stephanie then asked about activity centers. She wanted to know something about how they went about incorporating reading into the activity centers. Grace talked about the importance of the library and listening centers as contributing to reading, but she also said that children should "react to books by painting and puppets." Stephanie then asked about basal readers. She said that "you were supposed to hear every child read every day" and she didn't know how to do that without relying on the basal readers. She said she used the follow-up to stories and trips and making of books as added activities but that parents wanted to know an answer to a basic question "is my child reading?" (*Notes to file, November 4, 1981*)

Clearly, Stephanie had begun to engage in classroom planning but it was planning as curriculum inquiry. In this inquiry process, Stephanie asked questions about new materials and new practices and how she could use them in her program. But she was also asking questions about the way she had always taught reading. At the time of this meeting, Stephanie's reading program was based on a basal reading series. She worked with three groups, high, average, and low readers, and she made extensive use of what elementary teachers call "round robin reading" in which each child reads a passage from the basal reader each day. She supplemented the basal reading activities with field trips, stories, and having the children make small books as records of their experiences. But the backbone of her program was the basal reading program and the three instructional groups. As we shall see later, however, the supplemental activities of "making" were very important to the ways Stephanie knew and planned for her program. In the grade meeting, she called her old practices into question as she began to inquire into new practices such as Big Books and activity centers and how she could use them in her teaching.

In the next section, we follow Stephanie as she began to plan for language arts. In the planning process we see her engaging in curriculum inquiry and eventually in changed practices.

CURRICULUM PLANNING AS CURRICULUM INQUIRY

Here we learn about Stephanie's planning in language arts in November. In her involvement in the project, Stephanie learned about new ways of planning language arts, attended meetings in the Curriculum Resource Center, and asked to be released from teaching to visit other classes and to attend a conference. When we first met Stephanie in this chapter, she was asking questions about new practices and how they fit with, or were different from, her present practices. In this inquiry process, she asked questions about the ways she had previously taught language arts. In asking her questions, she was framing the way she both understood her present language arts practices and the way she would engage in planning new practices. Her questions were about her practices of using basal readers in her language arts program. She wondered how new practices such as Big Books and activity centers would work for her. The inquiry focussed not only on how to add new practices but also on her ongoing practices. We see Stephanie engaged in a kind of action research, an extension of the notion of curriculum inquiry, as she planned her language arts program.

To give a sense of Stephanie's planning, we provide a partial account of her process of planning. In her planning we see the inquiry extending both to the past, to the ways she had always taught reading, and to the future, to the possible ways that she might teach reading.

Asking Questions to Begin the Dialogue

Just prior to Stephanie's attendance at the grade meeting noted above, she was beginning to ask questions of other teachers about their language arts practices. She was also asking Clandinin, as a classroom participant observer, what Clandinin was doing in the language arts area with the children in her classroom. In asking these questions, Stephanie wanted to find out what other teachers, Clandinin included, were doing.

> Stephanie also asked Ellen, a Grade 3 teacher, if she used basal readers. Ellen said she did, she had tried on three different occasions to do individualized reading programs and she said she always had difficulty . . . . I told Stephanie that I would go on with the reading after recess unless she wanted to do the reading and I would go on with the other activities the students were doing. Her comment was that she wanted to learn from me. She asked what I had done. (*Notes to file, November 2, 1981*)

Later that same day, Stephanie wondered how different practices, such as the Big Book practices that the Curriculum Resource Teachers were suggesting, would work in her teaching. There was a tentativeness as she explored the ways she had known her teaching. With other teachers, she mostly asked for descriptions of their practices. But in the following questions, Stephanie was questioning her present practices, including the newly tried out activity centers; her past practices; and possible new practices being suggested by the Curriculum Resource Teachers. In addition, Stephanie wondered if the Curriculum Resource Teachers would "impose" new practices on her or whether she would be able to work the new practices out in her own teaching.

> She commented at one time that she had never been as organized as she was this year. We had another conversation about what she was doing and her concerns over the Curriculum Resource Teachers . . . . I told her that I did not think that they wanted her to throw out everything that she had done before. She then said that she supposed if the children needed structure then she would have to go back to having books like phonics books. She did talk a lot about the children's need

for structure . . . . She expressed concern that if the children were at
centers she would not know how they were coming along. She said she
needed to have them working in books. She needed to go through
things like having them write on lines, do every page and so on.
(*Notes to file, November 2, 1981*)

These notes show that Stephanie was asking questions that reached
into her past practices and her present practices, and suggested possibilities
for future practices.

Asking Planning Questions

A week later, after the grade meeting and when Stephanie had returned
from the conference, she talked about the new practices and how they would
work in her daily planning. The uncertainty that Stephanie felt as she began
her planning is well captured. She was assuring herself that if the new plans
did not work for her children, she could return to her old plans. She raised
issues about the importance of continuing to have students make certain
products in her classroom program, an important way in which Stephanie
knew her teaching. In the following notes, there is a sense of immediacy for
Stephanie. She had begun to focus on the new practices and to get ready to
try them out in her classroom.

At recess time Stephanie got the children sent out for recess and then
came right back in. She didn't suggest that we go down to the staff
room or that we take a break. She wanted to go right on talking
about what we would do in the program. She began to go through the
note cards (from the CAYC conference) she had made on Big Books. I
asked for some more explanation of how to go about it and she
started to tell me. She said she wants to start with a rhyme like
Humpty Dumpty and that she planned to do that tomorrow. She explained that first the children were called together on the carpet and
they did the chart together, then there was a follow-up booklet that
each student made. (*Notes to file, November 9, 1981*)

After telling Clandinin about the conference and about how she understood the new practice of using Big Books, she wanted to work out how she
could engage in the practice in her classroom. While the above notes do not
make reference to another practice, Uninterrupted Sustained Silent Reading
(U.S.S.R.), Stephanie had also learned about it at the Conference and from
the Curriculum Resource Teachers. She talked about the theoretical under-
pinnings, which she felt she were missing, of the new language arts practices.

In the notes, she describes these theories in terms of "books she wanted to read."

> When the students left at lunchtime, Stephanie came back to her desk and sat down. She commented that she had some things she had to do at lunchtime but we spent the entire lunchtime period talking over her program. She said she wanted to get organized and get her schedule made up. That was what we spent most of the day working on. She sat at her desk and I worked on the file folders for each child. . . . She showed me a list of books she wanted to read. She wanted to read them because the conference presenters had said that she was to be thoroughly grounded in child development. (*Notes to file, November 9, 1981*)

Her plans for her program occupied most of her work for that day. She spent time considering the variety of ways she could structure a language arts program and the ways she could schedule the program. She talked about the ways she had done the program, what she felt comfortable with, and how she felt about changes she had already made. Stephanie's program had been changing since September when she began to use activity centers. Her work with the activity centers, in the project, and with Clandinin had started to raise questions for her whole language arts program. The questions, however, were Stephanie's questions and she was both asking the questions and trying to come up with ways to understand the ways in which she knew her teaching. In the following notes she was trying to articulate various language arts possibilities for her classroom:

> Later that day, Stephanie tried to formulate how she had been working in her classroom. As we talked over the lunch period, the focus was basically the schedule. Stephanie thought through a couple of different approaches to the classroom. Finally she said she could see it in three different ways: the structured approach where it was into blocks of time and very teacher directed, the activity approach that we had started with in September, and something in between where there would be some activity centers but still individualized bins. We spent some time talking about each of those programs. Stephanie said that she is most comfortable with the very teacher directed program but that that is no longer "the thing" in Bay Street School. She said at one point during the morning she had never done the total activity center approach we had done in the fall and she had been very pleased with how that had worked out. (*Notes to file, November 9, 1981*)

By this time, there were two practices that Stephanie was planning to add to her language arts program. She had decided to try a Big Book program and U.S.S.R., a daily individualized reading time for all students and the teacher. In the following field note segment she talked about how she had made sense of the conference speakers on the U.S.S.R. practice and tentatively outlined how she planned to include the practice.

> One of the things that Stephanie decided to build into her program was U.S.S.R. When this had been mentioned at the conference, Stephanie said she didn't know what it stood for. She did understand, however, that they were talking about the silent reading time. Stephanie wants to make it more what the people at the conference were talking about, not just quiet reading but time when there would be sharing of books. The focus would be on books. (*Notes to file, November 9, 1981*)

Stephanie's early interpretation of the practice allowed her to see the practice as another way to share books, another practice that she saw as fitting into the ways she was now planning her program. Even though Stephanie felt she was going to proceed with the changes in her practices, she was uncertain about the response of the two school administrators. She related her concerns about her planned new practices to the conference proceedings and the ways in which her questioning had led her to reconsider her program and the school context in which she worked. Stephanie still needed to work the plans out in practice and she was still uneasy about how the practices would go.

> Stephanie commented several times that she hoped that Phil and Elizabeth would go along with the way she was running the program . . . . This came up in a discussion of the "round robin" that the CAYC speakers were apparently saying was not a good thing. They had pointed out that each student had very little time to read using such a program and it was in connection with that that Stephanie pointed out again how narrow the program had been that she was doing. (*Notes to file, November 9, 1981*)

Reflecting on Practice

The new practices, Big Books and U.S.S.R., were included in her program in the next few days. She paid particular attention to how the students handled the program and how she felt about the way the class had gone the first day. Her experience with trying the new practices led her to question other aspects of the program in a conversation with Clandinin.

Stephanie had actually gotten started on the Big Books. She had done Jack and Jill as a Big Book. There was an experience chart up as well as the dittoed books made. The students had worked in the books and they were quite delighted to show me their books.

After she told me about her helpers she told me that she had started U.S.S.R. yesterday. She was very happy with how the students had handled it and plans to go on doing it every day. She said that last night she had had a brainstorm about eleven o'clock. She said that she's been thinking about the room. She's decided that she wants to still have a math block and that will happen as it did this morning. After recess she wants to have the U.S.S.R. and then she wants to have a four-section reading program: first there would be time with her, listening, writing or printing, and stories. She started with the Big Books and she was very pleased to show me the books. She was very excited about David's book and showed me the artwork . . . . She plans to go on with the Big Books. She said that she wants to start a new one on Monday. (*Notes to file, November 13, 1981*)

The notes give a sense of the ways in which she was planning the language arts program. As Stephanie worked out the Big Books and U.S.S.R. in practice, she commented particularly on how she and the students felt about the experiences. But even as she tried out the practices, she continued to question her planning. The following notes describe her work with a Big Book and the children. After she had worked with the children, she talked about how she felt about the class. She recalled the discussion from the conference on Big Books and used that to ask more questions about her practice. It was a feeling that prompted her to ask a new question about how she had worked with the children. In many ways, it was her emotional sense that triggered new questions as she engaged in a dialogue with her practices.

After reading, Stephanie gathered the students on the carpet . . . . She had the students read the Big Book chart. She had the students pick out words that they recognized, she asked if they could find the word that rhymed with Jill and there was some discussion on the way the word looked. She commented later that Bob Barton had said that they should take an "holistic" approach and that they weren't to focus on individual words. She was very concerned that she had done that. (*Notes to file, November 13, 1981*)

Later that day she commented on how she saw the change process in which she was engaged.

We walked down the hall together. She stopped at one point and expressed concern about the program again. She said "it's just like trying to go into cold water" and she did this physically. She stuck one toe in and then pulled back and stuck it in again and pulled back. She said "I guess I just have to take the plunge." She made some comment about needing to see the underlying structure of the activity program. She said it's just like Grace says, you have to be aware of what the children are doing in the centers. (*Notes to file, November 13, 1981*)

Stephanie likened her planning process to jumping into cold water, to "taking the plunge." In her explanation she manages to convey a sense of the uncertainty involved in such a planning process. There is a process of questioning and working out in practice new ways of knowing. In the process, Stephanie looked for support for her actions by remembering the Curriculum Resource Teacher's comment from one of the grade meetings.

New Experience and More Questions

Stephanie's questioning about her planning did not end with the decisions to add the two practices nor with her first few days of practice. Four days later, she was released from a morning's teaching to visit another school. There she found a program that seemed like the program she was now questioning in her own classroom. She continued to question whether she should change and phrased her question in terms of what was right for the children. This time, however, she was able to look to the children's experience for confirmation of her planning.

She wanted to know if I thought she should go back to teaching the way they were teaching at the school she had visited that morning. She said when she had returned she had looked at the students' work from the morning and she was really pleased. The supply teacher had written her a note that said how nice her class was. She was really pleased by that. (*Notes to file, November 17, 1981*)

New Questions and Planning Changes

Stephanie and I had not talked about U.S.S.R. From my perspective, she was changing practice in the process of teaching. However, when I questioned her reasons and suggested alternatives, she articulated reasons that she had worked out for changing it. She also noted that she was working this out as she engaged in the practice with the children.

Stephanie settled the students down for U.S.S.R. She changed the rules slightly this time. She told them that they could get up and exchange their books if they wanted. The result was that a number of students wandered back and forth . . . . She told me they were tired of their library books and she wanted to use books from the library center. When I suggested she could have them get their books at the start of the period and bring them back and then share with other people at their table, she said she wanted to try it this new way. She commented on the way they had been shown at the Conference and how they didn't explain how to deal with situations like this. She said that she was glad that she had tried it. She also noted that this gave them reading in three different situations, the reading sessions with her, the reading they could do in the activity centers, and the reading during U.S.S.R. (*Notes to file, November 18, 1981*)

Stephanie needed to work the teaching of U.S.S.R. out in practice. The conference speakers had not, in her view, provided the necessary information. Stephanie felt the new practices allowed her and the children an opportunity to experience reading in different situations. This working out in practice was part of the planning process for both practices. In the following notes, she introduced a new Big Book. As she worked through the planned introduction, now fairly routine for the new practice, she introduced the idea of discussing ways to illustrate each line of the poem to the children. In introducing that change to the morning class, she made changes to her plan for the afternoon.

With the students on the carpet around her, Stephanie introduced the Humpty Dumpty chart. The students read it over a couple of times. They talked for some time about what Humpty Dumpty could be made of. Kevin suggested that he was an egg, someone else suggested that he might be made of what dishes were made of and there was a whole discussion about china and its origin. They talked about the king's horses and who had horses and men. The children said that it was now the police instead of the king who have horses. Stephanie had an illustrated story book and she showed them the picture. The children laughed at the picture of Humpty Dumpty represented as an egg falling into the frying pan. The whole discussion generated quite a bit of enthusiasm and they reread the poem several times. Stephanie also read the poem line by line and at the end of each line commented on what the picture might be to illustrate that line. Later when we talked about this she said that the idea just came to her and it seemed such a good idea. She outlined what she wanted them to do in the afternoon. She wanted them to choose their favorite line and illustrate it. When they had chosen their line, they could then have one of us underprint the line. (*Notes to file, November 18, 1981*)

Uncertainty in Planning as Inquiry

Even with what seems to be a successful language arts practice, Stephanie continued to question whether, with the addition of the practices, the program was coherent. A week later Stephanie was still questioning her planning and was not settled on the ways in which the practices were working in her program.

She told me that she had not slept that night until 5 a.m. trying to work out the program. She said that she still doesn't have it clear in her mind. (*Notes to file, November 25, 1981*)

Postscript on Planning

The U.S.S.R. program persisted for a time but became sporadic in early December and did not become an integral part of the classroom program. The Big Book program continued until mid-December. Stephanie encouraged the children to make their own small booklets; in fact, for Stephanie that was an important dimension of the program. Stephanie's Big Book program was, from its inception, a version of the original, for she created her own Big Books and had the students create their own booklets. When Clandinin returned to the room on January 4, 1983, almost 14 months later, she observed Stephanie creating a Big Book of "Alligator Pie," a Dennis Lee poem, and having the students create their own small booklets. The activity was preparatory to a class trip to view a play based on Lee's poetry. The Big Book program continued as a language arts practice. The resulting Big Books, her products, and the children's booklets were all used in classroom displays.

A NARRATIVE PERSPECTIVE
OR A TECHNOLOGY OF CHANGE?

Some readers may assume after reading this chapter presenting Stephanie's planning as a process of inquiry that curriculum developers and implementors need to work through such a process with teachers in order to have teachers implement new programs and policies. Indeed we are sure that some implementors and developers could imagine a more efficient inquiry process that could be set up for teachers than the one that Stephanie worked through. We might imagine that developers and implementors could devise strategies as part of a technology of change. But that would be a misreading of what was happening in Stephanie's classroom and what we intend to illustrate in this chapter. A narrative understanding of curriculum reminds us that Stephanie is a person, a holder and user of personal practical knowledge. Her personal practical knowledge is embodied in her classroom practices and shapes the ways in which she knows her classroom. We cannot give an account of Stephanie's personal practical knowledge here, but we have done so elsewhere (Clandinin, 1986). We do want to remind readers that old practices cannot be "strategized" away by replacing them, with new ones. Practices are expressions of a teacher's personal practical knowledge and are not without meaning in the way teachers know their teaching.

In our work with Stephanie, it was clear that she asked questions about her program in ways that allowed her to continue to express her personal practical knowledge in her classroom practice. The ways in which she knew her classroom practice shaped the ways in which she planned her program and the ways in which she shaped the inquiry. The curriculum situation, as we noted in Chapter 1, is a situation with a past and a present and is pointed into the future. A narrative understanding of curriculum gives us a different view of the ways in which we can understand classroom planning as inquiry and helps us see how inappropriate a technology of change is to our understanding of the process.

THE CURRICULUM RESOURCE TEACHERS AND STEPHANIE'S CURRICULUM PLANNING

It is also important to remind readers that the Curriculum Resource Teachers in their work with Stephanie had a sense of her personal practical knowledge and the ways in which she knew her classroom practice. They understood that they could not impose any classroom change on Stephanie without allowing her to work through an inquiry process. Furthermore, they had a sense that some practices would not be consistent with the ways in which Stephanie knew her teaching. The following discussion with the two Curriculum Resource Teachers and the school principal, Phil, gives a sense of their understanding of their work with Stephanie:

Grace, one of the Curriculum Resource Teachers, drew attention to the reference to Stephanie's personal practical knowledge. In connection with this, Grace told me that Stephanie had asked Grace to help her get things organized so that she would be able to have operating centers.

While we were having the discussion about Stephanie, Phil made a comment about Stephanie's classroom and how it used to drive Elizabeth crazy. They were all talking and chuckling about the amount of junk that Stephanie collected in the room. Clandinin pointed out that it used to be much more crowded and that she had actually cleared out a lot of the material. Clandinin commented that some things had more significance and Judy said something about not going in and just moving things. We talked about the importance of understanding the other person's perspective. (*Notes to file, May 21, 1982*)

With implementors who did not have a narrative understanding of curriculum, we might have imagined a much different process of working with teachers. We might have imagined they would mandate all of the practices used in the board's pilot school for all of the classrooms at Bay Street School. We might have imagined they would devise a strategy for ensuring that all teachers used the practices in their classrooms and a process in which all teachers were taught to use the practices in certain ways. This approach would not have allowed for a process of curriculum planning as curriculum inquiry and would not have allowed teachers such as Stephanie to work out new practices as expressions of their personal practical knowledge.

SUMMARY

In this chapter we explored how we might understand curriculum planning as curriculum inquiry and came to see how curriculum change occurs in a classroom through an individual teacher's curriculum inquiry. This view of planning acknowledges the centrality of a teacher's personal practical knowledge in a narrative understanding of curriculum.

In the chapter we developed the notion that curriculum planning as curriculum inquiry is temporal in nature. When Stephanie asked questions about her basal readers, she was asking questions about her past, and in asking the questions she brought her past forward to think about her work with Big Books and U.S.S.R. In the planning process, there was a reconstruction of her personal practical knowledge as she questioned old practices such as basal readers, tried out new practices such as U.S.S.R. and Big Books, and came to know her teaching and her practices in new ways.

We illustrated our view of planning from our work with Stephanie, a primary teacher working in Bay Street School. Stephanie's school was involved in a curriculum reform project, and we showed the ways in which she participated in the project. We followed her planning in language arts for a month. We began to follow Stephanie at a grade meeting in which she was questioning her past practices and asking questions about new practices. In the inquiry process, Stephanie initiated the dialogue by asking questions about other teachers' practices and by wondering how the new practices she was learning about fit with her ongoing work in the classroom. In this process, she was asking questions that reached into the past and the present and suggested possibilities for the future. Later Stephanie began to ask planning questions as she prepared to try out two new practices. After she tried out the practices, she began a process of reflection on the practices in her classroom. As she tried out the new practices, she worked out in practice new ways of knowing her classroom. We showed how this process of planning as inquiry is linked to her personal practical knowledge, and the ways in which a narrative approach to curriculum differs from a technological view of planning. Finally we saw how the curriculum reformers worked with Stephanie to facilitate her inquiry.

RECOMMENDED READINGS

There are two books that give careful accounts of teachers' work in their classrooms. We refer readers to Stephen Rowland's *The Enquiring Classroom: An Introduction to Children's Learning* and Michael Armstrong's *Closely Observed Children*. Each of these books gives an account of teachers' planning that is consistent with our view of curriculum planning as curriculum inquiry. For another account of the curriculum inquiry process, we suggest Donald Schon's two books, *The Reflective Practitioner* and *Educating the Reflective Practitioner*, which deal with ideas that are similar to those presented in this chapter.

14

Administering the Curriculum Narratively: A Principal's Personal Philosophy

There was a time in North America when the school principal was thought of as a "head teacher," and there are still places in the world where this is true. The idea was that the principal was a kind of master teacher chosen for his or her teaching abilities as a model and symbol of the best there is in teaching. One of the main functions of the principal's job was to teach demonstration lessons and to work supportively with teachers. This ideal is still alive in some measure in small elementary schools and, of course, in varying degrees elsewhere.

Mostly, however, the idea of school administration seems to have evolved to a point where the principal's role is distant from classrooms and from the curriculum. Administrators are often taught to be managers, and organizational principles seem to dominate their education. Aspiring principals read Thomas Peters and Robert Waterman's *In Search of Excellence* and study the staff training and management policies of successful organizations such as McDonald's. When schooling intrudes on this organizational perspective, it tends to be translated into such terms as "the principal as curriculum manager" or, in a somewhat less business-oriented way, "the principal as curriculum leader."

We feel uncomfortable with these modern ideas of administration. We mistrust the idea that the principal is primarily a manager of resources and people. We feel uncomfortable with the spirit of "objective scientism" that seems to come with the idea of principal as leader, manager, and organizational bureaucrat. Education is a people pursuit. In order to talk about schooling, curriculum, teaching, and classrooms, we need a language and point of view that are people oriented. We want a sense of our administrators as people who care and have personal experiences to which we can relate and from which they can communicate with us. We want people who have beliefs, values, and personal outlooks about schooling that we can agree with, disagree with, and deliberate upon. Instead, we tend to be given a value-free administration competent in skills, tactics, and strategies for managing and leading. Sometimes we wonder where the person is hidden in the thicket of strategies, tactics, implementation, management, and so forth.

The person, we think, is often in the office. We will tell you a little bit about an inner-city school principal, Phil Bingham, in a large urban board. Here is a principal who works in an era of applied organizational theory. His board has an elaborate plan for implementing many programs in the schools. We could describe him as a manager and organizational bureaucrat. But this does not fit him, for it is Phil's personal knowledge that stands out in any meeting with him. He has a personal philosophy evident not only in the way he runs his school but also in the way he chooses to present himself. It is not an elaborate philosophy in the sense of being connected with the great Greek philosophers, but is a personal philosophy of the sort described in Chapter 6. You may wish to reread Chapter 6 since it was also there that you first met Phil Bingham as we illustrated the idea of narrative unity through Phil's image of community.

We illustrated the idea of personal philosophy in Chapter 6 through Kroma's letters to a teacher, Bruce. In Chapter 14 we show how the idea of personal philosophy comes out a little differently for Phil Bingham, the principal. We will go on to show how a particular narrative unity in Phil's life is expressed in his administration. As you read through this material, keep the introduction to this chapter in mind since it is important to be able to contrast a narrative, personal history approach to the study of administration with an administrative organizational theory approach. We are not suggesting, of course, that there is nothing to be learned from an organizational and management theory approach. But we do not want, from our narrative point of view, to forget the person. The principal as a person is, after all, most important in the administration of curriculum, just as the teacher as a person is most important in the classroom. We might very well, if we were writing a book for administrators, have rewritten the idea of Chapter 3 to read "your personal curriculum as a metaphor for the administration of curriculum." Now let us spend a little time with Phil.

MEETING PHIL:
HINTS TO A PERSONAL PHILOSOPHY

On March 19, 1981, in our second meeting with Phil, we were introduced to teacher-members of the school cabinet who were central to the decision on whether or not to admit our research team to the school. We were asked to explain the purpose of our project and how this would translate into a way of working within the school. Our field records show that

> At the end of our conversation Phil pointed out that while he had not stressed it, our philosophy was clearly supportive of his philosophy . . . and he pointed out that his philosophy was very different from someone else he named. (*Notes to file, March 19, 1981*)

During the meeting, it was clear that he was lending his support to our application to work in the school; our notes show that "Phil emphasized several times that we would be a resource to the school." At the time we were, of course, gratified at this support since we had been turned down for a similar study in another school not far from this one. It was by no means clear that this staff would agree to work with us. Phil had made it clear to us that it was a staff choice, with the final decision to be made in cabinet. His reference to philosophy explained his support for us, but we were as yet in the dark as to what that philosophy was. Our best guess, fairly close to the mark as it turned out, was that we had "clicked" because Phil saw positive things for the school in the participant observation research process. We, as researchers, and Phil, as principal, saw us as yielding a classroom resource for participating teachers.

This may seem like a small point to a casual reader. But a big decision was involved and both parties realized this. Our research hinged on the willingness of a school's staff to work with us in ways that were unfamiliar to them. The study could very well have been blocked yet again. The failure to obtain a research setting would have ended it. From the school's point of view we were a risky unknown. One of the reasons we had been turned down in the other school was the fear that we would bring the school bad publicity. Our study was defined within the context of the board of education's policy on race relations, and the principal felt that our presence in the school might send a message to the community that the school had racial problems. Even without such extreme reasons, schools, for good cause, must be wary of visitors over whom they have no ultimate control and whose purposes are vague and unclear from the school's point of view. We might say we would be an asset to participating teachers, but more likely they would see us as an uncomfortable invasion of their classroom. Researchers, after all, tend to have a reputation not for "giving" to schools, but rather for "taking" through observations, the study of records, and the setting up of experimental situations. The stakes were high for all parties, and yet Phil's decision was made on what many would think of as nebulous grounds—his "personal philosophy."

We would like you to think about this decision for a moment and try to recover some of the sense of wonder we had and still have. There was no decision checklist, no concrete logic, that would lead to a "yes" or "no" on our application to work in the school. Information was sketchy at best. We presented a very brief abstract of the proposal and did our best to explain ourselves in the middle of a rather hurried meeting with teachers on the fly from place to place. At best, we could say that the situation "felt right." There was really only a kind of unspoken sense of agreement between what we saw ourselves doing and what we saw the school doing.

Personal philosophies have this kind of influence in our lives. In everyday life, when we are not consciously being "logical" or "scientific," most of us are quite comfortable saying "well, my philosophy is . . ." or "that fits with my philosophy." If pressed, the speaker may have trouble defining what he or she means and yet is reasonably confident that something truthful and reliable has been said. This is the way it was with Phil. He was quite confident in saying our philosophies matched and therefore he would like us in his school. Yet it is doubtful if he could have given a list of criteria or written out a set of logical reasons to support his feeling.

GETTING THE FEEL FOR THE PHILOSOPHY

Phil frequently uses a statement of his philosophy to present himself and the school to others. Before presenting the philosophy to you, however, we want you to get somewhat more of a feel for it. Besides, you will be able to retrace our own steps a little more closely by reading the next section before you read the full-blown statement of the philosophy.

A little more than a week later, on April 15, we had another meeting with Phil and a teacher-member of the school cabinet. The purpose of the meeting, according to our field records, "was to introduce us to the fact that we were 'in' the school." Phil used the half-hour meeting primarily to introduce his way of thinking as an administrator. According to our notes:

We spent a fair amount of time talking about his philosophy of the school and what he hopes to accomplish. Basically, he feels that he has a philosophical outlook, but with few detailed plans. Those fall into place. (*Notes to file, April 15, 1981*)

Our records show that he even ran through the details of his philosophy when he "recited four or five points." But, because we were as yet unaware of the significance of the details of the personal philosophy, we made no accurate record of it. It wasn't until later that its importance became apparent to us and we made proper notes. But, at that meeting, we learned a great deal about how this philosophy was translated into the problem of administering the curriculum. To begin with, it meant that his administration was not one to be burdened with a great deal of "detail." Rather, as problems emerged, such as our own application to work in the school, the philosophy functioned as a context for dealing with the problems. It was not necessary for him to have a specific policy on the role of outside research in the school.

Many other points emerged in that morning meeting. In the conversation "Phil said he had spearheaded renovation and redecoration of the staffroom and wanted to show us before and after pictures. He is a believer in raising morale through making surroundings more pleasant" (Notes to file, April 15, 1981). His emphasis on environment was, at that time, one of the most noticeable features of his style of administration and his "philosophy." Remember the concept of curriculum in Chapter 1. You will readily be able to place this aspect of Phil's philosophy within that context.

The concern for environment affected not only the comfort of the staffroom. Phil also applied it to a professional development day meeting tentatively scheduled for the following fall. Phil declined our offer in the April 15 meeting to house the professional development meeting at the university, in favor of a comfortable "pillow room" in a Toronto Harbourfront building. And, coming closer to curriculum, the philosophy also influenced his idea of the best environment for children. The following field notes record his comments on this matter as he walked us through the school following the meeting.

> Phil made comments as we walked. He pointed out the new lights in the senior school hallways. There had been only a single row of lights before. He said they had the senior school hallways and lockers painted. The lockers are always a mess. He pointed out there was no work displayed in the senior school and no use was made of the hallways for students. There was a student working on the discipline bench outside his office and he said that he has insisted that work be sent with students when they are sent out of the classroom. We stopped at the glass doors in the hallways and he said there had been a vandalism problem with the glass doors. We went through the doors and into the junior school. Phil said he was very pleased with the work displayed in the junior school. There was, according to Phil, a totally different atmosphere here already. (*Notes to file, April 15, 1981*)

When these notes were taken, Phil had been principal in the school for just over a year. Over the next four years, the school's physical environment was transformed. Light colors replaced dark ones in the halls, student work was everywhere, and the problem with graffiti was sharply reduced. The discipline bench outside the principal's office, referred to above, was removed. The very first place Phil took us in the school that morning was to a room where Cynthia, the school librarian, was supervising the construction of a large mural. This mural was later transferred to a prominent spot in the entrance hall and even now is a focal point in the hallways.

THE PHILOSOPHY
IN A PROFESSIONAL DEVELOPMENT CONTEXT

Sometimes one of the surprising things for researchers who keep detailed field records is how ideas and plans come to fruition even though there may be no written connection to link the time of the plan and the time of its execution. The planned professional development day Phil discussed in the April 15 meeting took place almost a year later, in February 1982. True to his words back in April 1981, Phil used the occasion for a discussion of school philosophy. This is all the more remarkable given some of the events that transpired in the interim. It is important that you know something of these events and try to put yourself in the place of the principal and school staff and consider how easy it would have been to avoid a discussion of "philosophy."

Phil is a community-minded principal. Throughout the year, he attended community meetings, invited parents into the school, encouraged teachers to do home visits, and established a school committee on community relations. A community issue had been bubbling beneath the surface for some time and it finally came to a head just a few days before the February 19, 1982 meeting. The details are not necessary for this particular account, but what is important to know is that different community ethnic groups were pitted against one another over certain school policies. The issue had reached the press and a rather spectacular public meeting was held in the school auditorium. Depending on how that meeting went, it was possible that Phil's job would be on the line and that much of what the school had been doing would be transformed. This was an issue that put tremendous pressure on the whole school staff. Under Phil's guidance, the meeting took place without bitterness, and the issue, if not resolved, was set on a course with which all parties were able to live. When the February 19 professional development meeting took place just two days later, all the staff, and Phil in particular, were in a relieved but drained state of mind.

Here is the scene on professional development day: The staff is away from the school in relaxed surroundings at the city's Harbourfront. The teachers are seated on chairs and on what the principal views as comfortable floor cushions arranged in a semicircle. Charts depicting the aims and goals of the project school are displayed on room dividers around the room. Phil is standing at the open end of the semicircle beside an overhead projector and a screen. According to our records:

Phil started the session by saying "thank you." He had put up the overhead that said "Bay Street Today For Our Children Tomorrow." With that overhead on the screen, he drew our attention to the automobiles passing on the Gardiner Expressway. They gave the illusion of being on the roof of the building. He said something about bringing children down and getting their impressions of what they thought it looked like.

He then said that he hoped that they would be able to relax today. He made a comment about them belonging together, working together to fulfill the mandates of the Board of Education and the Ministry of Education (the provincial government branch dealing with education). He said that the Bay Street staff was "here today for our children tomorrow."

He said that he had gone through what he planned to do that morning with about 300 people at the school's Open House but that the staff had missed it.

He started out by saying that he tried to base most of his planning and thinking on a set of guidelines. He made reference to them being "a set of fundamentals" that he took from E. C. Kelly in his book, *In Defence of Youth*. He said he found the book at a used bookstore when he was working with Hill Street (an alternative school) kids in the 1960s. He started out with a blank overhead and wrote the following points on it as he discussed them. He said that the following were his fundamentals for survival:
1. the importance of other people;
2. communication;
3. in a loving relationship or atmosphere (he said they could translate loving for caring);
4. a workable concept of self;
5. having the freedom to function (which Phil says stands for responsible action and interaction);
6. creativity (having the ability and the right). He said this is what we, as teachers, are trying to do with kids.

(Each point in the philosophy was repeated as each new point was introduced, so that by the time the sixth point was raised a long sentence containing the previous five points was stated.)

He said that "these fundamentals are in my mind when I work with you." He said it doesn't always work but that he does get satisfaction from trying to make them work. He then made an apology to those who have already heard it. (He was going to use the same overheads that he had used down in the cafeteria at the Open House).

He said that what he was going to present today is what "I've been working on for the past year at Bay Street School" and that he "felt that things were really moving in that direction." (Notes to file, February 19, 1982)

Clearly, the "philosophy" played a different role at the professional development meeting than it did either in the March 19 meeting, where it functioned as a guide to decision making, or later, when we walked through the halls and saw how it guided the school's physical environment for learning. In the professional development day meeting, the philosophy served as an instructional basis for staff development. And before this, as our field notes above show, Phil had given much the same presentation "with about 300 people at the school's Open House" in which he "explained" the school to parents. In sum, the philosophy is related to decision making, school environment, staff instruction, and explanations to parents and others.

The philosophy, therefore, is something quite pervasive and general. Yet, it is something that has an identifiable characteristic. Phil uses the philosophy, as he did in his introduction to us, in his meeting at the Open House with parents and in his work with staff, to carry a central understanding of the man and the school, whose "ethos" he believes he is structuring.

You will notice from the six listed points in the professional development meeting that the philosophy as expressed here has a more specific, self-conscious character than did the personal philosophy of the teacher Bruce in Chapter 6. As our account of Bruce illustrates, it is not necessary to be able to list points for a person to have confidence in saying he or she has a philosophy or for us to say of someone else "I think I understand what you are all about." But Phil's listing of the points in his philosophy illustrates that it is possible to be self-conscious about one's philosophy and to articulate it for purposes of discussion. Many of the "tools" for self-reflection described in Chapters 4, 5, and 6 can serve this purpose. The most direct route is, perhaps, through the exercises on personal rules and personal principles.

ADMINISTERING THE CURRICULUM NARRATIVELY

The professional development day illustrates the narrative administration of curriculum indirectly through the professional development of teachers. Phil's personal philosophy in effect defined the curriculum for the day. It is curricular in much the same way that Bruce's personal philosophy served curricular purposes for his classroom (Chapter 6). But for Phil we may also say that it is a "curriculum for the administration of curriculum" since his purpose is to have the philosophy pervade the school and influence the learning environment. He began the meeting, you will recall, with the overhead display "Bay Street Today For Our Children Tomorrow." His clear purpose at the professional development day meeting was to influence the students' curriculum through the administration of a curriculum of professional development for staff.

Phil did not, in this session, tell people specifically what to do, and we rarely saw him do so in subsequent years. It would not have been consistent with his "philosophy." He did not say "we will use this program or that program" nor did he say that he "planned to implement the board language policy by having everyone do this or that." Instead, he talked more generally about philosophy and purpose.

We are not saying that every teacher would be comfortable in such an environment. First of all, some would have philosophies that differed. How those differences were treated would be all-important to the question of whether the philosophy would eventually become a tyranny of ideas or a context for independence. Other teachers, perhaps used to a tradition of laid-on expectations, guidelines, and tasks, might feel dislocated in an environment where teachers were expected to work out their curriculum more independently. There are, however, a variety of ways in which a personal philosophy can relate to curriculum. Many different kinds of curriculum materials and actions, for example, would satisfy the community- child- environment-oriented philosophy expressed by Phil Bingham.

The management-oriented view of the administration of curriculum that we described in the opening paragraphs of this chapter would tend either to deny that what we have described was curriculum administration, or would see it as vague and impractical. Yet, we believe the influence of such a personal philosophy over the school curriculum is more pervasive and influential in the long run than are carefully designed and very specific goals, objectives, and administrative tactics and strategies.

SUMMARY

We began this chapter by contrasting two very general ideas of administration: one that viewed administration in terms of organization and management theory and the other that focussed on the administrator as a person. The two extremes, of course, will hardly ever exist in real settings, but they are useful for us in thinking about different approaches to the problem of how one may administer the curriculum. We then illustrated the personal narrative approach to the administration of curriculum by describing selected aspects of Phil Bingham's principalship of Bay Street School. Phil frequently refers to himself as having a "philosophy," which we, as researchers in the school, first encountered in our second meeting with him when the philosophy was central in his decision to let us work at Bay Street. Through selected examples of our field notes, we saw how the philosophy functioned in decision making, shaped the physical environment of the school, became the curricular content of the professional development day with teachers, and served as the basis for explaining the purpose and ethos of the school to parents. The philosophy both served as the basis of a curriculum for "teaching teachers" in professional development and, through the medium of the teachers, functioned as the administration of curriculum for school students. For Phil, then, administering the curriculum was not a matter of telling people what to do in detail or of having tactics and strategies for implementing policies and curriculum. Instead, administering the curriculum meant the narrative living out of a personal philosophy of education.

RECOMMENDED READINGS

You may be interested in following Phil Bingham's career in somewhat more depth than is provided in this chapter. One source is our article, "Personal Practical Knowledge at Bay Street School: Ritual, Personal Philosophy and Image," in which we show how Phil's personal philosophy can serve to reconfirm a school staff's belief in what they are doing. You will also see how this philosophy and the administration of Bay Street School are embedded in Phil's images of schooling (image is used in the sense described in Chapter 6). An unpublished resource, available from the authors, is a manuscript titled "Teachers' Personal Practical Knowledge: Image and Narrative Unity," in which Phil's imagery is explored in depth. There you will see how Phil has an image of a learning community, which is connected to his philosophy and which serves both to help him think of the school as a community of persons and also to think of the school in relationship to the community of parents, businesses, churches, and so forth, outside its walls.

15

Curriculum Planning with Your Students: Your Narrative as a Planning Metaphor

We have come to the end of this book on curriculum. Throughout its pages, you, the teacher/reader, have been central. We have asked that you think of the curriculum of your own education and have provided various tools to help you in your reflections. Chapter 3 introduced the idea of an individual's personal practical knowledge as it grows and develops through narratives of experience. These ideas help us talk about a person's curriculum in a way that is consistent with the experiential notion of curriculum set forth in Chapter 1.

Some might say that coming to understand ourselves is all very fine for us individually, but what good is it, professionally, to the business of teaching. Our first answer to this was given in Chapter 3 where we developed the idea of "your personal curriculum as a metaphor for curriculum and teaching." What this means is that in your role as teacher, you are a reflective learner for the eventual purpose of working with children. It is their curriculum, their personal practical knowledge and narratives of experience that fall within your guidance. This chapter turns to the place of students in your narratives of experience.

In this chapter, teachers tell stories of themselves as children and as students, and they consider the meaning of these stories for the kind of teachers they have become. You will also read teachers' stories of how they have learned about students through other teachers' stories. In all of these stories, both child and teacher as storyteller are learners. The narratives of experience of teachers and students interweave and mingle such that both are educated.

As you read this chapter, try to imagine the ideas of the book at work. Here the idea of curriculum as experience in a classroom situation (Figure 1.1) is expanded to include both teachers as learners and students. Throughout the book we have been concerned with the development of teachers' personal practical knowledge through narratives of experience. We have seen how past situations, the present, and future situations are connected. Temporality is at the core of our experience. We have seen interactions of persons, processes, and things in situations and have seen how teachers integrate theory and practice in their narratives, plan curriculum as inquiry, and administer the curriculum narratively. All of these matters are replayed in this chapter. There is nothing new except that in this chapter the key situational "interaction" is between teacher and student. Sometimes that student is the teacher at an earlier age, sometimes it is the teachers' students, and sometimes it is the students of yet other teachers or even another teacher as child and student.

As always throughout this book we can only provide narrative fragments. As a reader of the text, one of your purposes is to *recover* the meaning, as best you can, as it is expressed by the storyteller. The significant meaning, of course, is yours, and so you need to *reconstruct* a meaning for yourself. You may want to refresh yourself on the ideas of the recovery and reconstruction of meaning in Chapter 7. In general, you will need to do as Mary does in the last story, told as a journal, in this chapter. She says of the teacher's story she heard in a curriculum class, "Rosita's story was like reading a story in a history text. She made history come alive. You could read it in her face." You cannot, of course, "read it in Mary's face" or in the face of any other teacher in this book. But, with imagination and the use of your own experience, you can reconstruct the stories told as, to quote Mary, you "think of your own experience as the text."

Before turning to the stories themselves, two things need to be said. First, in this introduction we have used the word story in a general way to refer to the things teachers say. We have used not only stories but interviews teachers had with each other and one journal entry. The stories, interviews, and journals in this chapter, and throughout the book, were written by students in graduate courses on curriculum. We are indebted to them and think that you will feel the same indebtedness as you recover and reconstruct narrative, curricular meaning.

We have organized the material according to the commonplaces of curriculum described in Chapter 7: learner, teacher, milieu, and subject matter. Teachers tell how they learn about each of these commonplaces. We then conclude with a final section titled Learning from Curriculum as Narrative.

LEARNING FROM BEING A LEARNER

Teachers often tell stories about their own experiences as learners. They learn a great deal from reflecting, through their stories, on their experiences as children in their home, family, and community situations. They also learn about teaching from reflecting on their experiences as students in school. Often what they learn is not what we might imagine their own teachers had in mind. They also learn about the way they know their teaching from their experiences as adult learners in university, professional development, and inservice courses. Finally they learn from reflecting on their understanding of theories and research in education.

Reconstructing Being a Child

The first story is taken from an interview between two teachers, Martin and Gary. One of the teachers is reflecting on his experiences as a child and the ways in which he knows his teaching. Martin's question, "How did you become a doer prior to your teaching experience?" elicited the following response from Gary:

I think the idea of a doer has really developed from my childhood when my family had and still own a family business and this parallels what Rosita said about having to do certain jobs.

When I was 12 years of age my family owned a taxi business. As a family member you were expected to do certain things, such as gas up the cars on the simplest basis, wash cars, vacuum out cars. As you got a little older and your personal ability to respond to the public developed, you then became a dispatcher at the taxi business and you would work after four. Of course naturally once you became 16, you are then given major responsibility, that is drive taxi, or drive truck in our business, 'cause we had a delivery system as well. That developed into extra areas of responsibility because at the same time we had an ambulance business and also a busing business—school buses. The idea of having to do something, the responsibility of doing something on a set basis set the parameters for my whole educational background so that I was expected . . . I had the responsibility, I had to do it. Now when I look at responsibilities that we have, it has to be done. Setting the idea that there are jobs that have to be done in education and as a principal, if the idea of having to have them done is there, then your expectations of completing the job will be easy to attain. I often look at that attainment along the lines of my remembrance of driving truck when at 8 o'clock in the morning you left the town of Bracebridge with a load of freight on your truck. Your expectation was that when you came back that night at 5, 10, or midnight, your expectation was that the truck was empty and you were successful in delivering everything. I think the expectations that you have in education, as a student and as a teacher you can live up to them more easily but I admit as a student my experiences were not as successful as they have been as a teacher or as an adult student primarily because of the diversion of doing other things like driving truck and driving bus and so on, my education experiences were not positive ones.

In the second story, another interview fragment, Rosita also talks about her experiences as a child and the ways in which they shaped her knowledge of teaching.

> *Rosita*: I see myself as a worker. I think basically I've always enjoyed working as long as I had a specific goal. And that's probably why I went into teaching, because I realized there was a lot to be done in my line of interest.
>
> *Gary*: Your perception of yourself as a worker, you think that has come from your experiences in the past?
>
> *Rosita*: Very much so. I learned very young from my experiences on the farm that there were certain chores to be done on a regular basis. I think I developed fairly good work habits early on. Having a traditional background in school too really drilled the notion that you had to work. That came about in my summer employment with a person I worked very closely with, and when I discussed my ambitions I remember clearly her telling me whatever goal you set for yourself if you work hard enough at it you're sure to achieve. So I think my ambition stems from there.

Reconstructing Being a Child in School

In the following story, a teacher shares an experience she had in one of her early school encounters and through the story considers how the experience changed her teaching.

As a very young student (about 5 years old) at an old three-room country school in post-war England, I had an experience which rudely shattered my wonderful image of teachers. At the time, of course, I didn't realize what ramifications that experience would have for me as an adult, and particularly as a teacher, but it may have been the first of many which shaped my attitudes and thinking much later on.

My short little lifetime as a student up to that particular day had been filled with positive and pleasant experiences with school, with teachers, and with learning. School was a fascinating place to be, learning was fun, and teachers were warm and soft-spoken ladies who made you feel special. Because it was a rural school, our parents paid a small sum monthly which provided us with a hot noon meal, as travelling home and back was not feasible. The lunchroom was a small, dark building, separate and different from the school, not only physically but in atmosphere as well. Picture if you will, the one described by Dickens in Oliver Twist: It was poorly lit, complete with wooden tables and benches, steaming cauldrons at one end by which we filed in single, silent lines and our three teachers who, with the headmaster, patrolled the aisles and presided over our appetites and our manners.

The war had only been over for a short time and food was still bought with stamps from ration books. Perhaps because of this, or perhaps for other good reasons, we were constantly admonished to "clean our plates" and "remember that there are starving children in the world." Like most other five-year-olds, I did not have brussels sprouts high on my list of preferred foods, but being the model student that I was, I had cleaned my plate of all else and was slowly attacking the offensive sprouts one by one, diligently trying to get them past my gag reflex. This effort was consuming all my concentration and I was rudely startled by the hand of the headmaster on the back of my neck. He leaned close and said that as I was having so much trouble, he would help me. The hand that I had trusted calmly pulled my head back by the hair. By reflex, my mouth opened and more brussels sprouts than I could imagine immediately filled it.

Choking, crying, and thoroughly humiliated, I heard him say, "Trust me . . . I know what's good for you."

To this day I cannot eat brussels sprouts, and more than once as a teacher I have asked myself, "Can they trust me? Do I know what's good for them?"

Reconstructing Being an Adult Student

Stories about their own experiences as adult students are often shared by teachers. Many teachers tell stories about university undergraduate courses and particularly ones about student teaching. The following story is an account of one experience of being an adult learner:

As a student teacher, I'm sure I learned more from my students than they learned from me. One important lesson occurred in a Grade 9 class of what could variously be described as "disadvantaged" or "low level learners." For some reason, 9G had been intentionally set up to include the repeaters, the discipline problems, and other nonconformists. After two weeks of relatively pleasant experiences with two other Grades 8 and 9 classes, my cooperating teacher must have decided that it was time to test my mettle. She assigned me to teach "The Rime of the Ancient Mariner" to 9G.

Randy stood out the first day I saw the class. He was well into his sixteenth year, at least two years older than most of his classmates, and was taller than any of them by a good ten or twelve inches. He looked physically strong and well-muscled with a tough demeanor and that "show-me" look on his face. In physical stature at least, he was a man, surrounded by boys and girls. Aside from these attributes, I noticed that he was always personally unkempt: He wore faded, unpressed clothes, had shaggy hair and a bad case of acne. Randy never smiled. His eyes were clear blue, but tired and hurt, betraying his tough outward bearing. The other students cleared a path when he entered or left the classroom. He did not appear to have any friends and he did not participate in the "important" classroom gossip or power networks. Randy was a loner.

I intended to reserve further judgment but I was forced to skip the preliminaries and get to a one-on-one confrontation fairly quickly. Even though he was often late, his attendance was perfect . . . but Randy kept falling asleep in class. Perhaps it was "The Rime of the Ancient Mariner" or perhaps it was my teaching but I felt that there was more to it than that. After about the third incident, I asked him to stay after class. I had noticed a large roll of money in his shirt pocket and casually began our conversation with some comments about the inadvisability of carrying such a large wad to school. It turned out that Randy had good reasons for the money, the sleepiness, and his isolation from his Grade 9 classmates.

He had known no father. His mother had deserted him two years before, when he was 14; she just wasn't there one day when he came home from school. A neighbour lady had taken him in and he paid room and board to live in a small basement room in her home. Randy had a job as a milkman which required him to make deliveries from 4 to 8 A.M. every day before school. He supported himself this way and was determined to graduate from high school. No wonder he was managing poorly! It was a wonder he was managing at all!

What did I learn? I learned not to take anything for granted. I learned not to make judgments based on incomplete information. There is often a lot more going on in students' lives than is apparent to me in my class. I have to remind myself or be reminded of this from time to time.

Reconstructing Theory

Teachers learn a great deal from reconstructing the theoretical knowledge they meet in university classes, extra reading, and professional development activities. While we have many stories that we could share here, we feel that Sarah's story told by Elbaz in her book is the best illustration of learning in this way.

In the following interview fragment Sarah talks about the ways in which she learned from theory. In this fragment Sarah accepted the multiplicity and relativity of theories from which she had to work. She was willing to work from theory, taking the risks of choosing the appropriate theory and establishing her own criteria. We encourage readers to read Elbaz's full account of Sarah.

> When I tried to do professional reading, it was very often for a technique to use—one very isolated idea that would perhaps provide some interest to the kids.
>
> What I did a few months ago was to contact some people at the university who are combining these two things in workshops for kids—anxiety reduction and study skills—and I got hold of the articles that they were working from, 40–50 page articles, and when I get some time I'm going to try to look at it and try to get some teamwork going with the guidance department. (Elbaz, 1983, p. 109)

LEARNING FROM BEING A TEACHER

Teachers tell us that much of what they learn about teaching and what it means to teach is learned through being a teacher. They tell us they learn through the process of teaching, from students they work with in and out of their classes, and from other teachers.

Learning from the Process of Teaching

Many teachers who have helped us with this book, some of whom we have known for many years, talk about how they have changed as teachers over their teaching careers. Stephanie and Aileen in Clandinin's (1986) book both talked about changing as they taught. Sarah says the same in Elbaz's book. We sense it in ourselves as teachers.

The following story gives an account that illustrates how we learn as teachers through the process of teaching. The writer of this story, Kathleen, shares with us how she has learned about teaching through reconstructing theory, in this case, a new theory of literacy. The story is powerfully written as Kathleen brings together two experiences, climbing and teaching.

> The gloom of the underground parking garage was slashed by the white light of the August sun. The door lurched shut behind me.
>
> I drove through a city still in its summer sleep along empty streets and past houses closed against the heat of the day. It's still beach weather. I should be cycling or drinking iced tea on my balcony, watching my potted geraniums grow. But here I am driving to school with a churned-up feeling in my stomach.
>
> I am going to be teaching Grade 2 this year. I have been teaching 24 years but I have never taught a primary grade before. I am used to children who can read, who can find their way around a library, who can work on projects, who can discuss and even debate interesting topics. What can seven-year-olds do? I have no children of my own. I have neither nieces nor nephews. I have not spent time seeking out little ex-Grade 1s in shopping plazas or supermarkets to ask what their world is about, if they can read or write, or if they can even understand what I am saying.

> * * *

> I backed down over the cliff. The feed rope chafed my hand as I let it slide too fast through the carabiner. The belay rope pulled the harness taut around my waist. My climbing coach cautioned me to take it easy.

> * * *

> I recognized a few of the teachers' cars in the school parking lot. The office is just inside the front door of the school so I waved to the secretary, stopped for a chat with our principal, and exchanged summer news with colleagues gathered round the copying machine. I collected the sheaf of papers from my mailbox before I made my way to my teaching area.
>
> I climbed two flights of stairs before passing through the open areas that led to my own. Some teachers were busy moving furniture. Some were hunched over their desks preparing lesson plans for the first week. Other teachers had obviously come last week. Their areas were perfect with inspirational posters, completed bulletin boards, and mobiles from the teachers' store. I felt a little sick. I know how long it takes to do all that work.
>
> But this year for me is going to be different. I will be teaching the reading/writing process. Last winter I spent three months at the Uni-

versity of New Hampshire with Dr. Donald Graves. I have been converted. The writing process is the only way to teach language. Now all I need to do is make a beginning then prove that the theory really works.

* * *

I regained my balance, took a deep breath, and remembered the instructions: "Move slowly. Watch the cliff face for toe holds. Trust the equipment. Trust yourself."

* * *

I moved all the furniture into place. I displayed the 50 library books I had chosen from our school library. I put notebooks, paper, and pencils at the front of the classroom. I wrote the date on the blackboard. I still needed a story idea to share with the class at nine o'clock on Tuesday morning but there would be plenty of time during the three-day weekend to think about that.

Before I left my area, I took some time to think. My thinking was questions. Will the language resource team support this new program? Will my principal understand what I am trying to do? Will my colleagues be patient with me?

I could see in my mind twenty-eight seven-year-olds filing in— summer fresh, curious about me, and, perhaps, more nervous about themselves. Will my program be right for them?

* * *

I began to descend again. I searched for crevices on which to rest the toes of my climbing boots. I let the rope slide smoothly through my hand. I felt in control. It was a good feeling. My first free rappel had begun.

* * *

As I left, the other teachers were still lining up to use the ditto machine. They were counting textbooks. They were decorating bulletin boards—all the things I had done 24 times before to prepare for a new September class. But I continued walking. My resolve was solid. "Remember, Kathleen. No basal readers, no spellers, no phonics workbooks, and no ditto sheets."

It's going to be just me, the children, paper, pencils, and trade books. Like my free rappel down that cliff. Risky. Exciting. The belaying rope? My belief that what I have learned about the reading/writing process approach will take the weight when I falter.

Learning from Students

In our conversations with teachers and in thinking about our own knowledge of teaching, we often mention how much we have learned from our students. Sometimes our stories are about what we have learned from working with a particular class of students, other times what we have learned from our experience with one student or from a particular class incident with a student. We have included three such stories here. The first story, written by Martin, is about his experience with a particular group of students. The experience called into question many of Martin's ways of knowing curriculum.

It was Friday morning of the second week of September. Shortly after the lesson had begun, Marie-Therèse brought to my attention the fact that the class was quite boring. In fact, she had fallen asleep in Thursday's period. She was visibly frustrated with the Grade 13 Français class and she was letting me know how she felt.

At first I was speechless because I did not know if this was an outright confrontation or a desire for attention. There was a dead silence. I stood open-mouthed, not knowing what to answer. After regaining my composure, I asked her what she meant by her statement. By this time, she had gained the support of the other students and so decided to express her negative feelings about the class and about the way the material was being covered. I could see the heads nodding in agreement. The group had come to life. I had to think. "You know, we don't need this subject to get our diploma," struck me like a sledgehammer. Nothing was clear anymore. This had never happened to me before. Was it my teaching? What were they going to do? Had I lost control? The questions raced through my head. They were quite capable of leaving "en masse." (They had protested in the provincial parliament and I had seen them argue with the provincial Minister of Education.) Then Victor asked if we could discuss the course itself—the content and the strategies.

During that discussion, I remained silent, jotting down ideas and suggestions that the students were offering. The more they spoke, the more alive they seemed. As new strategies were being offered, they appeared more enthused.

I managed to camouflage my hurt ego and decided to explore with them, but only on a trial basis, the possibility of starting a new unit of study THEIR way. We negotiated certain standards and set certain objectives. I was somewhat apprehensive at first and wondered if the project would flop. We had decided to study techniques used in drama by trying them out with Grade 8 students. Certain concepts such as concentration, confidence, characterization had to be explored. In small groups of two or three, activity and strategy planning began. I was called upon for an opinion once in a while or when they wanted to try something to see if it would work on me. Once I had to encourage one group to continue by offering a couple of suggestions. Apart from that, I had faded into the background. I had the sensation that they didn't need me.

Finally, their units were ready to be tested. They shared them in class with me and we proceeded to meet the Grade 8 students. The experiment was very successful. The students were quite proud of themselves and I, too, had my eyes opened. They had covered much of the technical content of the course without much of my help. They had been active and enthused. Yes, there were little arguments and differences of opinion but these could be resolved.

The following week, we reacted to what had taken place and the students expressed the desire to try something else. This time the interaction had more of a consultative quality and was more respectful.

The strangest part of it all was that it took me three projects to realize that these kids were learning a lot more by having input and making some decisions about what they were doing than I could teach them. That was quite a blow to my traditional-parental "savant" approach. In fact, they were showing me new and fresh ways of looking at learning, but at the time, I remained somewhat cool to their approach and felt somewhat guilty because I felt that "my program content" (novel, drama, poetry, grammar) was not being covered.

The second story is about a teacher's experience with a student who was killed in a car accident during the year in which she was teaching him. The story is a powerful one for the teacher because it helps her see the importance of the relationship between herself as teacher and her students, a relationship crucial to teaching and learning.

The phone call came around 1:00. We had been out shopping and had grabbed a bit of lunch. Actually we had just got in the door.

It was Margaret on the line and what she had to tell me probably changed my life forever.

"Chris has been hit by a car and he's in the hospital. He's not expected to live."

Chris was probably the brightest boy I had ever had the privilege of having in my class. He was not only a scholar and a fantastic athlete, but a valued friend of the entire Grade 3 class. As far as I was concerned, he set the tone of the class and I had come to rely on his ready wit and mature attitude in the two short months that he had been in my class. With shaking hands I hung up the receiver and tried to look up the number of the hospital in the phone book but the task proved to be too difficult and I asked my husband for help.

I had not been teaching long and Dan did not yet comprehend the depth of affection that one developed for one's class. I sensed this lack of understanding as I asked for help but no words were spoken as I was concentrating on the heartrending task at hand.

Somehow I was able to dial the number and managed to ask for the emergency ward. When I asked for information about Chris, the nurse became very reticent. When pressed, she finally asked what my interest was in this case. With a shaking voice, I explained that I was Chris's teacher. Immediately her manner softened and with compassion she said "Chris died at 12:40 this afternoon."

I don't know how I ended the conversation, but as soon as the phone was out of my hand I broke into sobs. Dan just looked at me with absolutely no comprehension of what was happening.

How do you explain to an outsider, for that was what he was at that moment, this man who had been my closest friend for five years? How can you make him understand the smile, the twinkle in those blue eyes, the red jacket going down the hall not 24 hours before, the one that paused and looked back saying, "Have a good weekend, Mrs. Smith. See you on Monday!"?

For someone who has not taught, even though they have children of their own, cannot understand the part of you that bonds with the souls entrusted to your care for 10 months. They do not understand that the class becomes a part of you, that you and they have embarked on a journey together.

I had a number of tasks to attend to that weekend. I felt that I could not face questions on Monday so spent all of Sunday evening contacting the parents in my class to be sure that they spoke with their child before school on Monday. In the morning I went to school early to move the desk and belongings out of the room. Looking back, I'm not sure if I did the correct thing by making it appear that Chris had not existed. But this was my first brush with the death of a child and I was operating on instinct alone.

When the class entered the room I was surprised to hear very little talk about the accident. I'm not sure if the parents had suggested the matter not be brought up or if the entire incident was so beyond the understanding of these seven- and eight-year-olds that they had no vocabulary to bring to the situation.

When I look back on this time, 15 years ago, I now wish I had handled it differently. Now I would understand when Kim asked about a week after if Chris would come at Hallowe'en as a ghost instead of getting mad at her as I did then. I would encourage the children to talk and to cry as I so desperately wanted to that day in October. But I was young and inexperienced and afraid to appear human, I guess.

So instead, I remember and wonder if anyone else from that class does, that boy in the red jacket, forever in Grade 3.

The third story is about one particular experience a teacher, Mike, had with a class. One student stood out in this particular reconstruction of the event. The story highlights how the teacher learns to understand how his perspective on classroom time is different from his student's. The teacher's perspective is focussed on making a concept clear, while the student's, Robert's, is focussed on his rhythmic knowledge of time in the daily cycle.

Back to my first year. One day I had planned what I thought was a creative way to initiate a discussion about Baptism: I took my mug filled with water and sprinkled students as I walked around the room, asking what this reminded them of. (I had hoped it would be the times the priest sprinkles people with holy water at Baptism.) As I asked the question, Robert answered with a confident, "Baptism!" Just the answer I wanted! Then I asked him to explain why he thought my sprinkling them reminded him of Baptism. His answer as he pointed to the clock was, "it's time for religion class now, what else would it be at this time?"

Learning from Other Teachers

Many of the stories teachers tell of the ways they know curriculum are about other teachers. They come to know their own practices from their work with colleagues. The following story illustrates one teacher's, Sheila's, experience of learning from other teachers.

Grade 10 mathematics teachers in Ontario had to implement the new Ministry Curriculum Guideline courses this year. The guidelines for the advanced level courses at the intermediate level stress not only "what" we teach students but "how" we teach them—that is, the process components. There is strong encouragement to get students involved with some hands-on activities that use manipulative materials and an experiential approach. I think that this is a standard approach used by elementary teachers, but it is not common in advanced level high school mathematics classes.

I taught our Grade 10 enriched class. I haven't often used manipulative materials in an advanced level class (Have I ever? I can't remember.), especially one that was enriched, but a new unit on three-dimensional geometry was forcing me into unfamiliar territory. My comfort level was not high—unusual for me, since I consider myself to be an excellent teacher using the "regular" methods of teaching mathematics. I assembled the necessary equipment in the class—construction paper, scissors, rulers, protractors, scotch tape, glue— and gave the students a worksheet with a clear set of instructions. They were to work in groups of three to construct six specific three-dimensional geometrical models that had to be handed in. A short reading assignment introduced the idea of constructing a "net" as a first step in constructing the model.

I clarified the instructions and stood back, unsure of how things would go. (I guess that I like the feeling of being "in control.") There was some confusion as they sorted themselves into groups and gathered the necessary materials. But they settled down as they read and explained the introductory pages among themselves. And then the fun began. Desks were moved as students settled on the floor and worked cooperatively with their common goal. They worked actively until the end of the period. Even a chatty group seemed to be focussing on the task. When the next class started, students just got their materials from where they had stored them and got back to the activity. I stood back in amazement and watched them work. I wasn't really needed. And they will have a better concept of three-dimensional shapes than if I had prepared a super teacher-directed lesson.

I should have known that it would go well. I remember being impressed last year when my assistant head had developed and field-tested this particular unit. At that time I had visited his class and found it so interesting that I left during the class to invite the principal to drop in for a few minutes to see what was going on. The principal, a former mathematics teacher, seemed impressed that students were actively involved in a laboratory situation, but commented that it really didn't look like mathematics.

LEARNING FROM THE MILIEU

Teachers often tell stories about the ways they have learned from their curricular milieus. The following story, an interview fragment, is a particularly compelling instance of learning from a troubled school milieu. The interview fragment here is taken from the same interview with Rosita that we included in the section Reconstructing Being a Child. In the first part of the fragment presented earlier, the interviewer refers to Rosita's comments about seeing herself as a worker.

Gary: The image that you had of yourself as a worker originally came from your family tradition . . . and your own education, you carried into your teaching. Do you think that same image is still there only it is not book work? Is it still there? Are you still a worker?

Rosita: Yes. I still am a worker . . . I feel I'm a worker and I like to see justice done. And when I see that somebody is not given the justice entitled to them I feel the urge to step in and work at it. Maybe that's where I developed strength in the last several years with our school crisis. I'm not politically minded, but when I saw injustice being done to our students, I just felt that nobody was, hum, really pushing far enough. So that's when I decided well, there was something I could do, so I stepped in, from a very low-key point of view . . . but I really documented why things weren't going well. I tried to meet key people and explain to them why I thought things weren't right. The injustices of having teachers who are not competent in the French language for the French language school—it really hurt me . . . I always saw our community as a bilingual community and with equal rights. But when the rights were impinged upon, as a worker, I felt the urge to step in. I was very much involved in the French language advisory committee. I was involved in the . . . renegade school as an advisor on that board. I must say I worked really hard in many ways, because quite often I found that the whole mechanism was way too political and it wasn't doing justice to the students. I stepped in and that meant meetings every night, every night for at least six months—from 4 o'clock in the afternoon and sometimes we had dinner meetings that would continue till 10 or 11. And at least once a week we had meetings till after midnight. So I think if I hadn't been a worker, I'd have given it up. It all proved fruitful because eventually I was on the official French language committee and there I was vice-chairman and chairman of the Renegade Board for a while as well. I felt I had a lot of input on how things turned out. So I was happy with this.

Gary: So. I'm concerned with this image of a worker. You feel that when you were younger, you were a manual worker, a practical worker. You said you had chores and then you got into high school. Your first experience you did book work, a written type of work. Now you've changed your image, but it's still a worker. . . . It's a worker on the line of a consultant or of someone who voices an opinion . . . or it would be basically a consultant.

Rosita: Yes, and I think I've eventually worked my way up with my new position, now as a vice-principal. I think I'm in a position where I could often help out. Uh . . . like . . . this year I had new staff and with my experience at all levels of teaching, I was able to help this one particular teacher quite a bit. Sometimes it was only moral support but sometimes it meant going into his classroom or getting others to come in and help out. So, I see myself as a worker there. I believe that you can't tell people what to do but you can invite them to join you, and that's what I try to do. Uh . . . I think I'm much more tempted to go off and work and invite people to help out instead of dictating what needs to be done. Uh . . . I'm going back to your words, "Do as I do and not do as I say," as my motto.

Gary: To summarize, maybe could we refer to Dewey's experiential continuum? It appears that all of your knowledge has been based on that. You've gone from a practical worker to a written worker, to a consultant. What you're saying is: When you're involved in the aspects or the levels that you're involved in now, it's based on your past experiences. So your learning, which never stops in education, is an experiential continuum.

Rosita: Very much so. And I think this has been revealed in the last year more than ever. The school I'm at now is a very rapidly growing school. It's the only French language school in the community and a lot of people are seeing our school as a French immersion school. Rightfully, it is a French language school. Because of my experience of seeing how a similar situation worked in Penetang, I have concerns. We invited many English-speaking students into our school, and they are thrilled to be learning the language. At that time we were very happy to have them in the school but we didn't realize the influence or the secondary effects. In Penetang, the experience was negative. So in order to avoid a repetition of this, I was active this year in setting up the admissions committee so that we can sort out who are really francophone students and who are not, by rights, francophone students. This spills over. It worked.

Gary: Uh huh.

Rosita: It doesn't appear like much but there is a lot of work involved.

LEARNING FROM THE SUBJECT MATTER

Teachers also learn about their curriculum knowledge through learning from particular subject matter. One of the stories already presented in the section Learning from Other Teachers can be understood as a story of learning from the subject matter. In it the teacher, Sheila, tells about learning how to teach a particular mathematical concept. Because of the nature of the concept, the teacher felt it needed to be taught using a particular approach with which she was not familiar. You may now wish to return to Sheila's story and reread it from the point of view of learning from subject matter.

LEARNING FROM CURRICULUM AS NARRATIVE

We want to end the chapter and the book with a teacher's story, a journal entry, in which the teacher, Mary, writes about what she has learned from coming to understand curriculum as narrative. We and other teachers have said similar things, but Mary's journal captures the ways in which we can learn about our knowledge of curriculum from learning about curriculum as narrative.

When you think about your past, it is important to think about your own experiences as a text. Also, try to think about what has been observed in the classroom as a text. Look at what the teacher does— what the children do.

I found my work last year with a Grade 1 teacher and with her children most interesting. It would be good to think about their journal entries as a text. These entries are a daily record of what they did during class time and, in particular, Environmental Studies. It is their own curriculum book.

Again, I enjoyed hearing the biographies. Martin's and Rosita's stories really touched me. My husband is French Canadian and I have often heard his family speak about their lives and of the struggles they have had to keep their language and culture. The change and the growth that took place in Martin's life was certainly evident. He said it all when he spoke the words: "I'm Francophone. That's what I am. That's who I am."

Rosita's story was like reading a story in a history text. She made history come alive. I can't help but think that she must have had to have a lot of strength and courage. You could read it in her face. It had to be so difficult to be working for the board on the one hand and vice-chairman of the Renegade Board on the other. Now I'm beginning to see what is meant by: "Think of your own experience as a text." The more I reflect and write about these experiences, the more I understand.

References

Adler, M. J., & Van Doren, C. 1972. *How to read a book*. New York: Simon and Schuster.

Anyon, J. 1981. Social class and school knowledge. *Curriculum Inquiry*, *11*(1), 3–42.

Apple, M. W. 1979. *Ideology and curriculum*. Boston and London: Routledge & Kegan Paul.

Argyris, C., & Schon, D. 1974. *Theory in practice: Increasing professional effectiveness*. San Francisco: Jossey-Bass.

Aristotle. *Topica*. (W. A. Pickard-Cambridge, Trans.). In R. McKeon (Ed.), *The basic works of Aristotle* (pp. 187–206). New York: Random House, 1941.

Armstrong, M. 1980. *Closely observed children: Diary of a primary classroom*. London: Writers and Readers.

Ashton-Warner, S. 1964. *Teacher*. Toronto: Bantam Books.

Ausubel, D. P. 1960. The use of advance organizers in learning and retention of meaningful verbal material. *Journal of Educational Psychology*, *51*, 267–72.

Ausubel, D. P. 1968. *Educational psychology: A cognitive view*. New York: Holt, Rinehart & Winston.

Barone, T. 1983. Things of use and things of beauty: The Swain County high school arts program. *Daedalus*, *113*, 1–28.

Becher, T., & Maclure, S. 1978. *The politics of curriculum change*. London: Hutchinson & Co.

Belth, M. 1965. *Education as a discipline: A study of the role models in thinking*. Boston: Allyn and Bacon.

Ben-Peretz, M. 1975. The concept of curriculum potential. *Curriculum Theory Network*, *5*(2), 151–59.

Berk, L. 1980. Education in lives: Biographic narrative in the study of educational outcomes. *The Journal of Curriculum Theorizing*, *2*(2), 88–153.

Berman, P., & McLaughlin, M. W. 1979. *An exploratory study of school district adaptation*. Santa Monica, CA: Rand.

Bestor, A. E. 1955. *The restoration of learning: A program for redeeming the unfilled promise of American education*. New York: Knopf.

Boyer. E. L. 1983. *High school: A report on secondary education in America*. New York: Harper & Row.

Bruner, J. 1986. *Actual minds, possible worlds*. Cambridge, MA: Harvard Unversity Press.

Buber, M. 1965. *The knowledge of man*. New York: Harper & Row.

Bussis, A., Chittenden, E., & Amarel, M. 1976. *Beyond surface curriculum*. Boulder, CO: Westview Press.

Butt, R., & Raymond, D. 1985. "Individual and collective interpretations of teacher biographies." Paper presented at the Classroom Studies of Teachers' Personal Knowledge symposium, Toronto.

Clandinin, D. J. 1985. Personal practical knowledge: A study of teachers' classroom images. *Curriculum Inquiry*, *15*(4), 361–85.

Clandinin, D. J. 1986. *Classroom practice: Teacher images in action*. Barcombe Lewes: Falmer Press.

Clandinin, D. J. 1987. "Developing personal practical knowledge: Narrative study of beginning teachers." Paper presented at the annual meeting of the American Educational Research Association, Washington, D.C.

Clandinin, D. J. In press. Classroom research: Teaching and change. *Journal of Curriculum Studies*.

Clandinin, D. J., & Connelly, F. M. 1986. The reflective practitioner and practitioners' narrative unities. *Canadian Journal of Education*, *11*(2), 184–98.

Clandinin, D. J., & Connelly, F. M. 1986. Rhythms in teaching: The narrative study of teachers' personal knowledge of classrooms. *Teaching and Teacher Education*, *2*(4), 377–87.

Clandinin, D. J., & Connelly, F. M. 1986. *Teachers' personal practical knowledge: Image and narrative unity*. Working paper.

Coleman, J. S. 1966. *Equality of educational opportunity*. Washington, D.C.: U.S. Department of Health, Education and Welfare, Office of Education.

Connelly, F. M. 1972. The functions of curriculum development. *Interchange*, *3*(2/3), 161–77.

Connelly, F. M. 1979. Curriculum implementation and teacher re-education. In P. Tamir, A. Blum, Avi Hofstein, and N. Sabar (Eds.), *Curriculum implementation and its relationship to curriculum development in science*. Jerusalem: Israel Science Teaching Centre, Hebrew University.

Connelly, F. M., & Clandinin, D. J. 1984. Personal practical knowledge at Bay Street School: Ritual, personal philosophy and image. In R. Halkes and J. K. Olson (Eds.), *Teacher thinking: A new perspective on persisting problems in education*. Lisse: Swets and Zeitlinger B.V.

Connelly, F. M., & Clandinin, D. J. 1985. Personal practical knowledge and the modes of knowing: Relevance for teaching and learning. *NSSE Yearbook*, *84*(2), 174–98.

Connelly, F. M., & Clandinin, D. J. 1986. On narrative method, personal philosophy, and narrative unities in the story of teaching. *Journal of Research in Science Teaching*, *23*(4), 293–310.

Connelly, F. M., Dukacz, A. S., Quinlan, F. 1980. *Curriculum planning for the classroom*. Toronto: The Ontario Institute for Studies in Education.

Connelly, F. M., & Elbaz, F. 1980. Conceptual bases for curriculum thought: A teacher's perspective. In A. W. Foshay (Ed.), *Considered action for curriculum improvement*, ASCD Yearbook (pp. 95–119). Alexandria, VA: ASCD.

Crites, S. 1971. The narrative quality of experience. *Journal of the American Academy of Religion, 39*(3), 291–311.

Cusick, P. 1983. *The egalitarian ideal and the American high school: Studies of three high schools.* New York: Longman Inc.

Delamont, S. 1986. Two "new" sociologies of education: A comment on Heap's "Discourse in the production of classroom knowledge." *Curriculum Inquiry, 16*(3), 327–29.

Dewey, J. 1934. *Art as experience.* New York: Capricorn Books.

Dewey, J. 1938. *Experience and education.* New York: Collier Books.

Dewey, J. 1938. *Logic: The theory of inquiry.* New York: Henry Holt and Company.

Dewey, J. 1969. *The child and the curriculum* and *The school and society.* Chicago and London: The University of Chicago Press.

Doyle, W., & Carter, K. 1984. Academic tasks in classrooms. *Curriculum Inquiry, 14*(2), 129–49.

Eisner, E. W. 1979. *The educational imagination: On the design and evaluation of school programs.* New York: Macmillan.

Eisner, E. W. 1982. *Cognition and curriculum: A basis for deciding what to teach.* New York: Longman Inc.

Elbaz, F. 1981. The teacher's "practical knowledge": Report of a case study. *Curriculum Inquiry, 11*(1), 43–71.

Elbaz, F. 1983. *Teacher thinking: A study of practical knowledge.* London: Croom Helm.

Enns, R. J. 1982. *Crisis research in curriculum policy making: A conceptualization.* Unpublished doctoral dissertation, University of Toronto.

Enns-Connolly, E. 1985. *Translation as interpretive act: A narrative study of translation in university-level foreign language teaching.* Unpublished doctoral dissertation, University of Toronto.

Eraut, M., Goad, L., & Smith, G. 1975. *The analysis of curriculum materials.* Brighton, England: University of Sussex.

Feiman-Nemser, S., & Floden, R. 1984. *The cultures of teaching* (Occasional Paper No. 74). East Lansing, MI: Michigan State University, The Institute for Research on Teaching.

Flinders, D. J., Noddings, N., & Thornton, S. J. 1986. The null curriculum: Its theoretical basis and practical implications. *Curriculum Inquiry, 16*(1), 33–42.

Foshay, A. W. 1969. Curriculum. In R. I. Ebel (Eds.), *Encyclopedia of educational research: A project of the American Educational Research Association* (4th ed.) (pp. 5–119). New York: Macmillan.

Fullan, M. 1982. *The meaning of educational change.* Toronto and New York: OISE Press and Teachers College Press.

Gagne, R. M. 1964. The acquisition of knowledge. In J. P. DeCecco (Ed.), *Educational technology* (pp. 115–31). New York: Holt, Rinehart & Winston.

Glaser, B. G., & Strauss, A. L. 1967. *The discovery of grounded theory: Strategies for qualitative research.* Chicago: Aldine.

Goldstein, P. 1978. *Changing the American schoolbook: Law, politics, and technology.* Lexington, MA: D. C. Heath & Company.

Good, C. V. (Ed.). 1959. *Dictionary of education* (2nd ed.). New York: McGraw-Hill.

Goodlad, J., & Klein, M. 1970. *Behind the classroom door.* Worthington, OH: Charles A. Jones.

Grumet, M. Undated manuscript. Restitution and reconstruction of educational experience: An autobiographical method for curriculum theory.

Halkes, R., & Deijkers, R. 1984. Teachers' teaching criteria. In R. Halkes, & J. K. Olson (Eds.), *Teacher thinking: A new perspective on persisting problems in education* (pp. 149–62). Lisse: Swets & Zeitlinger B.V.

Halkes, R., & Olson, J. K. (Eds.) 1984. *Teacher thinking: A new perspective on persisting problems in education.* Lisse: Swets & Zeitlinger B.V.

Hammersley, M. 1987. Heap and Delamont on transmissionism and British ethnography of schooling. *Curriculum Inquiry, 17*(2), 235–37.

Hass, G., Bondi, J., & Wiles, J. 1974. Curriculum planning: A new approach. Boston: Allyn and Bacon.

Heap, James L. 1985. Discourse in the production of classroom knowledge: Reading lessons. *Curriculum Inquiry, 15*(3), 245–80.

Heap, James L. 1986. Assuming transmission or studying production: A reply to Delamont. *Curriculum Inquiry, 16*(3), 331–33.

Heap, James L. 1987. Sociologies in and of education: A reply to Hammersley. *Curriculum Inquiry, 17*(2), 239–42.

Holly, M. L. 1984. *Keeping a personal-professional journal.* Geelong: Deakin University Press.

Hopkins, D. 1985. *A teacher's guide to classroom research.* Milton Keynes: Open University Press.

Hunt, D. E. 1976. Teachers are psychologists, too: On the application of psychology to education. *Canadian Psychological Review, 17*(3), 210–18.

Hunt, D. E. 1987. *Beginning with ourselves: Practice, theory and human affairs.* Toronto: OISE Press.

Jackson, P. W. 1968. *Life in classrooms.* New York: Holt, Rinehart & Winston.

Jackson, P. W. 1986. *The practice of teaching.* New York: Teachers College Press.

Janesick, V. 1982. Of snakes and circles: Making sense of classroom group processes through a case study. *Curriculum Inquiry, 12*(2), 161–89.

Kelly, G. A. 1955. *The psychology of personal constructs.* New York: Norton.

Kermode, F. 1967. *The sense of an ending.* New York: Oxford University Press.

Kroma, S. 1983. *Personal practical knowledge in teaching: An ethnographic study.* Unpublished doctoral dissertation, University of Toronto.

Lakoff, G., & Johnson, M. 1980. *Metaphors we live by.* Chicago: The University of Chicago Press.

Lampert, M. 1985. How do teachers manage to teach: Perspectives on problems in practice. *Harvard Educational Review, 55*(2), 178–94.

Larsson, S. 1984. Describing teachers' conceptions of their professional world. In R. Halkes & J. K. Olson (Eds.), *Teacher thinking: A new perspective on persisting problems in education* (pp. 123–33). Lisse: Swets & Zeitlinger B.V.

Lawton, D. 1980. *The politics of the school curriculum.* Boston and London: Routledge & Kegan Paul.

Leithwood, K. A. (Ed.). 1982. *Studies in curriculum decision making.* Toronto: OISE Press.

Lightfoot, S. L. 1983. *The good high school: Portraits of character and culture.* New York: Basic Books.

Marland, P. 1977. *A study of teachers' interactive thoughts.* Unpublished doctoral dissertation, The University of Alberta, Edmonton.

McIntyre, A. 1981. *After virtue: A study in moral theory.* Notre Dame: University of Notre Dame Press.

McKeon, R. 1947. *Introduction to Aristotle.* New York: Random House.

McKeon, R. 1952. Philosophy and action. *Ethics, 62*(2), 79–100.

Mitchell, W. J. T. (Ed.). 1981. *On narrative.* Chicago: The University of Chicago Press.

Munby, H. 1983. "A qualitative study of teachers' beliefs and principles." Paper presented at the annual meeting of the American Educational Research Association, Montreal, Canada.

Nystrand, M. (Ed.). 1977. *Language as a way of knowing.* Toronto: OISE Press.

Olson, J. 1981. Teacher influences in the classroom. *Instructional Science, 10,* 159–75.

Parlett, M., & Hamilton, D. 1977. Evaluation as illumination: A new approach to the study of innovatory programs. In D. Hamilton (Ed.), *Beyond the numbers game* (pp. 6–22). Berkeley, CA: McCutchan Publishing Corp.

Peters, T., & Waterman, R. 1984. *In search of excellence.* New York: Warner Books.

Phenix, P. H. 1964. *Realms of meaning: A philosophy of the curriculum for general education.* New York: McGraw-Hill.

Pinar, W. 1975. Currere: Toward reconceptualization. In W. Pinar (Ed.), *Curriculum theorizing: The reconceptualists.* Berkeley, CA: McCutchan Publishing Corp.

Pinar, W. (Ed.). 1975. *Curriculum theorizing: The reconceptualists.* Berkeley, CA: McCutchan Publishing Corp.

Polanyi, M. 1962. *Personal knowledge: Towards a post-critical philosophy.* Chicago: The University of Chicago Press.

Pope, M., & Scott, E. 1984. Teachers' epistemology and practice. In R. Halkes & J. K. Olson (Eds.), *Teacher thinking: A new perspective on persisting problems in education* (pp. 112–22). Lisse: Swets & Zeitlinger B.V.

Progoff, I. 1975. *At a journal workshop.* New York: Dialogue House Library.

Ramsay, P. 1983. Fresh perspectives on the school transformation–reproduction debate: A response to Anyon from the Antipodes. *Curriculum Inquiry, 13*(3), 295–320.

Rowland, S. 1984. *The enquiring classroom: An introduction to children's learning.* London: Falmer Press.

Rugg, H. O. 1947. *Foundations for American education* (1st ed.). Yonkers-on-Hudson, NY: World Book Company.

Schon, D. 1983. *The reflective practitioner: How professionals think in action.* New York: Basic Books.

Schon, D. 1987. *Educating the reflective practitioner*. London: Jossey-Bass Limited.

Schutz, A., & Luckmann, T. 1973. *The structures of the life-world*. Evanston, IL: Northwestern University Press.

Schwab, J. J. 1962. The teaching of science as enquiry. In J. J. Schwab and P. Brandwein (Eds.), *The teaching of science*. Cambridge, MA: Harvard University Press.

Schwab, J. J. 1983. Personal communication.

Shipman, M. D. 1974. *Inside a curriculum project*. London: Methuen.

Smith, B. O., Stanley, W. O., & Shores, J. H. 1957. *Fundamentals of curriculum development*. New York: Harcourt, Brace and World.

Smith, L., Kleine, P., Prunty, J., & Dwyer, D. 1986. *Educational innovators: Then and now*. London: Falmer Press.

Spradley, J. P. 1979. *The ethnographic interview*. New York: Holt, Rinehart & Winston.

Spradley, J. P. 1980. *Participant observation*. New York: Holt, Rinehart & Winston.

Stake, R. E. 1978. Seeking sweet water. Case study methods in educational research. In R. M. Jaeger (Ed.), *Alternative methodologies in educational research*. New York: American Educational Research Association.

Sullivan, E. 1984. *A critical psychology: Interpretation of the personal world*. New York: Plenum Press.

Taba, H. 1962. *Curriculum development: Theory and practice*. New York: Harcourt, Brace and World.

Tamir, P., Blum, A., Hofstein, A., & Sabar, N. 1978. *Curriculum implementation and its relationship to curriculum development in science*. Jerusalem: Amos de Shalit Science Teaching Center, Hebrew University.

Tanner, D., & Tanner, L. N. 1975. *Curriculum development: Theory into practice*. New York: Macmillan.

Travers, K. J., & Westbury, I. In press. *The second international mathematics study: Curriculum analysis*. New York: Pergamon Press.

Tyler, R. 1950. *Basic principles of curriculum instruction*. Chicago: The University of Chicago Press.

U.S. Department of Education, National Commission on Excellence in Education. 1983. *A nation at risk*. Washington, D.C.: U.S. Government Printing Office.

Walker, R. 1985. *Doing research: A handbook for teachers*. Cambridge: Cambridge University Press.

Westbury, I., & Steimer, W. 1971. Curriculum: A discipline in search of its problems. *School Review, 79*, 243–67.

Wittrock, M. C. (Ed.). 1986. *Handbook of research on teaching* (3rd ed.). New York: Macmillan.

Yonemura, M. 1982. Teacher conversations: A potential source of their own professional growth. *Curriculum Inquiry, 12*(3), 239–56.

Zerubavel, E. 1979. *Patterns of time in hospital life: A sociological perspective*. Chicago: The University of Chicago Press.

Index

About the Authors

F. Michael Connelly, Ph.D., was educated at the University of Alberta, Canada; Teachers College, Columbia University; and The University of Chicago. He taught secondary school in Alberta, and held teaching positions at the Universities of Alberta, Illinois, and Chicago, before coming to Toronto, where he is Professor of curriculum and teacher studies at The Ontario Institute for Studies in Education and the University of Toronto. He coordinates the Canadian component of the Second International Science Study, is editor of *Curriculum Inquiry*, and is a member of the board of directors of the John Dewey Society for Education and Culture. He recently co-authored an Ontario government teacher-education policy paper. His research interest is in the study of teaching, and with D. Jean Clandinin, he is co-director of a long-term study of teachers' personal practical knowledge.

D. Jean Clandinin is an associate professor in the Departments of Curriculum and Instruction and of Teacher Education and Supervision at the University of Calgary, in Canada. A former elementary school teacher, counselor, and psychologist, she holds an M.Ed. from the University of Alberta and a Ph.D. from the University of Toronto. She is the author of *Classroom Practice: Teacher Images in Action*, and has authored or co-authored numerous articles on classroom practice, the reflective practitioner, and narrative study of teachers. Dr. Clandinin has participated in several research studies that develop ways of understanding teachers' personal practical knowledge.